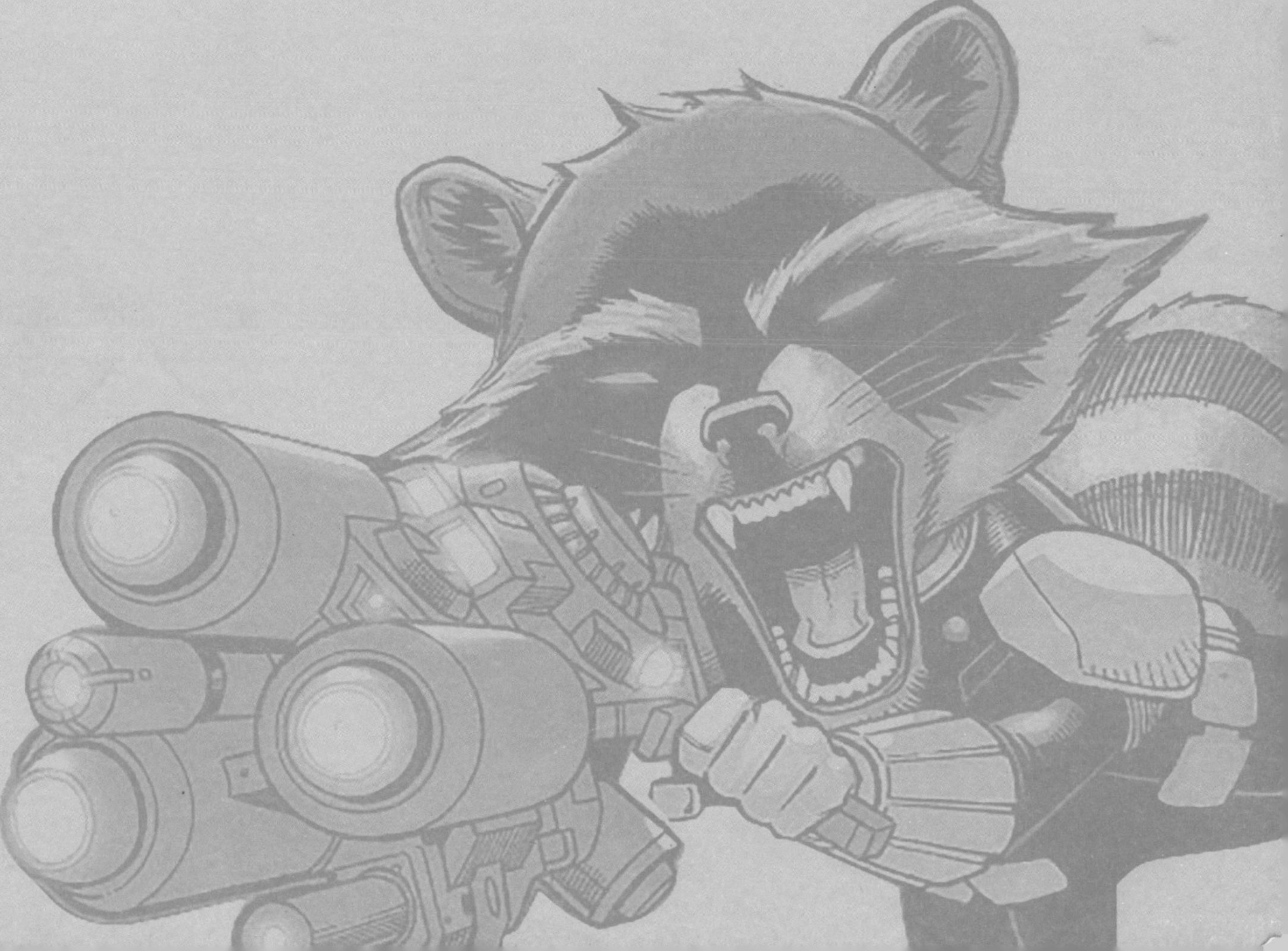

© 1993 MARVEL ENT. GROUP INC.

THE ULTIMATE GUIDE
TO THE COSMIC OUTLAWS

Senior Editor Elizabeth Dowsett
Senior Art Editor Clive Savage
Project Art Editor Paul Drislane
Picture Research Alex Evangeli
Pre-Production Producer Siu Yin Chan
Senior Producer Mary Slater
Managing Editor Sadie Smith
Managing Art Editor Ron Stobbart
Publisher Julie Ferris
Art Director Lisa Lanzarini
Publishing Director Simon Beecroft

Edited for DK by Simon Hugo
Designed for DK by Amazing15 Ltd.

First American Edition, 2017
Published in the United States by DK Publishing
345 Hudson Street, New York, New York 10014
Page design copyright © 2017 Dorling Kindersley Limited
DK, a Division of Penguin Random House LLC
17 18 19 20 21 10 9 8 7 6 5 4 3 2 1
001–299178–Apr/17

A catalog record for this book is available from the Library of Congress.
ISBN: 978-1-4654-5899-5

DK books are available at special discounts when purchased in bulk for sales promotions,
premiums, fund-raising, or educational use.
For details, contact: DK Publishing Special Markets,
345 Hudson Street, New York, New York 10014 SpecialSales@dk.com

DK would like to thank Sarah Brunstad, David Gabriel, Joseph Hochstein,
Brian Overton, and Jeff Youngquist at Marvel; Chelsea Alon at Disney; Vanessa Bird for
indexing and proofreading; and Natalie Edwards for editorial assistance.

Printed and bound in China

marvel.com
© 2017 MARVEL

A WORLD OF IDEAS:
SEE ALL THERE IS TO KNOW

www.dk.com

MARVEL
GUARDIANS OF THE GALAXY

THE ULTIMATE GUIDE TO THE COSMIC OUTLAWS

Written by Nick Jones

CONTENTS

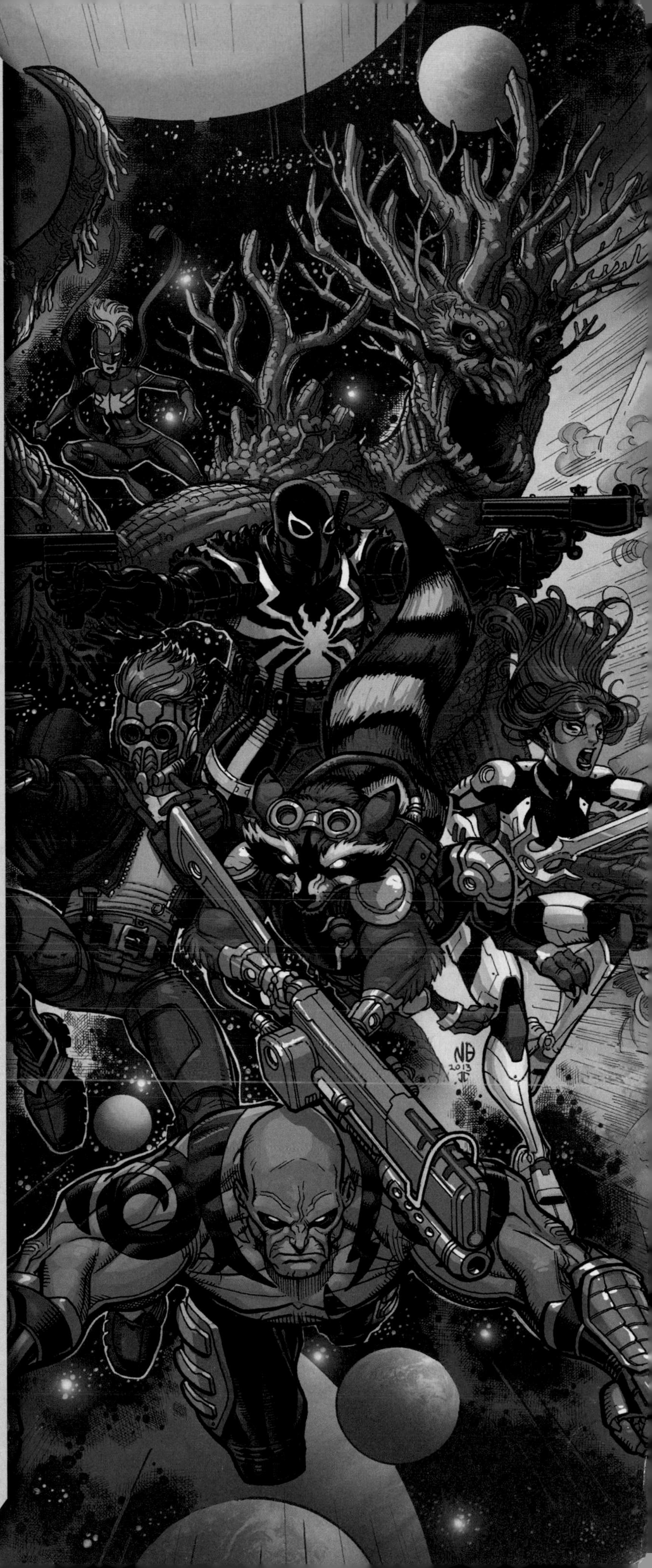

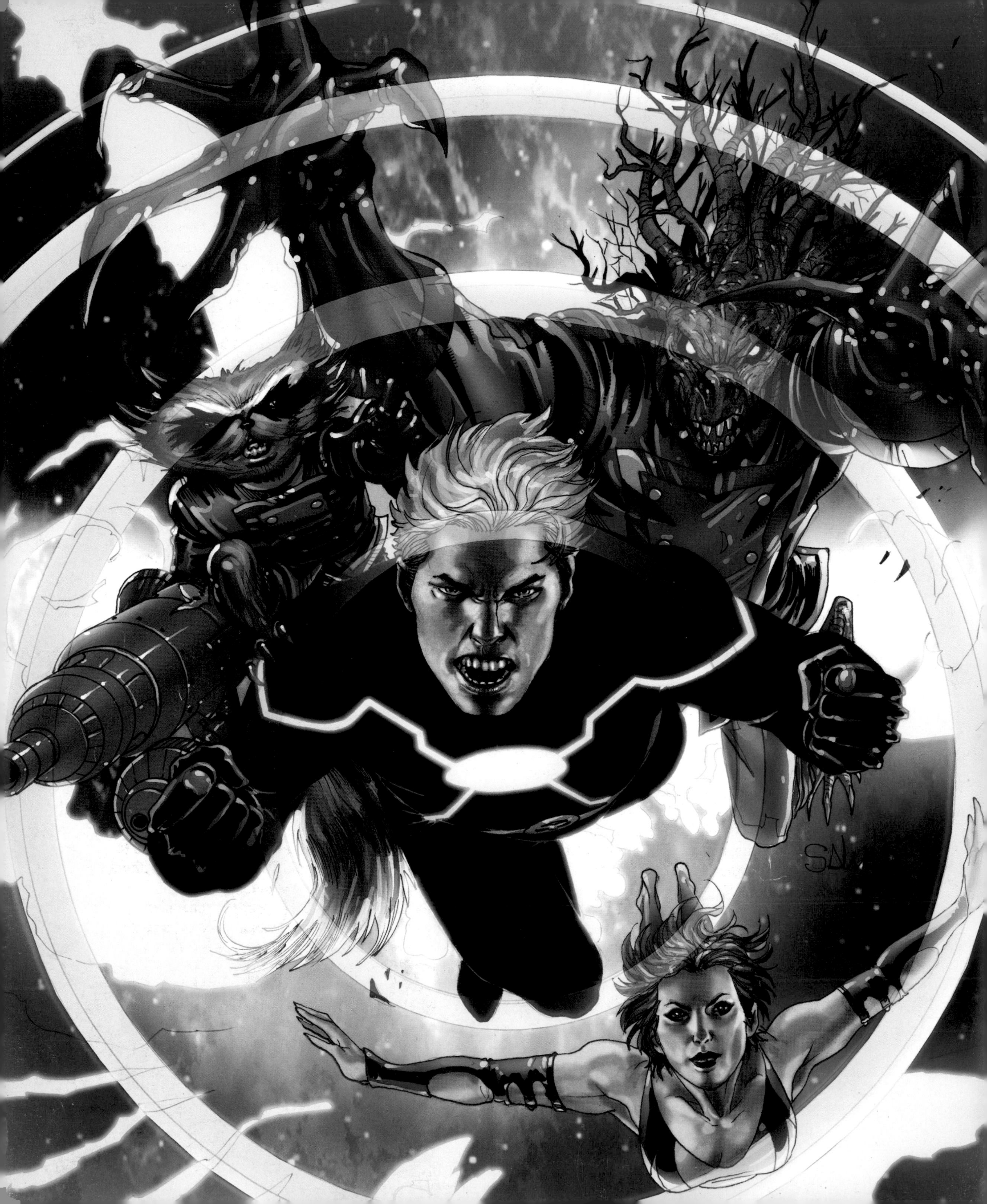

FOREWORD

You've got to put a team together to save the galaxy. The whole galaxy. You look at your checklist. Implacable destroyer—check. Deadliest woman in the Galaxy—check. Walking tree—

Wait. What kind of checklist is this? A talking raccoonoid with a giant blaster cannon? A smooth-talking pirate rogue who makes stuff up as he goes along? This is the crew you're putting together? These are the people you're pinning the fate of the whole galaxy on?

They call themselves the Guardians of the Galaxy, but that's a grand name for such a ragtag bunch of misfits. Yes, they have saved the galaxy a few times, so they kind of deserve the title, thank you very much, but it's also a bit of a joke. An overblown, spectacularly triumphant name for an improvised rabble.

The original Guardians of the Galaxy were a team of brave, idealistic freedom fighters who first appeared in Marvel Comics in 1969, thanks to the imaginations of Arnold Drake and Gene Colan. The Guardians were never a first-tier Marvel super-team, but they were the only one around in the year 3000AD to fight the good fight, and they fought it well. And thanks to the high jinks of time travel, they visited the present day, helping out the mighty heroes of the Marvel Universe. So much so, they were all made honorary Avengers.

In 2008, I was writing cosmic stories for Marvel, and my editor suggested that it might be fun to have a team book in the mix. We ransacked the Marvel vaults for old, forgotten, D-list Marvel heroes from the cosmic canon. These were characters who had never made it big, but I was certainly very fond of them—I'd always been a fan of Marvel Cosmic. There was Star-Lord, the space-faring rogue, the deadly Gamora from Jim Starlin's amazing Warlock stories, the destroyer Drax, the irrepressible Rocket Raccoon, and Groot, the walking tree. Wouldn't it be fun, we speculated, to make a team out of these... losers? They don't get on with each other, they're massively outclassed by all the big cosmic threats, at least two of them are pretty much villains, and the rest have only a passing familiarity with the right side of the law. Wouldn't it be fun if it was these guys who ended up being in the right place at the right time to make a difference? Wouldn't it be a riot if, for better or for worse, the fate of the galaxy was in their hands? Or, in some cases, paws. It seemed like too good an idea not to run with it.

That's when they stole the name. They wanted something epic and dramatic to lend themselves the confidence and importance that they otherwise lacked. So they "borrowed" the name of the original team (a move that came full circle when Vance Astro and other members of the original line-up voyaged through time and joined their ranks).

Led by Star-Lord, they were the "new" Guardians (who were actually the "old" Guardians because they adventured a thousand years before the original team...oh, the headache of time travel!). They proved to be a greater whole than the sum of their parts and went on to save the galaxy several times (and of course, as suits such a bunch of maverick nobodies, got no recognition for it at all). Oddly, though they hadn't been created as a team, they fitted together really well, the characters bouncing off each other in entertaining ways, especially the double act of Rocket and Groot.

Then the comic became a movie. The ragtag bunch of nobodies that no one had ever heard of suddenly became household names worldwide. Characters that had been overlooked for so long were abruptly elevated onto the A-list.

There's a lot to love about the Guardians of the Galaxy in every incarnation of the team, most of all that blend of strong character, serious fate-of-the-cosmos drama and snappy humor that James Gunn's movies showcase so well, and you can find out everything you wanted to know about them in this book. Thanks to the Guardians, the Marvel Universe got a whole lot bigger.

So if your universe is in peril, grab that checklist. They may not look like it, but these are the guys to go for. They'll guard your galaxy, whether your galaxy wants to be guarded or not.

As Groot might say, "I am Groot." And I think you know exactly what I mean.

Dan Abnett

Dan Abnett
Writer of Marvel's 2008 comic
The Guardians of the Galaxy

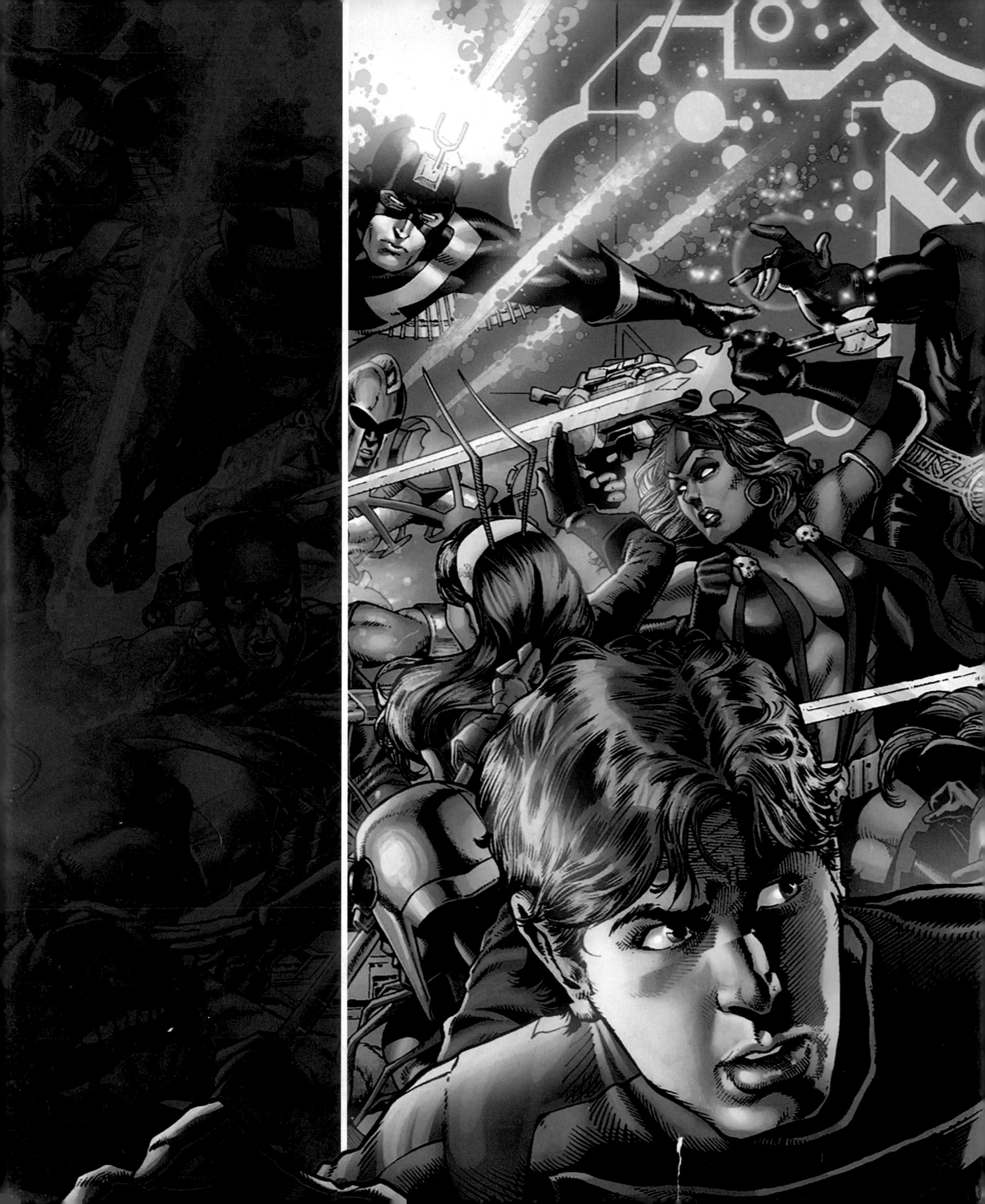

INTRODUCING THE GUARDIANS OF THE GALAXY

In 1969, writer Arnold Drake and artist Gene Colan introduced a new team of heroes to the Marvel Universe—of the future! They were the Guardians of the Galaxy: thousand-year-old astronaut Vance Astro; super-strong Jupiter colonist Charlie-27; diamond-skinned Martinex from Pluto; and noble savage Yondu from Centauri-IV. These 31st-century freedom fighters had numerous thrilling adventures—both in their far-flung era and the modern one—over ensuing decades, gaining their own series in 1990 before disappearing from view.

Then, in 2008, writers Dan Abnett and Andy Lanning and artist Paul Pelletier launched a new team of Guardians. Spinning out of cosmic events Annihilation and Annihilation: Conquest, and building on the cosmic legacy of creators like Jim Starlin, Bill Mantlo, Steve Englehart, Keith Giffen—and, of course, Stan Lee and Jack Kirby—this modern-day team was composed of the unlikeliest of heroes: rogues, assassins, manhunters, a raccoon—even a talking tree!

It was a stroke of genius. The exploits of Star-Lord, Gamora, Drax, Rocket Raccoon, Groot, Adam Warlock, and Phyla-Vell soon became legendary. Their story has expanded across multiple media—comic books, animation, movies, and more—but their mission remains the same: to protect the downtrodden, to ward off threats to the very fabric of space—to be the Guardians of the Galaxy!

START

Groot is exiled from Planet X.

Groot arrives on Earth, calling himself the Monarch of Planet X and wreaking havoc.

Mistress Death appears before the young Thanos for the first time, leading him down an ever-darker path.

Surviving the crash that killed her mother and father, Heather Douglas is raised on Titan by the Shao-Lom monks.

J'Son of Spartax crash-lands on Earth and is rescued from the wreckage of his ship by Meredith Quill.

Arthur Douglas is killed when his car is blasted by Thanos; Arthur is resurrected in a new body, becoming Drax the Destroyer.

Mantis is raised by the Kree Priests of Pama at their monastery in the Vietnamese jungle.

Thanos forges an alliance of convenience with Annihilus.

Negative Zone tyrant Annihilus leads his Annihilation Wave forces in a galactic invasion.

Peter Quill is imprisoned in galactic jail Kyln and meets Thanos for the first time.

Phyla-Vell and Moondragon meet on Earth and become lovers.

Peter Quill, Gamora, Drax, Phyla-Vell, Moondragon, and Nova join forces to battle Annihilus' Annihilation Wave.

The Nova Corps is wiped out by the Annihilation Wave. Richard Rider is the last surviving Nova.

A prison ship carrying Drax crash-lands on Earth; the Destroyer is reborn in a new form.

Peter Quill gives up the mantle of Star-Lord after thousands die during a battle with the Fallen One.

During the Annihilation War, Drax fights Thanos and tears out the Titan's heart, killing him.

The Phalanx conquer the Kree Empire.

On the run from Phalanx Selects Gamora and Drax, Nova discovers Knowhere and meets the station's chief of security, Cosmo.

Annihilus is killed by Nova.

Phyla-Vell acquires Wendell Vaughn's Quantum Bands, becoming the new Quasar.

Star-Lord leads a team—including Rocket Raccoon, Groot, and Mantis—against the Phalanx.

Moondragon is killed by Ultron, leader of the Phalanx.

TIMELINE

The present-day Guardians of the Galaxy's story intertwines with that of the 31st-century Guardians'—past, present, and future colliding, diverging, and reconnecting across the two teams' timelines.

Timeline key

▷ Present-day Guardians

⬡ 31st-century Guardians

◗ Both groups team up

Peter Quill is orphaned when Badoon troops murder his mother, Meredith.

Gamora is adopted by Thanos and undergoes a brutal training regime and physical augmentation.

Adam Warlock encounters the Magus for the first time.

Peter Quill is bequeathed a Spartoi Element Gun belonging to his father, J'Son.

Drax learns that Moondragon is his daughter.

In the 31st-century Guardians' timeline, Vance Astro leaves Earth on a mission to deep space.

Peter Quill steals a Kree starship and sets out for space, becoming Star-Lord.

The 31st-century Guardians travel back in time in their space station, Drydock, and help the Avengers to defeat Korvac.

The 31st-century Guardians of the Galaxy make their first journey back in time, encountering the Defenders.

Adam Warlock, Gamora, Drax, Moondragon, Thanos, and others form the cosmic team Infinity Watch.

Rocket Raccoon leaves Halfworld to seek his destiny in space.

Vance Astro triggers his younger self's latent telekinesis, creating a divergent timeline where he grows up to be a Super Hero rather than an astronaut.

As the conflict with the Phalanx ends, Star-Lord decides the galaxy needs a team of Guardians.

The Guardians discover Major Victory from the 31st-century Guardians frozen in a block of ice.

The Guardians rescue Star-Lord from the Negative Zone, along with Jack Flag, who joins the team.

Half the Guardians travel to 3009 and experience a succession of alternate futures.

The newly formed Guardians of the Galaxy battle the Universal Church of Truth for the first time.

A Skrull Secret Invasion on Knowhere causes a split among the Guardians.

Moondragon is resurrected by Drax and Phyla-Vell.

The Guardians are embroiled in the War of Kings between the Inhumans/Kree and the Shi'ar.

TIMELINE

Adam Warlock succumbs to his dark alternate future self, the Magus.

Drax is killed by Thanos. Star-Lord and Nova are trapped in the Cancerverse battling the Mad Titan.

Rocket Raccoon rescues Groot from the Isle of Punishment on Planet X.

In the Cancerverse, Nova sends Star-Lord, Thanos, and a resurrected Drax back to their own dimension.

Thanos is resurrected by the Universal Church of Truth and kills Phyla-Vell.

The Magus opens a dimensional rift, allowing an invasion from the Cancerverse.

Cosmo forms the Annihilators—successors to the Guardians team.

The Thing joins the Guardians.

In the year 3007, the Brotherhood of Badoon conquer Earth and its colonies.

In the 31st-century Guardians' timeline, Earth is riven by global warming, Bionics Wars, Martian invasion, and war between the Techno-Barons.

After a thousand-year voyage, Vance Astro arrives on Centauri-IV—decades after humanity colonized the planet.

Genetically adapted humans colonize the Solar System and beyond. The United Federation is established.

Rocket Raccoon, Drax, and Groot encounter Guardians from the 31st and 11th centuries.

The Guardians aid former team member Captain Marvel against another former team member, Iron Man.

Martinex wages a one-man war of resistance against the Badoon on Pluto.

Captain America, S.H.I.E.L.D. agent Sharon Carter, and the Thing travel to 3014 and help the Guardians defeat Badoon Lordsire Drang.

Nikki joins the Guardians of the Galaxy.

Charlie-27 returns from Space Militia duty to find Jupiter overrun by the Badoon.

Vance Astro, Charlie-27, Martinex, and Yondu form the Guardians of the Galaxy to combat the Brotherhood of Badoon.

The Defenders join the Guardians in 3015 and drive back the Badoon.

Thor travels to the 31st century and helps the Guardians fight Korvac, who then flees to the past.

The Guardians help the Avengers to defeat Thanos, who has a Cosmic Cube.

Iron Man joins the Guardians.

Thanos invades Earth; the Guardians disable orbital station the Peak to break his blockade.

The Guardians help Jean Grey of the All-New X-Men, who faces trial by the Shi'ar.

Kitty Pryde comes to Star-Lord's rescue when he's captured by J'Son (alias Mister Knife) and the Slaughter Squad.

The Guardians of the Galaxy re-form.

J'Son of Spartax manipulates the Guardians into becoming Spartax's sworn enemies.

Angela joins the Guardians.

Agent Venom and Captain Marvel become Guardians.

Star-Lord and Groot play a crucial role in defeating Doctor Doom and reconstituting reality.

All of reality is destroyed, despite the efforts of the Guardians and Earth's heroes.

Kitty Pryde joins the Guardians.

Hala, the Kree homeworld, is destroyed by J'Son.

Peter Quill briefly becomes president of Spartax, and Kitty Pryde replaces him as Star-Lord.

Star-Lord locates the Guardians on Battleworld, the patchwork planet created by Doctor Doom.

To stop reality being rewritten, the 31st-century Guardians and Geena Drake travel back in time and team up with the present-day Guardians.

The Guardians and the X-Men unite to prevent J'Son from acquiring the Black Vortex.

The Guardians triumph over Dormammu, but at the cost of their ally the Ancient One (Doctor Strange).

Korvac is still a threat. The Guardians pursue his essence across time and space.

The Guardians encounter the Stark, and Firelord joins the team.

Talon, Krugarr, and Hollywood become Guardians.

Vance Astro assumes a new identity—and look—as Major Victory.

The Guardians visit the past to cure Talon of a disease, and wind up battling the Masters of Evil.

FINISH

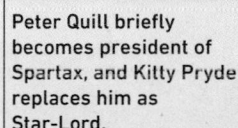

Aleta becomes a member of the Guardians in her own right.

Replica, Phoenix, and the Spirit of Vengeance all become Guardians.

Martinex resigns as leader of the Guardians of the Galaxy.

On Mainframe's world, Martinex establishes sister team the Galactic Guardians.

Yellowjacket travels from the past with the Guardians and joins the team.

Blasting into action in 1969's *Marvel Super-Heroes* #18, the first Guardians of the Galaxy—Major Vance Astro, Charlie-27, Martinex, Yondu, and latecomers Starhawk and Nikki—appeared in an array of different comics over the next dozen years. They battled the Badoon in their native 31st century, but spent almost as much time in the present day.

31ST-CENTURY GUARDIANS

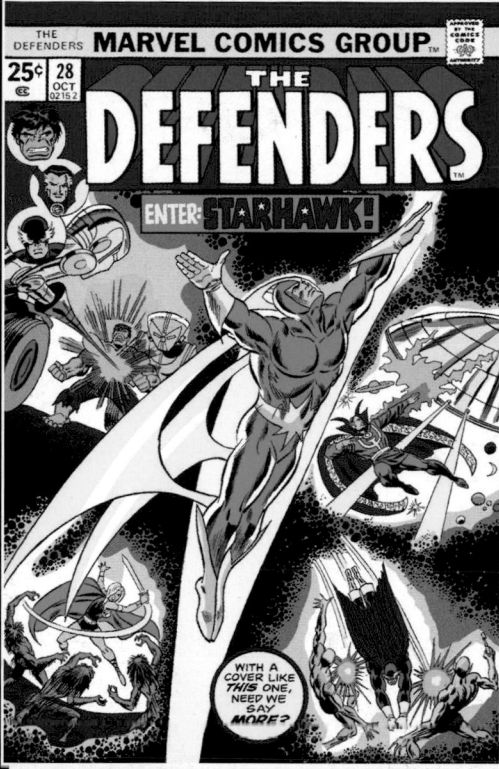

DEFENDERS (VOL. 1) #28 (OCT. 1975)
The mysterious Starhawk blazes into the lives of
the Guardians (and the Defenders), manipulating
events right from the off.

MARVEL PRESENTS (VOL. 1) #12 (AUG. 1977)
The end of the Guardians' ten-issue run in *Marvel
Presents* also marks a beginning, as the team chance
upon long-lost space station Drydock.

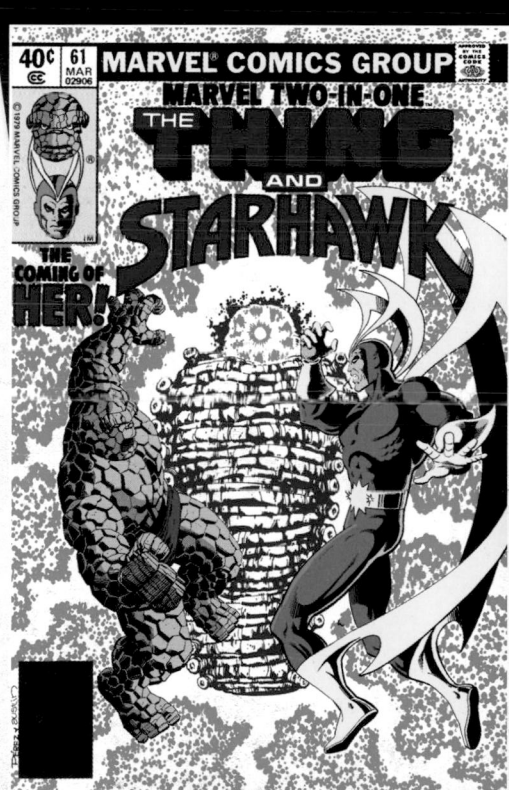

MARVEL TWO-IN-ONE (VOL. 1)
#61 (MAR. 1980)
Starhawk meets a hero who will himself
one day become a Guardian of the
Galaxy—the Fantastic Four's Thing!

MARVEL TWO-IN-ONE (VOL. 1)
#69 (NOV. 1980)
The 31st-century Guardians' future timeline
diverges from the regular Marvel timeline, as
Vance Astro changes his own past.

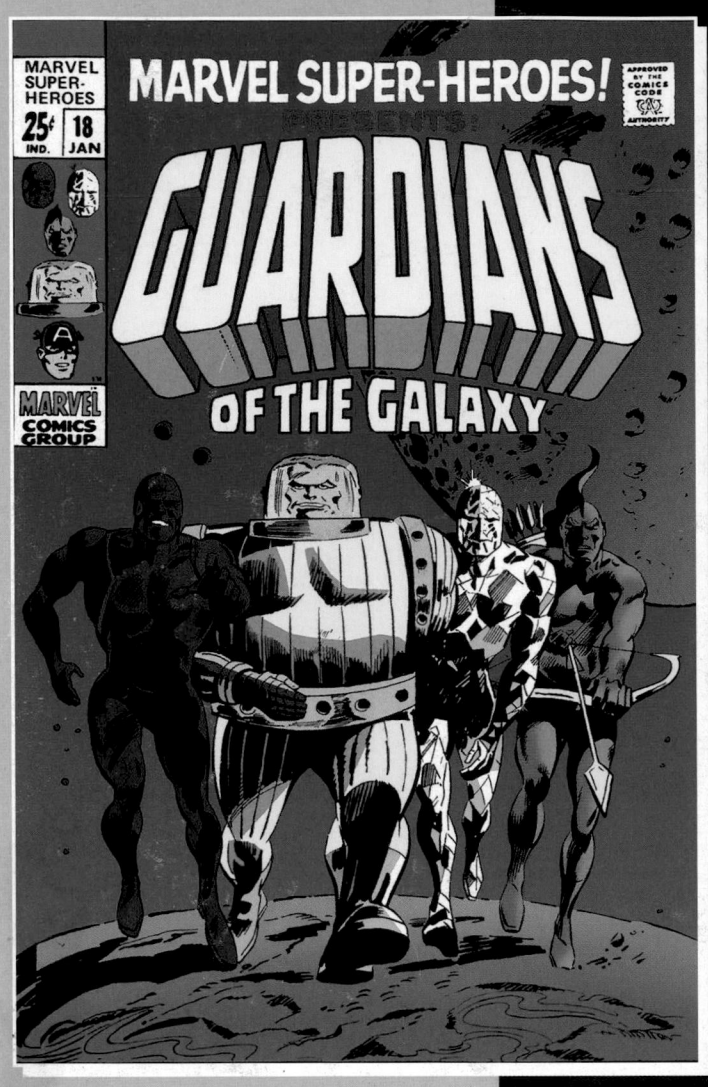

JANUARY 1969

MAIN CHARACTERS
Charlie-27 • Martinex •
Major Vance Astro • Yondu

SUPPORTING CHARACTERS
Brotherhood of the Badoon •
Drang—Supreme Commander
of the Eastern Sector of the
Badoon Empire

MAIN LOCATIONS
Jupiter • Pluto • Earth •
New New York

MARVEL SUPER-HEROES (Vol. 1) #18

THE RAMPAGING BADOON CAUSE FOUR STRANGERS TO UNITE AS THE GUARDIANS OF THE GALAXY.

The year is 3007. Humanity has established one single government—the United Lands of Earth (U.L.E.)—and expanded into space, colonizing dozens of worlds under the banner of the U.L.E. Federation. In the outer Solar System, a lone ship rockets through the void, carrying its occupant back to his home colony.

1 After six months of Space Militia duty, the fifth-generation Jupiter colonist Charlie-27 is finally back home. To his alarm, he finds the Badoon have overrun Jupiter. He does his best to fight the invaders, but even with his genetically enhanced physique, he is outmatched. He escapes via the Tele-Tran (Living Matter Transmitter).

2 Charlie-27 arrives on Pluto only to find that it too has been conquered by the Badoon. He meets Martinex, a crystalline Pluvian who is descended from Humans. When Pluto was evacuated two months ago, Martinex stayed to wage a campaign of sabotage. Together, the pair dart for the Tele-Tran.

"Earth shall overcome! Earth shall overcome! Earth shall overcome— **someday***!!"*

GUARDIANS OF THE GALAXY (ALL TOGETHER)

3 On Earth, Major Vance Astro—a time-displaced astronaut and famed hero from the 20th-century—is being held captive by the Badoon. Drang, Supreme Commander of the Badoon, orders Vance to execute his fellow captive, Yondu, of the planet Centauri-IV. Vance insists upon using Yondu's own weapon—a bow and Yaka Arrow. He knows Yondu has the power to control the arrow sonically—and turn it back on the Badoon!

4 As the Yaka Arrow blasts the Badoon, Vance and Yondu escape. They arrive at the Tele-Tran just as Charlie-27 and Martinex teleport in, and mistake the newcomers for Badoon guards. A battle ensues, but Vance realizes his mistake as the Badoon show up, and the four unite against their common enemy.

5 With their combined powers, Vance, Charlie-27, Martinex, and Yondu quickly make mincemeat of the Badoon, then teleport to the shattered colony of New New York. As the colony burns behind them, they determine to fight the Badoon wherever they find them, together, as the Guardians of the Galaxy!

When Krugarr's magic began to fade, Vance started to age rapidly. He was saved by a new symbiotic suit with the same Captain America-inspired color scheme.

Vance adopted his blue-and-white costume after he was freed from his containment suit by Sorcerer Supreme Krugarr, who used an enchantment to stop him ageing.

Advice From the Future

During the 31st-century Guardians' first visit to the past, Vance Astro met his younger self, Vance Astrovik. While keeping his identity secret from young Vance, he told him about the dark future that awaited mankind. The boy was upset, until the elder Vance pointed out that, while he couldn't alter his past, young Vance could change his future.

Marvelous Meeting

While in the past with the Guardians, Vance met Ms. Marvel (Carol Danvers), who would go on to be Captain Marvel. Abducted by the villain the Faceless One, Ms. Marvel was taken to the Guardians' orbital station, Drydock. Vance initially mistook her for an intruder, before then helping her to defeat the Faceless One.

HERO OF THE HOUR

Rocketed into space from Earth in the 20th century, Major Vance Astro awoke from suspended animation to find mankind had colonized the stars in his absence. Unable to take off his containment suit lest he crumble to dust, he felt an overwhelming loneliness, despite being hailed as a pioneer. When the Badoon invaded, he found new purpose as a founding member of the Guardians of the Galaxy, and put his newly developed psychokinetic powers to use battling the Badoon.

VANCE ASTRO

Blasted a thousand years into the future, Major Vance Astro is a man out of time. An astronaut from the 20th century, Vance became a hero of the 31st century. That heroism was put to the test when the Brotherhood of Badoon conquered Earth and its colonies. To counter the invaders, Vance helped form a band of freedom fighters: the Guardians of the Galaxy!

Vance went on a long, arduous quest to find Captain America's long-lost shield. He then used it as a symbol to rally humanity against its Badoon conquerors.

ORIGIN

Growing up, Vance Astrovik wanted to be an astronaut so much that he shortened his last name to "Astro." As an adult, he achieved his dream and was given the ultimate mission: a 1,000-year voyage of space exploration. To stop him from growing old during the trip, he was sealed in a copper containment suit and placed in suspended animation. During his epic journey, Vance developed advanced mental abilities that enabled him to emit psychokinetic blasts. When he finally got to his destination—the planet Centauri-IV—he found humans already there, Earth having discovered the secret of faster-than-light travel just two centuries after Vance left!

Timelines Diverge

Vance sought out his younger self for a second time while in the past. He told him that he would spend a thousand years in suspended animation and be one of the loneliest people alive, and pleaded with the boy not to become an astronaut. He also inadvertently set off Vance Jr.'s latent telekinesis. With this new power, young Vance resolved to be a super hero rather than an astronaut. He grew up to become Marvel Boy, and a whole new timeline was established.

*"The future has **more** than **one** course—it's possible to **alter** what's in store for you!"*

VANCE ASTRO

Mighty Monster Mashers

The Guardians received a boost in their battle against the Badoon in the shape of Captain America, Sharon Carter, and the Fantastic Four's Thing, who had all traveled to the future. Charlie-27 had an affinity for fellow powerhouse the Thing in particular, and the pair combined their strength to bring down a mighty Badoon Monster!

JOVIAN GOOD FELLOW

Like all Jovians, Charlie-27 has been genetically engineered to withstand the immense gravity and deadly radiation of Jupiter, giving him great strength and durability. He is steadfastly devoted to the cause of the Guardians and has been a calming presence on the team. Stout and reliable, his great intelligence and eloquence are a surprise to those who would judge him by his brutish appearance.

Charlie-27's skin is dense enough to withstand bullets, so he doesn't need to cover his body in protective gear.

Savage Time

When the Guardians traveled into the past in pursuit of a Badoon device, Charlie-27 was surprised by mankind's savagery. In a New York back alley, he chanced upon a violent mugging. After dealing with the assailants, who were armed with knives and clubs, Charlie reflected that there was a little bit of the Badoon even in his ancestors.

DATA FILE

REAL NAME: Charlie-27

OCCUPATION: Soldier, adventurer

BASE: Mobile

HEIGHT: 6ft

WEIGHT: 555 lbs

EYES: Blue

HAIR: Brown

FIRST APPEARANCE: *Marvel Super-Heros* (Vol. 1) #18 (Jan. 1969)

Solo Mission

When the Guardians chanced upon Drydock—a space station believed lost in the war with the Badoon—they were seized by the onboard computer, which had gone mad. Only Charlie escaped, battling through lasers, giant spikes, a hydraulic press, electrified cables, and construction robots to rescue his team! Once secured by Charlie-27, Drydock became the Guardians' base.

> *"We're the last free men of Jupiter and Pluto, and we're lookin' for a fight."*
>
> CHARLIE-27

ORIGIN

Charlie-27 grew up in a mining colony on Jupiter. As soon as he was old enough, he joined the Space Militia and climbed his way through the ranks to become a captain. Returning home from a mission that had seen him spend six months in deep space, he found that his planet had been conquered by the Brotherhood of Badoon—along with every other Earth colony. On Jupiter, he saw his father taken away by Badoon forces. Unable to do anything to help, he made his escape to Pluto via the Tele-Port system. On Pluto, Charlie met another fugitive from the Badoon—the Pluvian Martinex. It would not be long before the two of them would come to be known as Guardians of the Galaxy!

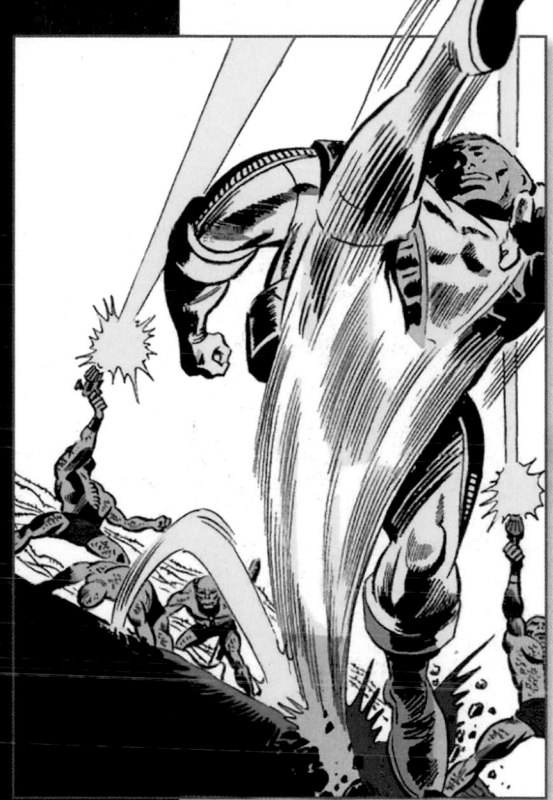

Jovian genetic engineering gives Charlie-27 more than 10 times the muscle mass of human beings raised on Earth.

CHARLIE-27

The super-strong and super-resilient Charlie-27 is the Guardians' resident powerhouse. Hailing from the Earth colony on Jupiter, he was among the four original Guardians who came together to fight for the freedom of Earth and its colonies. Since then, he has become the solid, sturdy backbone of the team.

MARTINEX

Genetically engineered to survive on the frozen Earth colony of Pluto, Martinex is the Guardians' silicon-based warrior-scientist. With his heat-generating and cold-emitting powers, he is a force to be reckoned with in battle. Yet his fellow Guardians prize him just as much for his scientific mind.

Martinex's silicon eyes are highly adaptable, allowing him to see in dazzlingly bright light or near-total darkness.

> *"I am **not** an alien. You're aware that my grandparents were **carbon-based** humans like yourself?"*
>
> MARTINEX

A silicon body enables Martinex to draw heat from his surroundings and stay warm in the coldest environments.

Formative Influence

When the Guardians traveled to the past to find a piece of Badoon technology, their ship was found by Vance Astrovik —Vance Astro's younger self. Alone on the craft, Martinex refused to answer the boy's questions when he came on board. Even so, young Vance proudly proclaimed that one day he would be an astronaut, and would change his name to "Astro," to make it sound more like "astronaut."

ORIGIN

In common with other Pluvians, Martinex was biogenetically engineered to survive amid Pluto's harsh conditions. He had an untroubled adolescence, characterized by a passion for all science and technology. However, all that changed when the Brotherhood of Badoon invaded Pluto and all Earth's other colonies. While his fellow Pluvians were evacuated, Martinex remained with a mission to sabotage the planet's industrial complexes. He spent months fighting the conquerors as a one-man resistance, but then met another freedom fighter, Charlie-27. Teaming up, the pair headed for Earth to continue the struggle.

Like his fellow Guardians, Martinex wears a G-Star that acts as a long-range communicator, tracking device, and teleportation trigger unit.

DATA FILE

REAL NAME: Martinex T'Naga

OCCUPATION: Scientist, adventurer

BASE: Mobile

HEIGHT: 6ft 1in

WEIGHT: 455 lbs

EYES: Black

HAIR: None

FIRST APPEARANCE: *Marvel Super-Heroes* (Vol. 1) #18 (Jan. 1969)

THE CRYSTAL MAN

A scientist who became a freedom fighter, Martinex is perhaps the most cerebral of the Guardians. Born on the Earth colony on Pluto, the crystalline structure of his body enables him to fire blasts of extreme heat or cold from his fingertips. As formidable as those abilities are, his brainpower has been just as important to the Guardians, from piloting and maintaining their ship to briefly taking command of the team.

Finger of Fate

Though he is a man of science, Martinex can be as ruthless as a freedom fighter needs to be. During the final battle with the Badoon for control of Earth, he left the main action and found the Badoon Governor of Earth, Koord. With one finger, Martinex unleashed a jet of extreme heat, setting Koord aflame. Slipping away, Martinex smiled grimly at the summary execution.

Human Touch

After Earth was freed from the Badoon, Martinex worked to recover as much of the planet's shattered technology as possible. In Berlin, he and a fellow scientist found little worth saving. When Martinex lamented the loss, the scientist reached out to comfort him... but then withdrew his hand, repelled by the Pluvian's crystalline nature. This taught Martinex a bitter lesson about humanity and appearance.

YONDU

A noble, blue-skinned savage from the planet Centauri-IV, Yondu is the last of his people. A seasoned hunter, he is highly skilled with his bow and Yaka Arrows. Yondu has pledged this talent and his many other skills to the Guardians of the Galaxy—to fight the Badoon and similar oppressors across the cosmos in the name of his ancestors.

Savage Awakening

After the Badoon were defeated, Yondu headed for one of the few pieces of woodland left on Earth. With his own people killed by the Badoon, he wondered whether it was his time to die, too. Then he was attacked by a savage human. Defending himself, Yondu knew that if he had truly wanted to die, he would not have fought to live. He therefore determined to seek his destiny with the Guardians.

"More than once I have felled a foe not by my *aim*... but by my *whistle*..."

YONDU

ORIGIN

Born and raised on Centauri-IV—the first planet to be colonized by humans outside the Solar System—Yondu spent his early years living a simple existence as part of the native Zatoan tribe. He grew up to be an expert hunter but, like all Zatoans, had no time for technology. Yondu's hunting skills were his salvation when a Badoon invasion force slaughtered the rest of his people. When he was captured and taken to Earth, he escaped along with another prisoner: astronaut Vance Astro. The pair then forged an alliance with their fellow freedom fighters Charlie-27 and Martinex.

PRIMAL FORCE

Primitive and spiritual, Yondu is burdened with the knowledge that he is the last of the Centaurians. Yet, instead of being crushed by this weight, he has channeled his despair into the fight against the Badoon—and into protecting the galaxy alongside his fellow Guardians. An expert with primitive weapons, he is especially proficient with his bow and arrow. Molded from Yaka—a metal found only on Centauri-IV—Yondu's arrows can be sonically controlled in flight by whistling.

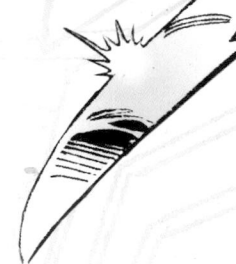

As well as his bow, Yondu wields razor-sharp knives forged from the same Yaka metal as his arrows.

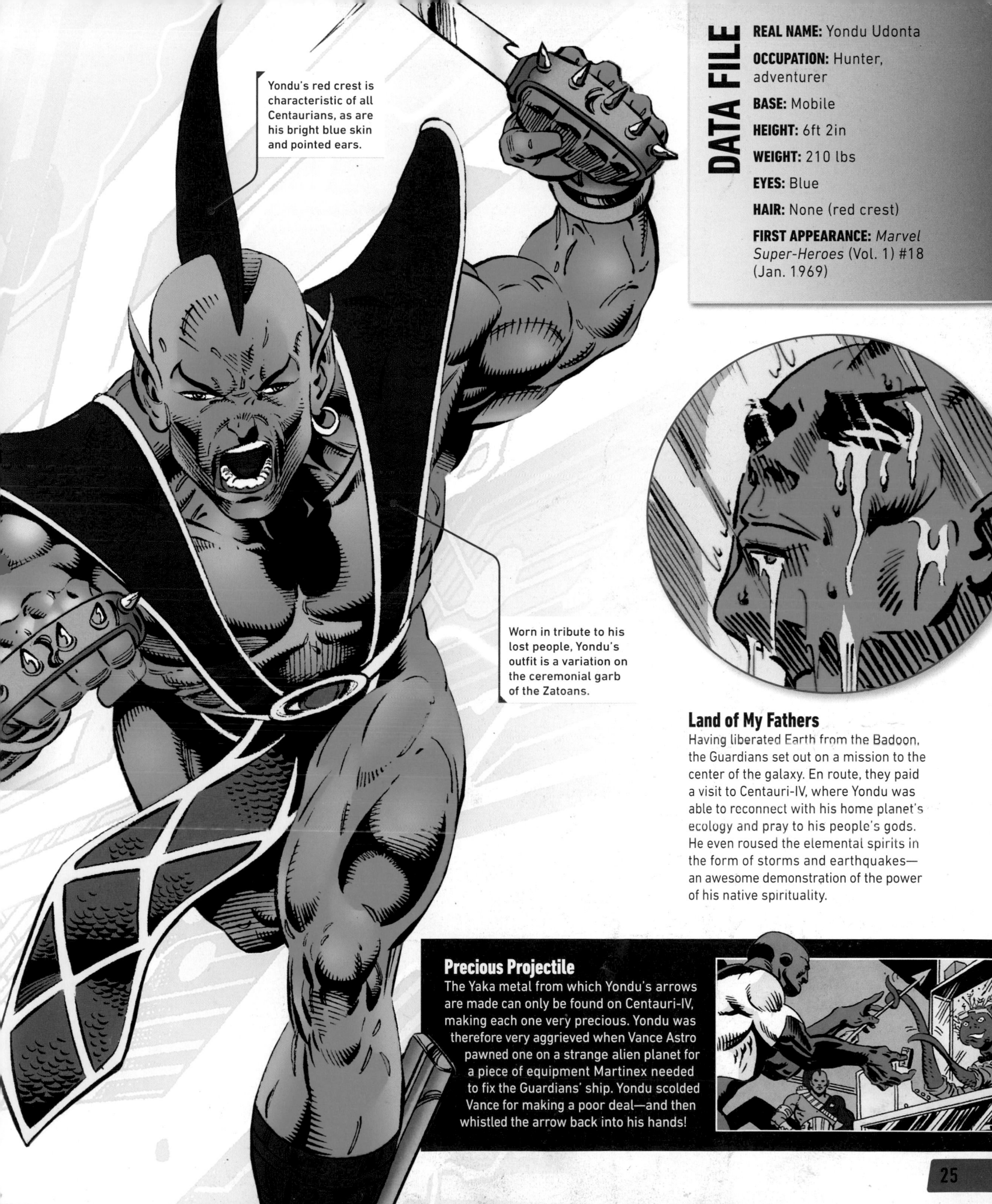

Yondu's red crest is characteristic of all Centaurians, as are his bright blue skin and pointed ears.

DATA FILE

REAL NAME: Yondu Udonta

OCCUPATION: Hunter, adventurer

BASE: Mobile

HEIGHT: 6ft 2in

WEIGHT: 210 lbs

EYES: Blue

HAIR: None (red crest)

FIRST APPEARANCE: *Marvel Super-Heroes* (Vol. 1) #18 (Jan. 1969)

Worn in tribute to his lost people, Yondu's outfit is a variation on the ceremonial garb of the Zatoans.

Land of My Fathers

Having liberated Earth from the Badoon, the Guardians set out on a mission to the center of the galaxy. En route, they paid a visit to Centauri-IV, where Yondu was able to reconnect with his home planet's ecology and pray to his people's gods. He even roused the elemental spirits in the form of storms and earthquakes—an awesome demonstration of the power of his native spirituality.

Precious Projectile

The Yaka metal from which Yondu's arrows are made can only be found on Centauri-IV, making each one very precious. Yondu was therefore very aggrieved when Vance Astro pawned one on a strange alien planet for a piece of equipment Martinex needed to fix the Guardians' ship. Yondu scolded Vance for making a poor deal—and then whistled the arrow back into his hands!

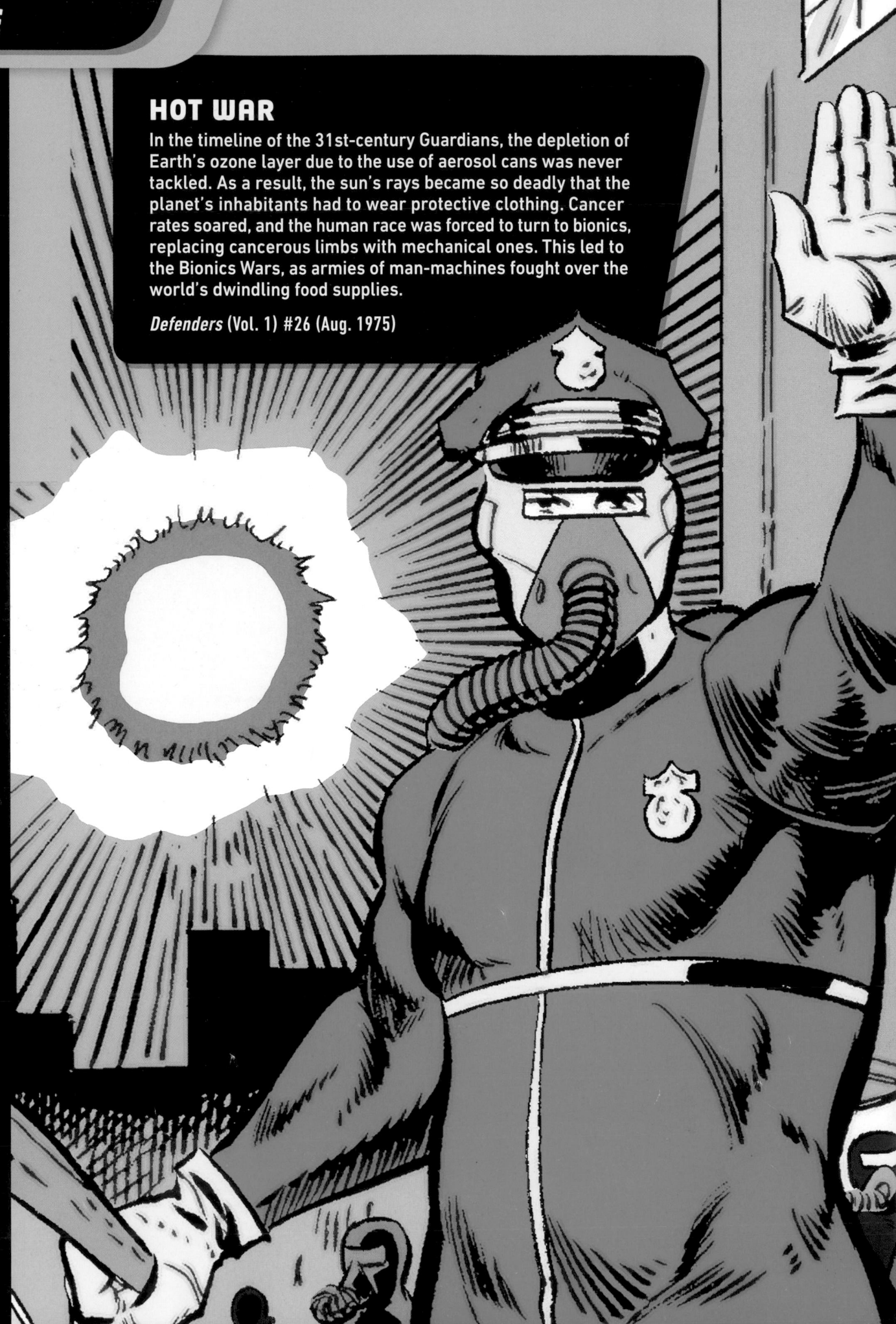

A SHORT HISTORY OF ONE FUTURE

HOT WAR

In the timeline of the 31st-century Guardians, the depletion of Earth's ozone layer due to the use of aerosol cans was never tackled. As a result, the sun's rays became so deadly that the planet's inhabitants had to wear protective clothing. Cancer rates soared, and the human race was forced to turn to bionics, replacing cancerous limbs with mechanical ones. This led to the Bionics Wars, as armies of man-machines fought over the world's dwindling food supplies.

Defenders (Vol. 1) #26 (Aug. 1975)

It is said that future is unwritten—that unlimited potential futures await mankind. In one of those myriad possible futures, the Guardians of the Galaxy will come together to defend the citizens of the 31st century from the Brotherhood of Badoon. The road to that particular future will see humanity rise and fall again and again.

MARS ATTACKS!

After a nuclear disaster left half of North America uninhabitable, the Bionics Wars ended and humanity came to its senses. The first Confederation of Nations formed, and mankind began to rebuild. The peace was short-lived, however, as Earth was invaded by Mars. Martian war machines conquered the planet, razing the recovering cities. But a resistance formed against the invaders—the Freemen, led by the fearsome Killraven. By 2025, the Martians had been defeated.

Killraven (Vol. 2) #1 (Dec. 2002)

RISING FROM THE WRECKAGE

Centuries of barbarism followed the defeat of the Martians. Wars raged between feudal Techno-Barons over ownership of the Moon. Finally, in the year 2525, the last Techno-Baron—the tyrant Kwaal—was executed. A World Federation was established, and mankind set out for the stars. Genetically adapted humans colonized the solar system's planets, from scorching Mercury to ice-cold Pluto. A vast fleet of starships was built, and by 2960 mankind had made contact with the inhabitants of the nearest star system, the Zaloans of Centauri-IV.

Defenders (Vol. 1) #26 (Aug. 1975)

ROCKET FROM THE PAST

In the year 3000, every human colony and numerous alien races came together as the United Federation. Six years later, a rocket landed on Centauri-IV bearing a human astronaut. This was Major Vance Astro, who had been placed in suspended animation one thousand years before and dispatched on a mission of interstellar exploration. Ironically, humans had beaten him to his destination by almost 50 years, and were there on Centauri-IV to greet him.

Defenders (Vol. 1) #26 (Aug. 1975)

RISE OF THE GUARDIANS

Mankind had reached a golden era of peace and prosperity—yet it was not to last. In the year 3007, civilization was again crushed by an alien invader, as the Badoon conquered Earth and its colonies. The survivors were turned into zombie-like slaves or imprisoned in labor camps, but a team of brave souls from across the colonies would come to the aid of a desperate humanity—the Guardians of the Galaxy!

Defenders (Vol. 1) #26 (Aug. 1975)

THE BADOON

In the year 3007, Earth and its colonies were conquered by the baleful Brotherhood of Badoon. In the years that followed, the Guardians of the Galaxy led the fightback against these alien oppressors, along the way learning much about their history and customs.

> "Cut them down! Your Lordsire commands!"
> LORDSIRE DRANG

BROTHERHOOD OF BADOON

The Badoon are aggressive reptiles bent on conquest. One of the earliest recorded encounters with them came when the Silver Surfer prevented their Brotherhood from invading Earth in the modern era. One thousand years on, they had grown sufficiently in strength to conquer Earth and all of its colonies. They killed millions and enslaved the rest, turning many into mindless "Zoms". An exclusively male order of Badoon, the Brotherhood sees the female of their own species as little more than breeding stock.

SISTERHOOD OF BADOON

The Guardians became aware of the Sisterhood of Badoon when Vance Astro and Valkyrie of the Defenders teleported to the Badoon homeworld. They were attacked by savage female Badoon in a swamp, before encountering Starhawk for the first time. He guided them to Venesia, the city of the Sisterhood of Badoon. There, Queen Tolaria, leader of the peaceful Sisterhood, explained how the Brotherhood subjugated the women of their species, confining them to the homeworld. Only once in a Badoon's lifespan do males and females mate, becoming savage when they do so—which accounted for the female Badoon in the swamp.

LORDSIRE DROOM

When the Defenders accompanied the Guardians to the year 3015, they ran afoul of Badoon Lordsire Droom. He disrupted the teleport systems of the Guardians' ship—sending members of both teams to far-flung planets—while his Badoon troops captured Charlie-27, Martinex, and Defender Nighthawk. It fell to Vance Astro and Defender Valkyrie to save the day, after which Nighthawk felled Droom with a single punch.

LORDSIRE DRANG

When Vance Astro and Yondu were first caught by the Badoon in the year 3007, they were brought before Drang, commander of the conquered Solar System. However, they escaped his clutches and joined up with Charlie-27 and Martinex to form the Guardians. Seven years later, aided by Earth's resistance—along with Captain America, Sharon Carter of S.H.I.E.L.D., and the Thing of the Fantastic Four—the Guardians finally defeated Drang and freed New York from his clutches.

QUEEN TOLARIA

Confined to the homeworld, Queen Tolaria of the Sisterhood of Badoon was shocked to learn that the Brotherhood had built an interstellar empire, having assumed that both female and male Badoon had evolved along similarly peaceful lines. At the climax of mankind's rebellion against the Badoon, Starhawk brought the Queen to Earth, and she promised to remove the meddlesome Brotherhood from Earth forever.

MONSTERS OF BADOON

These mindless, hulking beasts are the Badoon's ultimate weapons on the ground, with incredible strength and metal jaws and teeth. When Captain America, Sharon Carter, and the Thing used Doctor Doom's time machine to travel to the year 3014, the super-strong Thing was knocked out by a single Badoon Monster!

HEROES ACROSS HISTORY

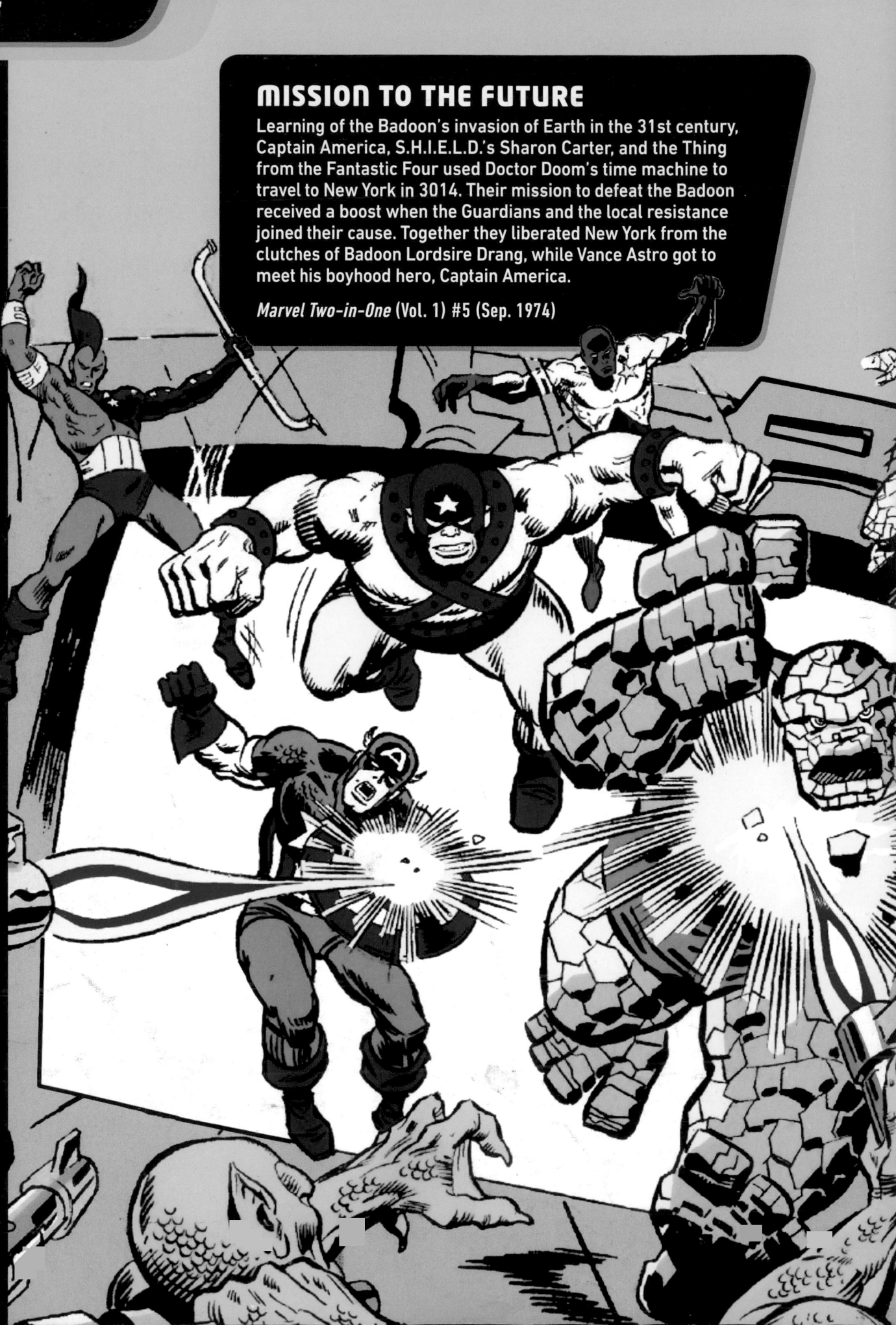

MISSION TO THE FUTURE

Learning of the Badoon's invasion of Earth in the 31st century, Captain America, S.H.I.E.L.D.'s Sharon Carter, and the Thing from the Fantastic Four used Doctor Doom's time machine to travel to New York in 3014. Their mission to defeat the Badoon received a boost when the Guardians and the local resistance joined their cause. Together they liberated New York from the clutches of Badoon Lordsire Drang, while Vance Astro got to meet his boyhood hero, Captain America.

Marvel Two-in-One (Vol. 1) #5 (Sep. 1974)

The 31st-century Guardians encountered heroes from their own past many times. Sometimes those heroes traveled to the far future; on other occasions Vance Astro, Charlie-27, Martinex, Yondu, Starhawk, and Nikki found themselves in the distant past. Each time, alliances were forged, and friendships made.

BACK TO THE PAST

The 31st-century Guardians traveled back in time in their ship, the _Captain America_, on the trail of a powerful Badoon device. Unfortunately, the device was used as a nest by an electric eel, which mutated into the man-eel! With the aid of the Defenders—Doctor Strange, Hulk, Valkyrie, and Nighthawk—Eelar was captured and returned to its original state. Meanwhile, Martinex encountered a present-day Earth boy—Vance Astrovik, Vance Astro's younger self!

Giant-Size Defenders
(Vol. 1) #5 (Jul. 1975)

DEFENDERS OF TOMORROW

To assist them in their battle against the Badoon, the Defenders accompanied the Guardians on their return to the Earth of 3015. However, Badoon Lordsire Droom disrupted the Guardians' time-travel technology, sending various Guardians and Defenders to distant planets. On the swamp world Lotiara, Vance Astro and Valkyrie learned of the existence of the peaceful Sisterhood of Badoon, and met Starhawk, who would soon become a Guardian himself. Meanwhile, on the Goozootian homeworld, Yondu and the Hulk were forced to compete in gladiator games!

Defenders (Vol. 1) #26–29 (Aug.–Dec. 1975)

GALACTIC THUNDER

While trying to stop a nuclear reactor overloading, Thor was flung into the far future. There, he floated in space, frozen, until he was found by the Guardians. Together, they tackled the villain whose tampering had resulted in Thor's time-displacement—the cyborg Korvac. Though the Guardians and the God of Thunder defeated Korvac's Minions of Menace, the cyborg himself escaped by teleporting into the past.

Thor Annual
(Vol. 1) #6 (Dec. 1977)

SPECTACULAR TEAM-UP

When the Guardians traveled back in time to stop the nefarious Deterrence Research Corporation (DRC) from acquiring their future tech, they ran into Spider-Man. At first, Spidey and the Guardians fought, but then Martinex explained they were on a vital mission. The heroes then teamed up to defeat DRC thugs Hammer and Anvil. The Wall-Crawler also kept the Guardians' presence in his era secret by destroying the photographs that had been taken of them.

Marvel Team-Up (Vol. 1) #86 (Oct. 1979)

STARHAWK

Starhawk is, in his own words, "one who knows." A blazing bright cosmic being composed of two people, he is gifted with precognition, guiding the Guardians of the Galaxy toward what he determines to be their destiny. Because of this, his motives are not always discernible—and his actions can appear questionable, even to his teammates.

ORIGIN

Long ago, on the planet Arcturus IV, a mutant baby was discovered by Ogord, a member of the warlike, mutant-slaying Reavers of Arcturus. Ogord adopted the boy, calling him Stakar and raising him alongside his own daughter, Aleta. As a youth, Stakar always felt there was something missing in his life, and so he began to explore the forbidden areas of Arcturus. He found the hidden temple of the Hawk God, and was followed there by Aleta. She was taken over by the robot embodiment of the Hawk God and launched into a power-crazed rampage. To stop this, Stakar merged his mind with Aleta's, causing an explosion. This fused the pair together permanently, turning them into one cosmic being: Starhawk!

Starhawk's retractable wings are built in to his suit. They harness the power of solar winds, augmenting his innate ability to fly.

Guiding Light

The first Guardian to encounter Starhawk was Vance Astro. He and Valkyrie of the Defenders found themselves on a strange planet, surrounded by savage female Badoon, when Starhawk made himself known to them. The planet turned out to be the homeworld of the Badoon, and Starhawk was there to deliver the pair to Tolaria, Queen of the Sisterhood of Badoon. Why he did this only became clear later, when Tolaria intervened on the Guardians' side in the final battle to free Earth from the Badoon.

> "I am the **light**... and the **giver** of light... but I can also steal that light **away**."
>
> STARHAWK

POWER OF THE HAWK

Mysterious and enigmatic, Starhawk is part prophet, part demigod. Created when Stakar and Aleta Ogord were merged with the spirit of the Arcturan people's Hawk God, he is possessed of vast power, including knowledge of the future. How he uses that power is often a source of great frustration to his fellow Guardians, who can feel manipulated into doing his bidding. To add to the ambiguity around their teammate, Starhawk also has a habit of transforming into Aleta and back again.

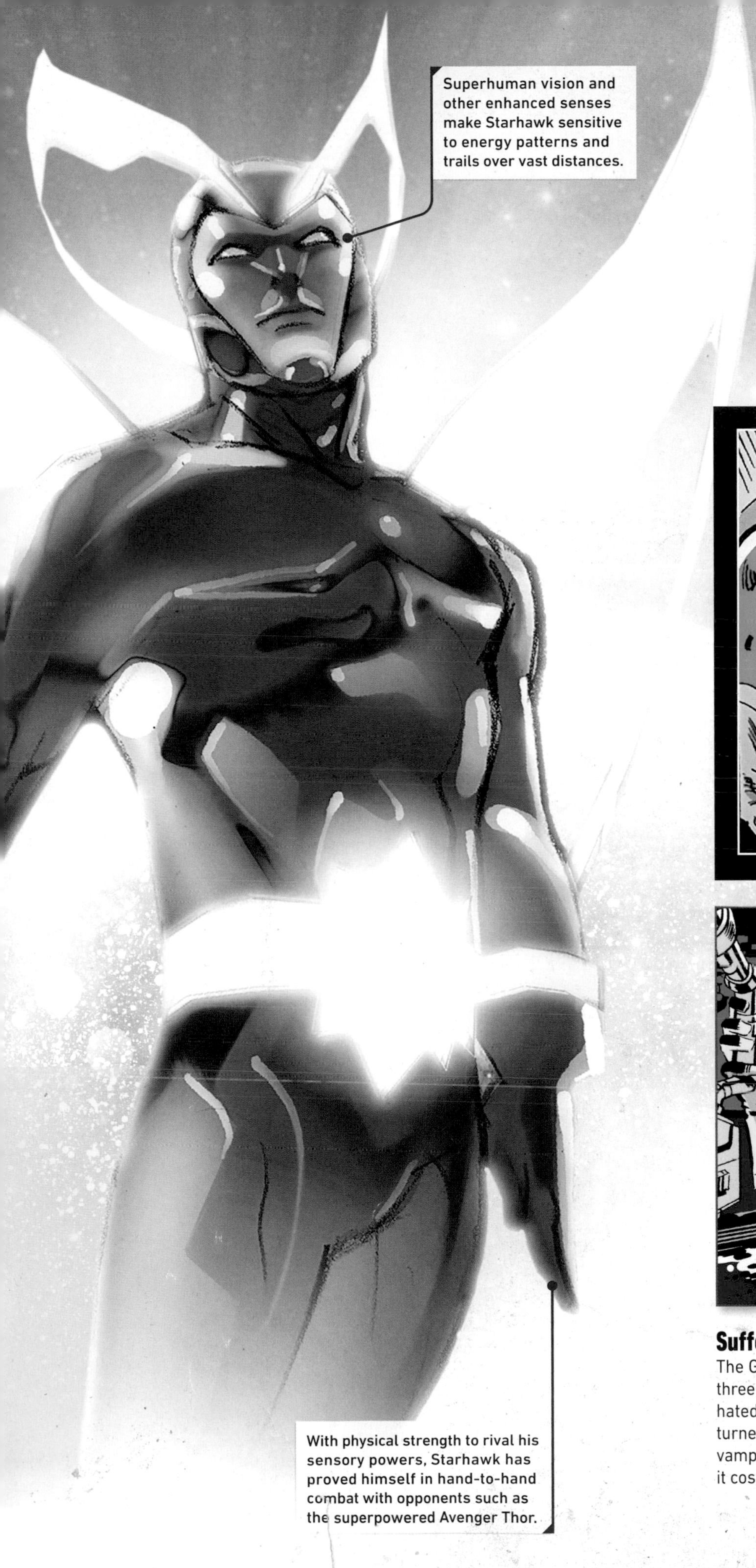

Superhuman vision and other enhanced senses make Starhawk sensitive to energy patterns and trails over vast distances.

With physical strength to rival his sensory powers, Starhawk has proved himself in hand-to-hand combat with opponents such as the superpowered Avenger Thor.

DATA FILE

REAL NAMES: Stakar and Aleta Ogord

OCCUPATION: Cosmic protector

BASE: Mobile

HEIGHT: 6ft 4in

WEIGHT: 450 lbs

EYES: White

HAIR: Red

FIRST APPEARANCE: *Defenders* (Vol. 1) #27 (Sep. 1975)

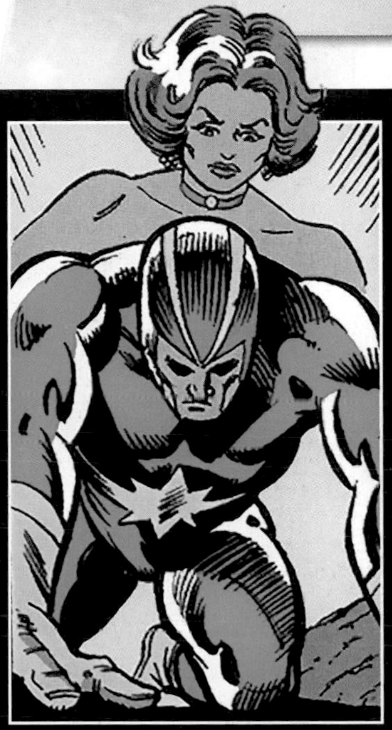

Two into One

Not long after Starhawk joined the Guardians of the Galaxy, he began to reveal his dual nature. First to experience this was Vance Astro, who was bemused when he bumped into Aleta just after Starhawk turned into her. Vance was left wondering just who the mystery woman could be. Later, Martinex saw Starhawk change into Aleta. She revealed that she and Starhawk had three children, and they were in danger!

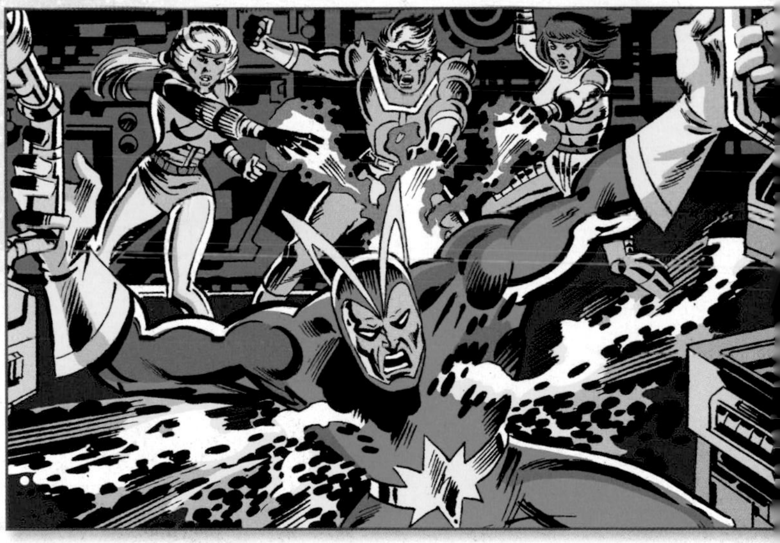

Suffer Little Children

The Guardians learned Starhawk and Aleta had children when all three youngsters were kidnapped by Ogord, their grandfather. Ogord hated Starhawk for refusing to ally with the Arcturan Reavers, and turned the children against him, using their innate power as psychic vampires. The Guardians broke Ogord's control over the youths, but it cost all three of them their lives, leaving Starhawk devastated.

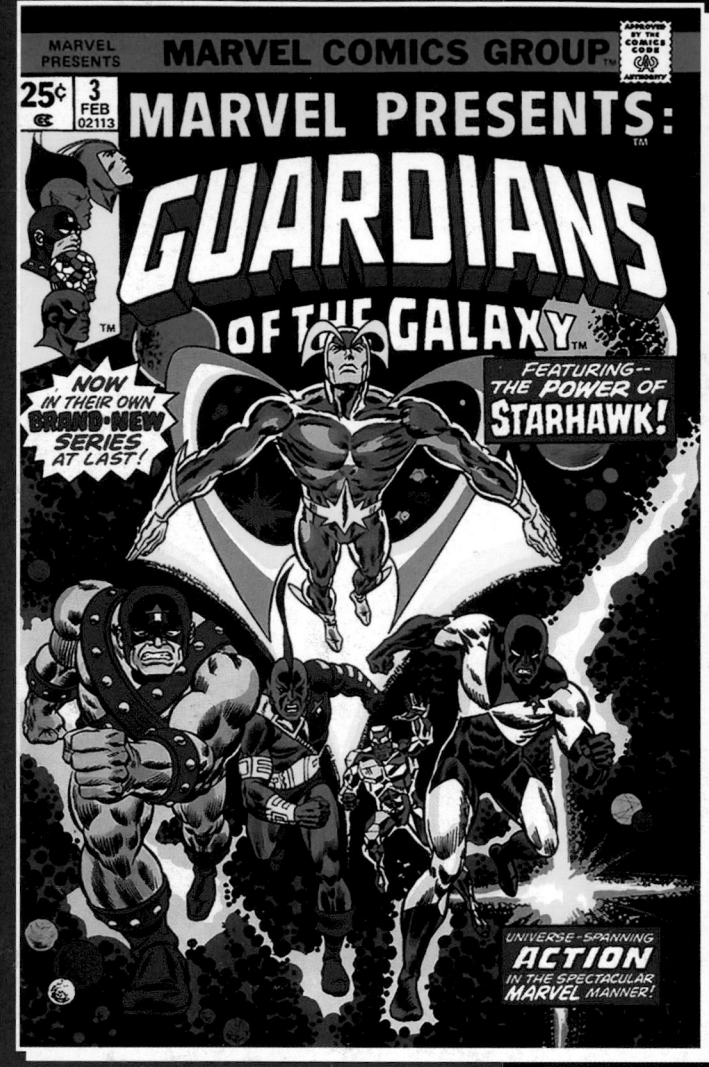

MARVEL PRESENTS:
GUARDIANS OF THE GALAXY (Vol. 1) #3

AS THE BADOON WAR COMES TO AN END, CAN EARTH AND THE GUARDIANS FIND PEACE?

Earth, 3015. For eight long years, the Guardians of the Galaxy have led the resistance against the occupying Brotherhood of Badoon. Now, on the streets of New Moscow, the final reckoning is underway, as the Guardians and a motley band of human slaves battle the alien oppressors to regain control of the planet.

FEBRUARY 1976

MAIN CHARACTERS
Vance Astro • Charlie-27 • Martinex • Yondu • Starhawk

SUPPORTING CHARACTERS
Koord—Badoon Governor of Sol III • Queen Tolaria

MAIN LOCATIONS
New Moscow • Berlin • Los Angeles • San Francisco

1 As New Moscow burns, the struggle for control of Earth nears an end. With help from Vance Astro's mental powers, Charlie-27's physical strength, and Yondu's Yaka Arrows, the tide finally turns humanity's way. Koord, the Badoon Governor of Sol III (alias Earth), faces the Guardians' leader Martinex—who executes him.

2 Charlie-27 proclaims Earth free! The surviving Badoon are all rounded up by their former slaves—but as Starhawk looks on, the humans decide to exact revenge by maiming and even murdering their prisoners. The mysterious Guardian silently vows that they will do neither, and signals a fleet of starships in orbit to land. Charlie-27 is furious and yells that Starhawk has betrayed the Guardians—and must have been a Badoon agent all along!

*"We've done it! The last of the Badoon are being rounded up in the streets! The Earth is **free**!"*

CHARLIE-27

3 The occupants of the newly arrived ships emerge. It is the peaceful Sisterhood of Badoon and their leader, Queen Tolaria. She explains that they have come to take away the aggressive male members of their species. However, the humans are having none of it, and start attacking both the male and female Badoon. Once again, Starhawk intervenes, with a blinding burst of energy that stops the fighting. The Sisterhood takes its males and departs—a scenario that repeats across the globe.

4 A week later, the Badoon are gone. With no reason to stay together, the Guardians go their separate ways. In the months that follow, each seeks a fresh purpose. Yondu retreats to the wilderness, but cannot find solace. Martinex heads to Berlin to assist with tech salvage, but finds only prejudice. Charlie-27 turns his strength to rebuilding San Francisco, but is brought low by insults about his appearance.

5 In a San Francisco bar, Vance Astro tortures himself by watching an exotic dancer. Trapped in his containment suit, he will never again feel a woman's touch. He brawls with a drunk, then returns to the Guardians' ship... where he finds Martinex, Charlie-27, and Yondu. All have decided there is nothing for them on Earth. Starhawk arrives, and suggests that they embark on a new mission—a journey to the center of the galaxy...

Genetically engineered to withstand the harsh conditions on Mercury, Nikki's hair is always aflame as it burns off her excess heat.

Survival Specialist

After escaping Mercury and its Badoon invaders, Nikki piloted her craft until the generator gave out. Spotting a derelict cargo vessel, Nikki boarded it, only to find the crew dead, killed by a failed life-support system. Nikki commandeered the ship and spent the next seven years surviving all alone. In that time, she educated herself, reading the ship's library twice over.

Nikki's skin is scalding to the touch and she must take cold baths in order to touch normal humans safely.

Trial by Fire

After joining the Guardians, Nikki's greatest test came when the galaxy was threatened by a gigantic cosmic being known as the Topographical Man. Nikki submitted to a mystical process that saw her body set aflame in order for her soul to ascend and oppose the entity. She defeated it with some psychic help from Vance Astro, leaving the pair with a new connection.

FLAME RESISTANCE

When 18-year-old Nikki teamed up with the Guardians of the Galaxy, she brought youthfulness, energy, and a sense of fun to the team. All these qualities were much needed by the Guardians, but just as valuable were the skills Nikki had developed while on her own in space for seven long years—evading the enemy and surviving against the odds. Since joining the team she has displayed a talent for handling firearms, while her Mercurian heritage gives her the ability to withstand extremes of heat.

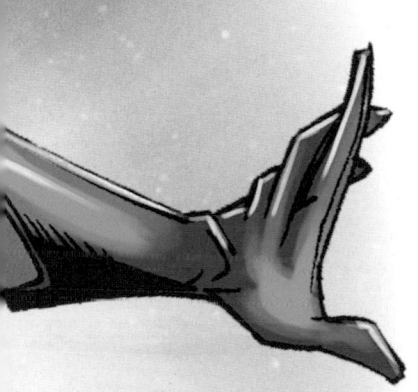

ORIGIN

Nikki was just 11 years old when the Badoon crushed the Mercurian mining colony that she called home. Her mom and dad were cut down before her eyes, swiftly followed by the rest of the colonists. Unwilling to meet the same fate, Nikki made her escape in her family's private spacecraft. But while she had transport, she had no set destination —correctly reasoning that if the Badoon had conquered Mercury, it was a safe bet they'd conquered Earth, too. Eventually her ship's generator blew, and Nikki was left adrift...

> "**I'm** as qualified to guard the galaxy as any of you clowns. Maybe **more** so."
>
> — NIKKI

Romantic Spark

After the ordeal she went through to defeat the Topographical Man, Nikki shared a tender moment with Vance Astro, briefly holding hands with him. Later, her impetuous nature led her to steal a kiss from Vance. Trapped inside his containment suit, unable to feel another's skin, Vance accused her of mocking him. Nikki countered that she thought their situation was a romantic one—"a guy who'd turn to dust for love of li'l ole me!"

NIKKI

Flame-haired and hot-headed, young Mercury colonist Nikki has been a vital and exuberant addition to the Guardians. Encountered by chance after the defeat of the Badoon, she joined the Guardians' mission to the center of the galaxy, swiftly proving her worth as a raw but enthusiastic fighter.

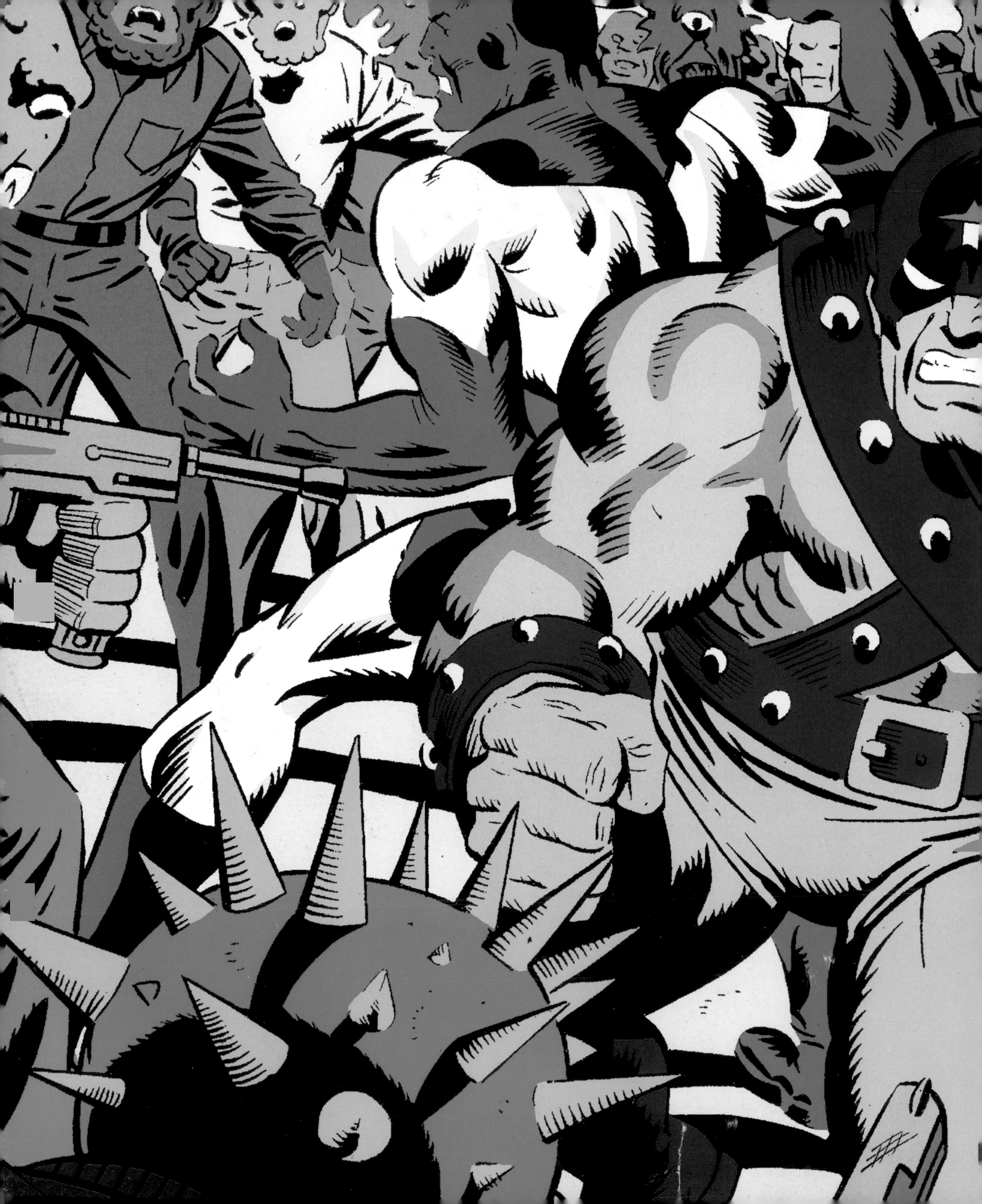

MARVEL PRESENTS (VOL. 1) #5
JUNE 1976

On a voyage to the center of the galaxy, the
Guardians' ship sustained damage, forcing the team
to teleport to a nearby planet while Martinex worked
on repairs. The bizarre world—which bore a striking
resemblance to 20th-century Earth—turned out to
be a planetary asylum. Its alien inmates became
violent, prompting a swift retreat by the Guardians.

Michael Korvac was a 31st-century computer technician embittered by his superiors always overlooking his abilities. When the Badoon conquered Earth and its colonies, Korvac became a willing collaborator. He was put in charge of the computer systems of entire planets, but collapsed due to overwork. To punish him, the Badoon replaced his lower body with a special systems module, turning him into a living computer. Korvac overcame his masters and escaped, seeking a way to conquer the galaxy for himself.

Menace to the Galaxy

To assist in his schemes to take control of the universe, Korvac established a base on a barren planetoid and assembled a team of mercenaries from across the galaxy—his Minions of Menace. However, his plans were foiled by the Guardians and Thor, who had been transported to the 31st century by accident. Teleporting away, Korvac swore vengeance.

"All shall pay homage to the glory of Korvac!"

KORVAC

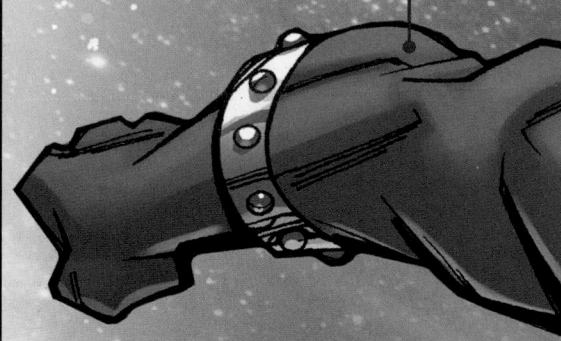

Korvac's clothing predates his cyborg conversion, being only a slight variation of the 31st-century suit he wore when he was a servant of the Badoon.

The computer unit that replaced Korvac's legs enabled him to fly even before he acquired his godlike powers.

Love Conquers All

After teleporting back in time, Korvac siphoned knowledge and power from the world-devourer Galactus, becoming virtually a god. This drew the attention of the cosmic being known as the Collector, who feared that Korvac would eventually pose a threat to him. The Collector sent his own daughter, Carina, to spy on him, but, Korvac and Carina fell in love, and she chose to combine her power with his.

KORVAC

Michael Korvac has been a recurring thorn in the side of the Guardians of the Galaxy. His pursuit of power has driven him to seek galactic supremacy in different eras, pitting him against the Guardians, the Avengers, and other heroes. It is a quest that has seen him elevated from lowly technician to something approaching godhood.

Despite his distinctive cyborg physiology, Korvac can easily disguise himself as fully human using the cosmic power that he siphoned from Galactus.

DATA FILE

REAL NAME: Michael Korvac

OCCUPATION: Would-be god

BASE: Mobile

HEIGHT: Variable

WEIGHT: Unknown

EYES: Blue

HAIR: Blond

FIRST APPEARANCE: *Giant-Size Defenders* (Vol. 1) #3 (Jan. 1975)

IN PURSUIT OF POWER

Transformed into a brilliant cyborg by the Badoon, Michael Korvac was consumed by an insatiable lust for power. His dreams of conquest have seen him travel through time in search of ways to rule the universe. They have also put him at odds with the Guardians, who have pursued him across the ages in order to stop schemes.

Korvac Lives!

Though Korvac was eventually killed in an encounter with the Guardians and the Avengers, that was not the last of him. Not only did his consciousness survive to infect some of his descendants, he was also resurrected by cosmic games-player the Grandmaster, who made Korvac and the Silver Surfer fight for his amusement.

THE KORVAC SAGA

When Thor was flung into the 31st century, he and the Guardians fought tyrannical cyborg Michael Korvac. His dreams of conquest thwarted, Korvac then teleported to the past, where he drew godlike powers from the world-devourer Galactus...

TWO TEAMS COLLIDE

In the present day, the Avengers investigate a huge space station that has suddenly appeared in Earth's orbit. There, Beast encounters the Guardians of the 31st century—and attacks them, believing them to be invaders! Captain America and Thor, who have met the Guardians before, set him straight. The Guardians have tracked Korvac to this era, and are out to find him before he does anything to affect the future!

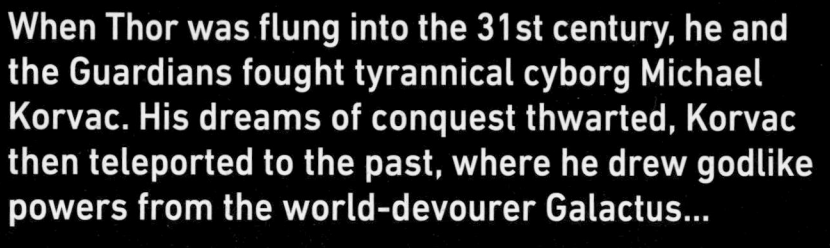

The Avengers (Vol.1) #167 (Jan. 1978)
The Avenger Beast lashes out at Charlie-27, having mistaken him for an alien invader!

The Avengers (Vol.1) #168 (Feb. 1978) *Korvac reels through planes of existence after a mighty blow from Starhawk's fist.*

The Avengers (Vol.1) #173 (Jul. 1978) *Korvac contemplates the nature of Eternity from the comfort of his living room.*

BATTLE IS JOINED

Now almost omnipotent, Korvac has taken on human form. He has fallen in love with a model called Carina Walters, and the pair has set up home in Forest Hills, a suburb of Queens in New York. When they are traced by the Guardians' Starhawk, Korvac tries to keep his location secret. In a titanic struggle that rages across realities, Korvac kills Starhawk. He then recreates him in a way that means Starhawk can't see or hear him, thereby protecting his human cover.

The Avengers (Vol.1) #177 (Nov. 1978)
In suburban Forest Hills, Korvac and Carina stand united against the Guardians and Avengers.

SHOWDOWN IN SUBURBIA

Using the heightened senses of Moondragon—and with the help of Captain Marvel, who has detected disturbances in space—the Avengers follow clues that lead them to Forest Hills. With Starhawk by their side, the heroes converge on Korvac's home, only to find it inhabited by an ordinary man. But when Starhawk says he cannot see who the Avengers are talking with, they realize they are being tricked. With Carina by his side, Korvac declares war on them all!

KORVAC ATTACKS!

Martinex, Charlie-27, Nikki Gold, and Yondu join the Avengers' battle with Korvac. Korvac demonstrates his power by destroying the Guardians' space station, killing Vance Astro, who is on board. One by one, Korvac begins to kill Guardians and Avengers and is winning the fight—until the combined might of Starhawk, Vision, Iron Man, and Thor stuns him. Reeling, Korvac reaches out to his beloved Carina for strength. Sensing her horror at the carnage, Korvac uses the last of his energy to restore to life all those he has killed, and then dies.

"Your meddling heroics have destroyed the hopes of a universe, the dreams of a god!"
KORVAC

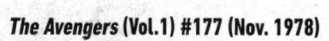
The Avengers (Vol.1) #177 (Nov. 1978)
Korvac's immense power reduces the Guardians' space station to a flaming ball of 31st-century scrap metal.

In 1990, after two decades of guest appearances and short runs in other comics, the Guardians of the Galaxy got their own series. With it came new threats, new team members, a vastly expanded universe to explore, and a kinetic new look, courtesy of writer/ artist Jim Valentino.

GUARDIANS OF THE FUTURE

GUARDIANS OF THE GALAXY (VOL. 1) #6 (NOV. 1990)
With the Guardians' help, Vance Astro acquires an
iconic piece of equipment—Captain America's
thousand-year-old shield!

GUARDIANS OF THE GALAXY ANNUAL (VOL. 1) #1 (JUL. 1991)
Aleta officially joins the team; Vance Astro's divergent
timelines explained; plus the story of how the team got
their ship, *the Captain America.*

GUARDIANS OF THE GALAXY
(VOL. 1) #13 (JUN. 1991)
The Guardians meet the Spirit of Vengeance—
the 31st-century's Ghost Rider—who later
joins the Galactic Guardians.

GUARDIANS OF THE GALAXY
(VOL. 1) #20 (JAN. 1992)
After years trapped in his containment suit,
Vance Astro gets a brand new look—and a brand
new codename: Major Victory!

JUNE 1990

MAIN CHARACTERS
Vance Astro • Starhawk/Aleta •
Charlie-27 • Martinex • Nikki

SUPPORTING CHARACTERS
Taserface • The Stark

MAIN LOCATIONS
Courg • *Freedom's Lady*—
the Guardians' starship

GUARDIANS
OF THE GALAXY
(Vol. 1) #1

THE 31ST-CENTURY GUARDIANS SEEK A LEGENDARY SHIELD, BUT FIND A DEADLY NEW ENEMY!

After a series of adventures in the 20th century alongside the Avengers, Spider-Man, and the Thing, the Guardians of the Galaxy (Major Vance Astro, Charlie-27, Martinex, Yondu, Nikki, and Starhawk/Aleta) return to the year 3017. On his home planet, Yondu discovers the Book of Antag, a mysterious tome containing strange prophecies.

1 Yondu finds a chapter in the Book of Antag that describes a colorful disk with the power to grant its possessor invincibility in battle. Though most of the team dismiss this as superstition, Vance Astro is convinced that the disk is the long-lost shield of Captain America. Vance persuades the Guardians to follow the clues to the location of the disk.

2 The clues in the book direct the Guardians to a string of planets that all prove to be dead ends. On one backwater world in the Bledsoe System called Courg, they come under attack from a doomsday machine that is clearly not native to the planet. They destroy the machine, but it sends a distress signal into space.

> *"Your lives are **forfeit** for having the **temerity** to harm a member of... the Stark!"*
>
> THE STARK

3 The machine's signal is received by a heavily armed and armored being named Taserface. Furious to learn that someone is trespassing on his territory, he sets out for Courg. On his arrival, he demands that the Guardians leave, before blasting Vance with the laser cannon built onto his right arm. A fierce battle ensues as the team comes to Vance's defense.

4 Eventually Taserface is felled by the combined might of Vance, Martinex, and Charlie-27. While the Guardians try to work out who Taserface is and why he attacked them, a second signal travels into space. When it is received, it tells the occupants of a vessel that their most powerful scout has been defeated.

5 Vance Astro points out that Taserface's armor and blasters are similar to those of the 20th-century Avenger Iron Man. As Nikki wonders how a far-flung alien could have gotten hold of Iron Man's ancient tech, the beings who received Taserface's signal arrive. Armored in a similar manner to Taserface, the alien newcomers declare war on the Guardians. They are the Stark!

THE STARK

When Mars attacked Earth, Tony Stark sent his Iron Man armor into space to keep it out of Martian hands. It found its way to a species who then turned themselves into the Stark.

STARK INVASION FORCE

The primitive Stark were corrupted when a rocket containing Iron Man's suits of armor crash-landed on their world. The inhabitants of this planet studied the armor and developed a technologically advanced society based upon it, coming to worship Tony Stark and naming themselves after him. Eventually, the Stark used up their own planet's resources and set out to find other worlds to plunder and enslave. This is what took them to the planet Courg, where the Guardians first encountered them.

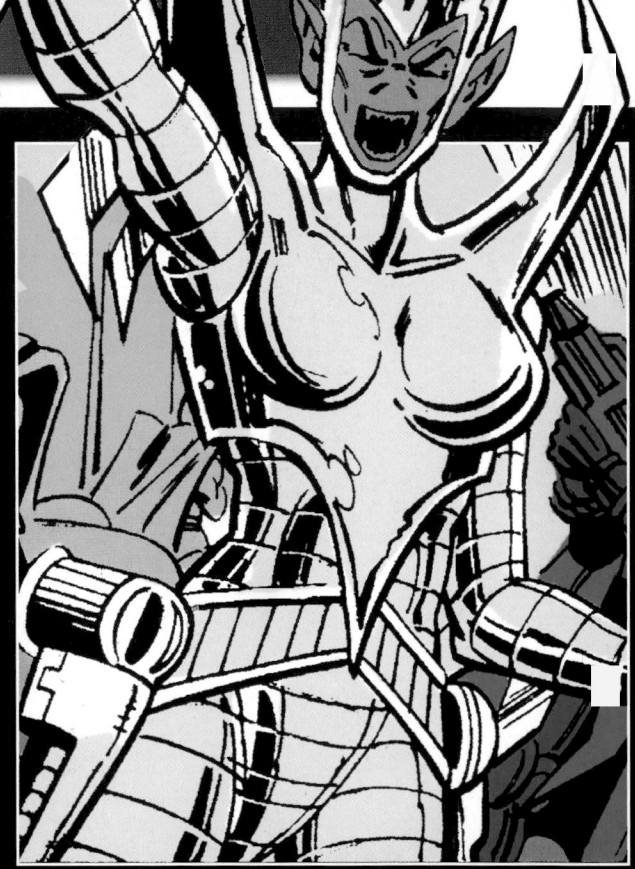

COMMANDER BLACKHAND

Stark society is organized along matriarchal lines, with the females ruling over the males. Blackhand was in charge of Stark forces on the planet Courg, directing the initial assault on the Guardians of the Galaxy before she retired to a command vessel in orbit. Considered to be an exceptional commander by High Sister and the Council of Elders, she proved herself by destroying the Guardians' ship. However, Commander Blackhand and her forces were finally defeated by the Guardians and their newfound ally, Firelord, former Herald of Galactus.

TASERFACE/OVERKILL

A cyborg scout tasked with identifying planets for plunder, Taserface was the first Stark the Guardians encountered. He attacked the team after they interfered with his machinery on the planet Courg, before calling in reinforcements. Taserface was torched by Firelord, who joined the Guardians in their fight against the Stark on Courg. The Stark retrieved their scout and took him back to their homeworld, where he was subjected to a reconstruction procedure. He emerged in a new, more heavily armored form, now going by the name of Overkill.

> "Are you prepared to **lay down your life** for the greater glory of the **Stark**?"
>
> HIGH SISTER

HIGH SISTER

The supreme leader of the Stark presides over the Council of Elders on the species' homeworld. Having entrusted the battle on Courg to Commander Blackhand, High Sister was furious when the Guardians defeated the Stark. She retrieved the only survivor of the battle—the badly burned Taserface—and had him tortured for his failures. Then, rather than have him killed, she ordered that he be taken to the reconstruction chamber. Once he was recreated as Overkill, High Sister ordered him to reclaim his lost honor.

STARK GENERAL

Directing the Stark's ground forces on Courg, the Stark General became enraged when Lieutenant Darkeyes was killed. She grew even angrier when she discovered that Darkeyes had been killed by another woman—something strictly forbidden in Stark society. The General was captured by Charlie-27 and taken aboard the Guardians' ship. When Commander Blackhand destroyed the Guardians' vessel, the Stark General was killed while teleporting from the ship to the surface of Courg.

LIEUTENANT DARKEYES

Darkeyes commanded the airborne wing of the Stark forces on the planet Courg. As soon as Charlie-27 realized that the female Stark were the ones giving the orders, he hollered at Starhawk to change into Aleta, figuring the male Stark serving under Darkeyes would be unwilling to attack her. His hunch was right, leaving Darkeyes to launch her own solo assault. Aleta killed her with a hard-light blast, prompting the Stark General to swear vengeance.

THE KORVAC QUEST

As the villainous Korvac faced defeat at the hands of the Guardians and Avengers, Galactus sent out a beam to reclaim the power Korvac stole from him. Sensing the beam's approach, Korvac transmitted his power to one of his ancestors, and then died.

*"My mind and power lives on now in **this**, the body of my **ancient ancestor**!"*

KORVAC

SOUND OF THUNDER

Using Reed Richards' device, the Guardians track Korvac's power to the year 2591, where it now inhabits Varley, a downtrodden and bitter mail supervisor at a big corporation. Reveling in his newfound power, Varley runs amok, bending reality to his will. As the Guardians struggle to contain him, they are joined by that era's Thor, the God of Thunder, who helps them to trick Varley into blasting himself with his own power. Varley crumbles to dust—but Korvac's power escapes once more.

Thor Annual (Vol. 1) #16 (Jul. 1991) Martinex, Charlie-27, and the 26th-century Thor break free from a trap set by Varley, a mail room supervisor and ancestor of Korvac.

Fantastic Four Annual (Vol. 1) #24 (Jul. 1991) Infused with the power of Korvac, Jaboa Murphy stands atop the grounded Guardians and fallen Fantastic Four!

FANTASTIC VOYAGE

In the 31st century, Starhawk senses that reality is about to unravel—and Korvac is somehow the key. The Guardians travel back in time to the period where they and the Avengers defeated Korvac, then seek out the Fantastic Four, whom Starhawk believes can help. Reed Richards of the Fantastic Four builds a device to track Korvac's power, and locates it in Australia— in a young woman named Jaboa Murphy. After a fierce battle, Korvac/Murphy defeats the Guardians and the Fantastic Four; but then Korvac's essence departs, sensing the approach of Galactus' beam.

Silver Surfer Annual (Vol. 1) #4 (Jul. 1991)
*The Silver Surfer unleashes his cosmic
powers against the Guardians in defense
of his adopted home.*

Guardians of the Galaxy Annual (Vol. 1) #1 (Jul. 1991) Martinex presents
Aleta with a G-Star, signifying her membership of the Guardians.

SURFER'S PARADISE

The Guardians next pursue Korvac's power to a verdant
and peaceful planet. Its leader, Marshach, gained Korvac's
power long ago, and used it to create a paradise for his
people—and for the immensely powerful Silver Surfer, who
has made his home there. The Guardians ask Marshach
to yield his power, but the Silver Surfer intervenes, and
an almighty battle ensues. When two young children are
caught in the crossfire, Marshach reluctantly surrenders
Korvac's power. It flees once again, leaving
Marshach's world with
an uncertain future.

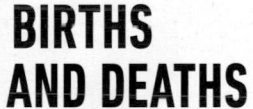

*Guardians of the Galaxy Annual
(Vol. 1) #1 (Jul. 1991)* Korvac's
father acquires his son's power.

BIRTHS
AND DEATHS

Korvac's power takes
refuge in his own father,
Jordan—whose wife, Myra,
is about to give birth to their
son! To protect his wife and
unborn child, Jordan engages
the Guardians in fierce battle,
threatening to destroy their vessel.
Starhawk transforms into his Aleta
persona to save the ship, using her
hard-light powers. The fight ends when
Michael is born and takes back his power,
killing his father in the process. All seems
lost until the Ancient One—sorcerer Doctor
Strange—and his acolyte Krugarr arrive,
responding to an SOS sent by Starhawk.

TEAM BUILDING

Doctor Strange and Krugarr magically ensnare
the newborn Korvac and transport everyone to
Galactus' Worldship. Galactus takes back his
stolen power, but leaves the fate of the now-
normal baby to the Guardians. Knowing who
the child will grow up to become, most of the
Guardians agree that he must die, but Aleta
convinces them to let him live. The team go
home to their own time, leaving Korvac's
mother swearing that she will never let her
son forget the day the Guardians killed his
father. Later, the Guardians realize Aleta
has never been officially inducted into the
team. Presenting her with a star badge,
they invite the delighted Aleta to become
a Guardian of the Galaxy.

HONORARY GUARDIANS

As the Guardians of the Galaxy continued their adventures in the 31st century, their roster expanded to include some of the heroes they met along the way. They also welcomed a hero who had been in their midst all along...

ALETA

Aleta Ogord is one of the two beings that make up Starhawk (the other being her adopted brother (and, er, ex-wife...) Stakar Ogord). She rarely made an appearance during the Guardians' war against the Badoon, but became a member of the team in her own right after playing a key role in stopping Michael Korvac's essence infecting his ancestors. Though Aleta does not possess Starhawk's powers herself, she can manipulate hard light. When she and Starhawk became two separate beings, Starhawk was forced to reabsorb her in order to save his own life. This incensed Vance Astro, who had fallen in love with Aleta. She later separated from Starhawk and became her own person again.

FIRELORD

Once a Herald of Galactus, now Protector of the Universe, Firelord helped the Guardians battle the Stark on the planet Courg, scorching their advance scout, Taserface, with cosmic flames. He never became a full member of the team, but he did accept a Guardians' communicator star. The team later came to Firelord's aid when he was attacked by the reconstructed Taserface— now called Overkill—whose new armor drained Firelord's energy. Starhawk flew Firelord into a nearby sun, replenishing his depleted power. After this, Firelord helped out the Guardians on a number of occasions.

REPLICA

Teenager Replica was a member of the human resistance on Haven, a lost colony ruled over by a mutant elite, headed by Rancor, a descendant of the X-Man Wolverine. A shape-changing Skrull, she knew that her species was hated throughout the galaxy, and learned from her parents never to reveal her true heritage. She was one of the only survivors when the resistance was all but wiped out by the Mutants, and escaped Haven by stowing away on the Guardians' ship. She later joined the team, but her Skrull nature was discovered. She later joined Martinex's Galactic Guardians.

KRUGARR

A member of the wormlike Lem species, Krugarr succeeded Doctor Strange as Sorcerer Supreme—the galaxy's greatest magical protector. His biggest challenge came when he and the Guardians faced the demonic Dormammu —a titanic struggle that led to the death of Doctor Strange. It took the combined might of Krugarr and his former apprentice Talon to banish Dormammu back to the Dark Dimension.

YELLOWJACKET

Rita DeMara became Yellowjacket in the present day, when she stole Hank Pym's Yellowjacket costume, which gave her the power to shrink and shoot disruptor stings. She was a villain at first, joining the super-powered criminal gang the Masters of Evil. This was how she crossed paths with the Guardians, who had traveled back in time from the 31st century to battle the Masters of Evil in Avengers Mansion. Yellowjacket switched sides during this battle, before following the team back to their century. She joined their ranks after shrinking to dislodge a clot in Charlie-27's throat, saving his life.

TALON

An Inhuman with razor-sharp claws and enhanced catlike abilities, Talon was the apprentice of Sorcerer Supreme Krugarr. He was on Earth in the 31st century when he met the Guardians, who were there fighting alongside new allies the Commandeers to defeat a deadly street gang known as the Punishers. When Vance Astro was shot in the head doing battle with the gang, a watching Talon ran to fetch Krugarr. As the Sorcerer Supreme worked to save Astro's life, Talon assisted the Guardians in their war against the Punishers. He went on to become a full-fledged member of the Guardians' team.

GUARDIANS OF THE GALAXY (VOL. 1) #11
APRIL 1991

To end revolutionary war on the unstable planet
Haven, Starhawk convinced freedom fighter Giraud
to bond with the cosmic entity the Phoenix. Using
the Phoenix's power, Giraud turned the tide against
Haven's oppressors, before the Phoenix consumed
the disintegrating world (once Starhawk had
teleported its population to safety).

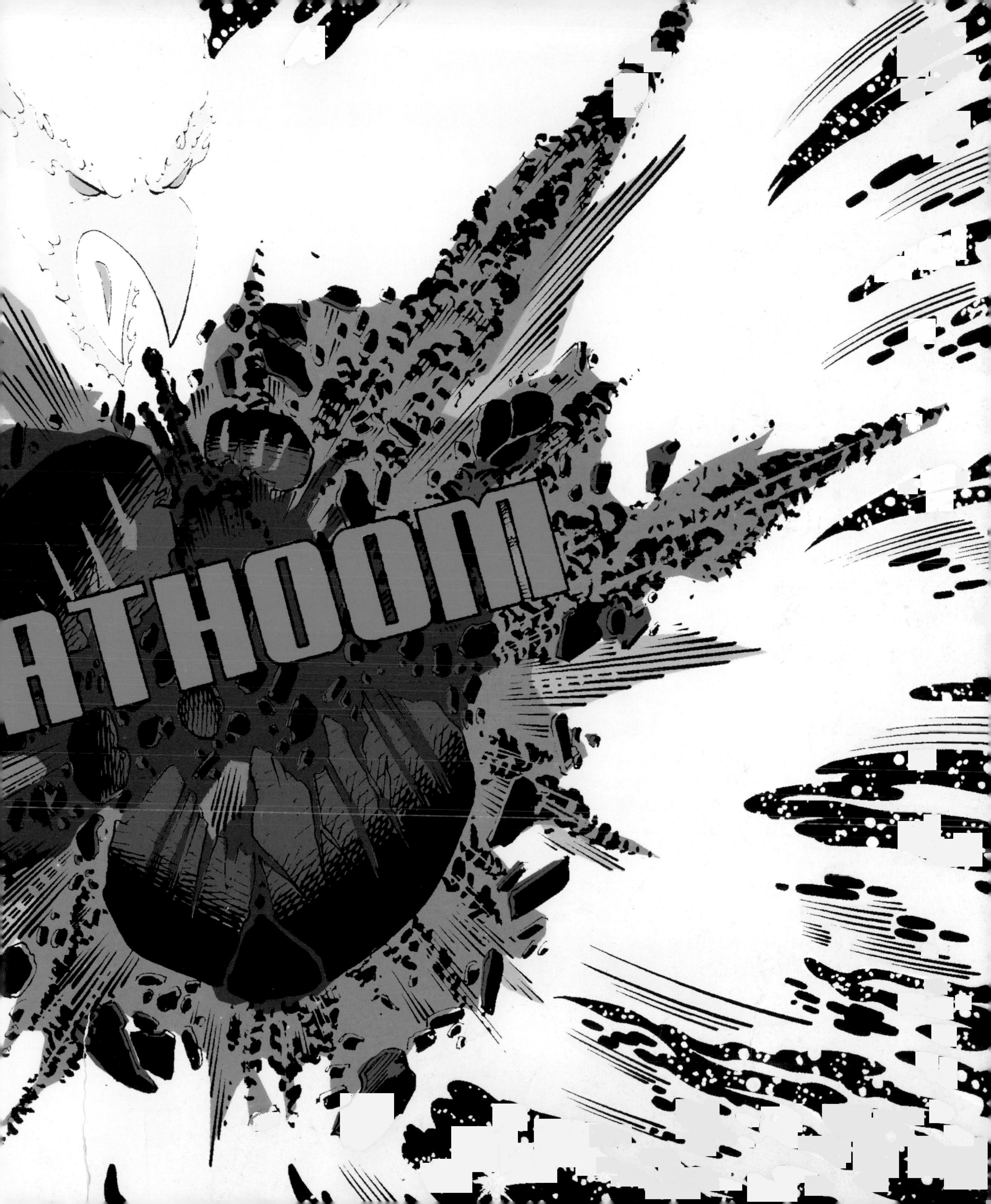
ATHOOM

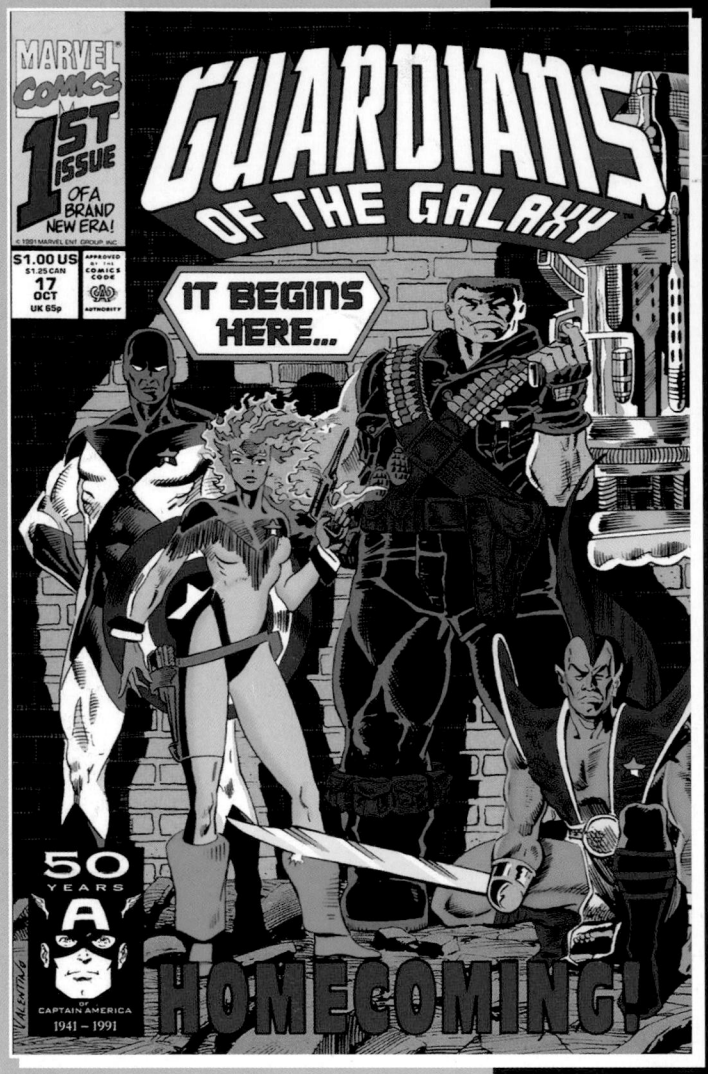

GUARDIANS OF THE GALAXY (Vol. 1) #17

THE 31ST-CENTURY GUARDIANS RETURN TO EARTH—AND ARE SHOCKED BY WHAT THEY FIND.

Four years ago, the Guardians freed Earth from Badoon rule. Not long after, the team left the planet to explore deep space. Many adventures later, they are finally returning to Earth, though in far from ideal circumstances. Angry at Starhawk's actions, Vance Astro has demanded that they go there—otherwise he'll quit the team!

OCTOBER 1991

MAIN CHARACTERS
Vance Astro • Charlie-27 • Martinex • Nikki • Yondu

SUPPORTING CHARACTERS
Tarin • Old Redd • Gabrielle • Crazy Nate • Inez • Hollywood • Belle • Punishers

MAIN LOCATIONS
New York • U.S.S. *Captain America II*—the Guardians' starship

1 Having become demerged from his "other half" Aleta, Starhawk has forcibly reabsorbed her. This has enraged Vance Astro, who is in love with Aleta. As the Guardians' ship, the U.S.S. *Captain America II*, heads toward Earth, Vance demands that the absent Starhawk be thrown off the team. The others concur, except for current team leader Martinex. Eventually, he too agrees with Vance.

2 As the ship arrives at Earth, Martinex and Nikki punch up visuals on screen. The whole team is alarmed to see the Australian city of Sydney in ruins—and then Tokyo and Beijing in a similar state. The team speculates that there must have been a war in their absence, before teleporting to New York. They find the city crumbling and cut off, with the bridges in and out of Manhattan utterly destroyed.

*"They learned about **Frank Castle** from me, didn't they?"*

VANCE ASTRO

3 Though the city seems to be deserted, that illusion is shattered when a gang of warriors leaps down from above, guns blazing. After a brief tussle, the leader of the group, which calls itself the Commandeers, presents himself. It is Tarin, who is known to the Guardians. He introduces the team to the rest of the Commandeers: Old Redd, Gabrielle, Inez, Crazy Nate, Belle, and the silent Hollywood.

4 The Commandeers take the Guardians to their HQ: the sub-sub-basement of the old Avengers Mansion! There, Tarin explains what has befallen Earth. While the Guardians were away, an entire generation became so addicted to an immersive video game that they died in front of their screens. Their offspring then took to the streets, starting bloody turf wars that lay waste to entire cities. The victors were the most violent and ruthless gang of all: the Punishers.

5 Vance realizes that the Punishers must have been inspired by his own records of a vigilante from 1,000 years ago: Frank Castle, the Punisher. The Guardians commit to joining the Commandeers' war against the Punishers—with the sole exception of Martinex. Instead he quits, intending to start a new team—the Galactic Guardians—to deal with the galaxy's bigger threats. Vance leads the remaining Guardians to the surface—and straight into the gunsights of the Punishers...

GALACTIC GUARDIANS

A sister team to the Guardians of the Galaxy, the Galactic Guardians are composed of a number of ex-Guardians along with various allies. They formed after Martinex resigned as leader of the main team, believing that the galaxy needed an expanded version of the original Guardians.

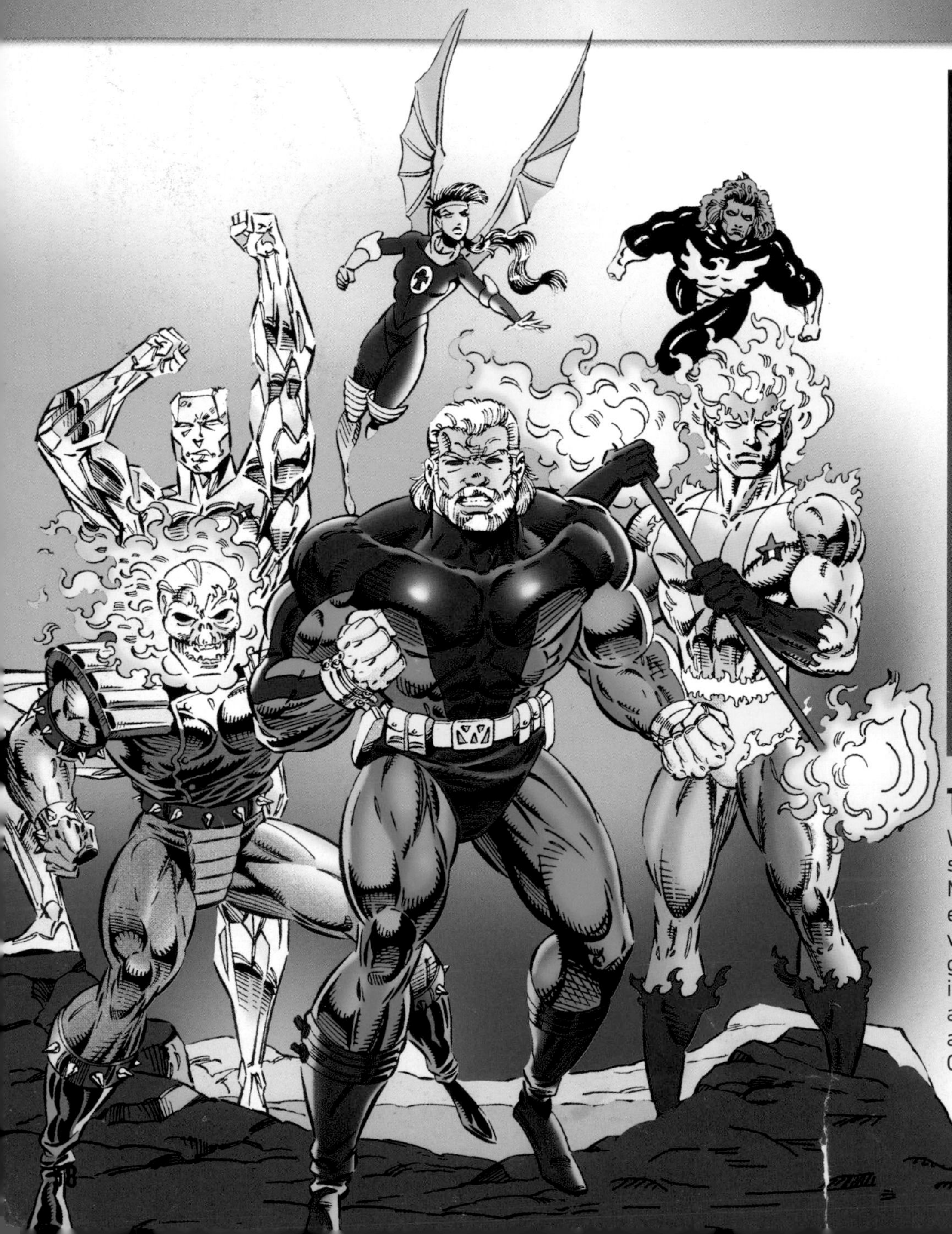

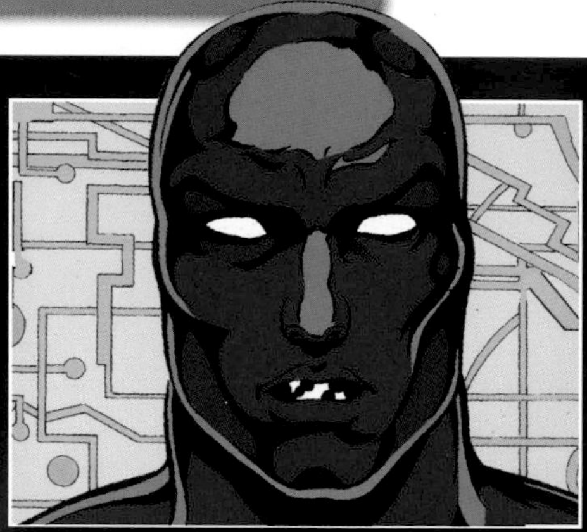

MAINFRAME

Mainframe was the android Vision—a mainstay of the Avengers—evolved into the sentient operating system of an entire planet. The Guardians met him when they came to his world in search of Captain America's shield. After overcoming a virus that turned him into an amalgam of himself and the villain Korvac, he joined the newly formed Galactic Guardians, who set up their base on his planet.

THE B-TEAM

When the Guardians of the Galaxy opted to stay on Earth to help fight the Punishers, Martinex realized that his destiny lay elsewhere. He told the Guardians of his vision for a thousand-strong team of galactic protectors, then set about making it a reality. He summoned Guardians past and present to Mainframe's world to battle a resurrected Korvac, then formed the Galactic Guardians with Spirit of Vengeance, Firelord, Phoenix, Replica, Hollywood, and Mainframe.

PHOENIX—GIRAUD

Giraud was a survivor of the ill-fated human resistance on Haven, a colony on a world riven by ground-quakes and ruled by a mutant elite. When the Guardians joined the fight against the mutants, Giraud was taken by Starhawk to one of the planet's volcanoes, where he joined with the cosmic Phoenix Force and was reborn as the immensely powerful Phoenix. With Starhawk's guidance, and using Mainframe's computational abilities, he teleported the entire population of his doomed planet to Mainframe's world, later joining the Galactic Guardians.

> "I have a vision for a truly galactic group of Guardians..."
>
> MARTINEX

SPIRIT OF VENGEANCE

The last priest of an outlawed faith on the planet Sarka, Autolycus used the Flames of Kauri (Hades) to transform himself into the Ghost Rider-like Spirit of Vengeance. Spotting the Guardians' ship near his planet, he mistook them for his enemies the Black Knights from the Universal Church of Truth and confronted them. After Aleta convinced him of who they were, the team helped him fight the Universal Church on Sarka. He later responded to Martinex's summons to Mainframe's world to join the Galactic Guardians.

HOLLYWOOD

The Guardians met the mysterious, super-powered Hollywood on Earth, where he was a member of the Commandeers, the freedom fighters battling the street gang the Punishers. When Vance Astro was shot, the Ancient One (Doctor Strange) used Hollywood's ionic blood to save Vance's life. A revived Astro realized that Hollywood was in fact Simon Williams—formerly Wonder Man of the Avengers—whose ionic nature granted him extended life. Though he stayed on Earth when the Guardians left, Hollywood heeded Martinex's call for heroes that brought about the Galactic Guardians.

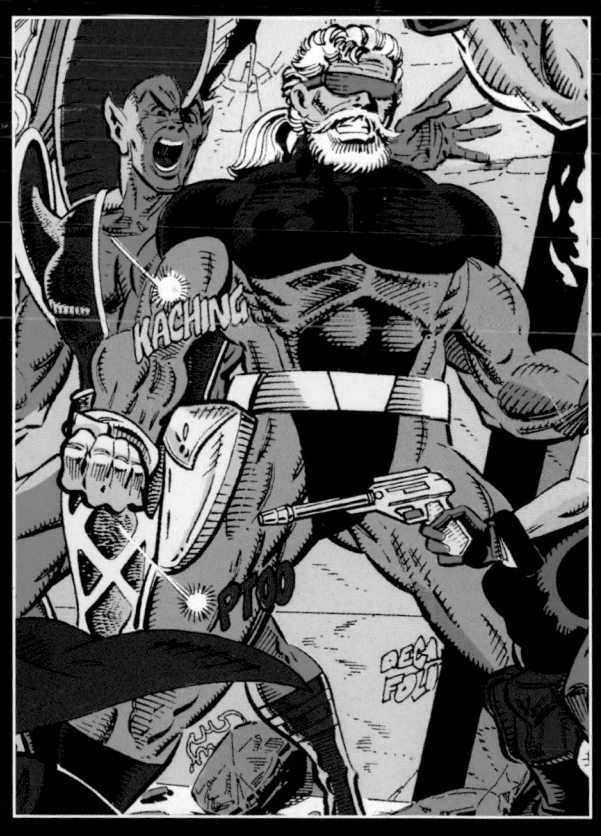

In the 2000s, Marvel rejuvenated their cosmic characters with a series of cataclysmic intergalactic conflicts, written largely by Keith Giffen, Dan Abnett, and Andy Lanning. In the thick of the action were a bunch of edgy, unconventional (anti-)heroes who would go on to form a new team of present-day Guardians of the Galaxy...

GUARDIANS BEGIN TO GATHER

THANOS (VOL. 1) #12 (SEP. 2004)
Peter Quill gets firsthand experience of the
duplicitous, volatile villain who will one day
become the Guardians' greatest enemy: Thanos.

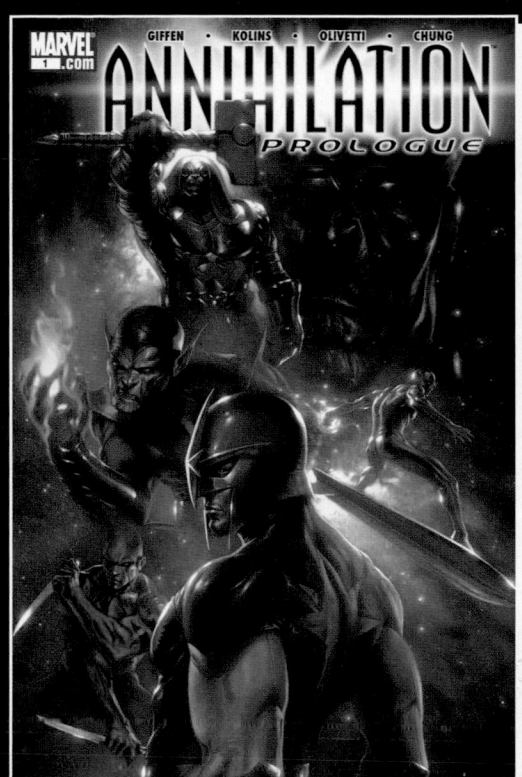

ANNIHILATION: PROLOGUE (VOL. 1) #1 (MAY 2006)
The war with Annihilus, cruel dictator of the
Negative Zone, begins—the catalyst for a
gathering of Guardians-to-be.

ANNIHILATION: CONQUEST
(VOL. 1) #1 (JAN. 2008)
The big bad behind the Phalanx invasion
of the Kree Empire is revealed: Ultron, the
crazed robot nemesis of the Avengers.

ANNIHILATION: CONQUEST
(VOL. 1) #6 (JUN. 2008)
As the war with Ultron and the Phalanx
concludes, the idea for a new team of
Guardians of the Galaxy is born...

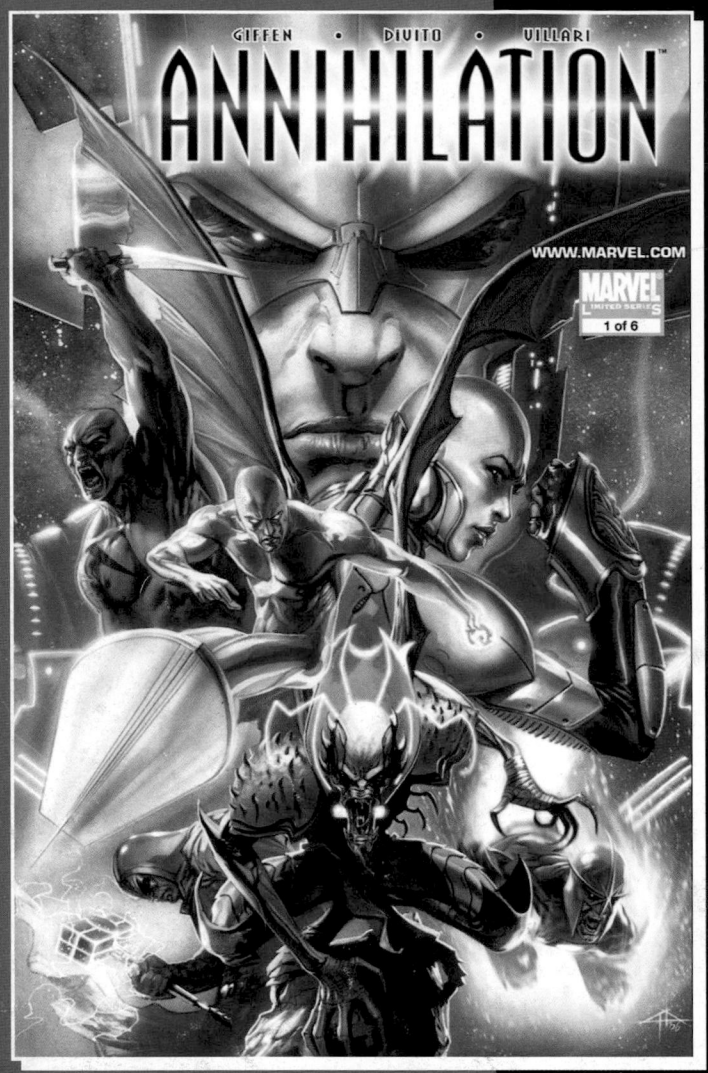

ANNIHILATION (Vol. 1) #1

A MAKESHIFT ALLIANCE TRIES TO HOLD THE LINE AGAINST A FLEET OF INSECTOID SHIPS.

Annihilus, ruler of the Negative Zone, has launched a devastating assault on the galaxy. His colossal fleet of starships, the Annihilation Wave, has wiped out entire civilizations, including the Skrull Empire and galactic cops the Nova Corps. Now, friend and foe must join forces to halt the relentless advance.

OCTOBER 2006

MAIN CHARACTERS
Nova—Richard Rider •
Peter Quill—Star-Lord
• Drax • Cammi

SUPPORTING CHARACTERS
Gamora • Ronan • Annihilus
• Extirpia • Thanos • Ravenous •
Firelord • Red Shift • Stardust
• Silver Surfer • Galactus •
Tenebrous • Aegis

MAIN LOCATIONS
Daedalus 5 • Daedalus Prime
• Annihilus' Flagship, in
orbit around Rhianda 9

1 It's been 206 days since Annihilus made his move, and resistance movement the United Front holds firm against overwhelming odds. With a command center on Daedalus 5, the Front is marshaled by Nova Corps' sole survivor, Richard Rider (Nova Prime), and his second-in-command, Star-Lord.

2 Among Rider's troops is Drax the Destroyer, with whom he formed an uneasy alliance after the destruction of the Nova Corps. The ferocity shown by Drax as he combats the Annihilation forces has proved an inspiration for Rider and the rest of the United Front. Unknown to Nova, however, Drax has an ulterior motive for taking up arms against the Annihilation Wave...

> *"If we don't hold them here, **it's over.**"*
>
> NOVA

3 In a brief but welcome respite from the fighting, Nova finds comfort in the arms of another unlikely ally—Gamora. She is proving to be a vital asset in the campaign, running black ops against Annihilation command centers. As Nova muses, "Guess it's true that war makes for strange bedfellows. No pun intended."

4 As night falls on Daedalus 5, the weary United Front troops are resting up. Among them are Drax and his young friend Cammi. A runaway Earth girl, Cammi has guessed Drax's real reason for joining the resistance: Annihilus has allied with Thanos the Mad Titan, and Drax has seen an opportunity to kill his sworn enemy.

5 Just as Nova thinks the United Front might have a chance against the Annihilation Wave, he discovers that Annihilus and Thanos have forged a new alliance with the godlike Ancient Ones, Aegis and Tenebrous. Together, they have enslaved the cosmic being Galactus. With his awesome power at their disposal, it seems the war is lost...

Pirate Pursuits

No sooner had young Star-Lord blasted into space than he and his stolen ship were captured by the space pirate Yondu and his Ravagers. Using his ingenuity, Peter turned the tables on the pirate and almost managed to steal his vessel. This impressed Yondu so much that he let Peter stay on board. Despite starting out as the ship's cleaner, Peter determined to learn all he could from the Ravagers. He became involved with Yondu's business dealings—and the hair-raising getaways that followed!

ORIGIN

As a boy growing up on Earth, Peter Quill had no clue who his father was. But then his mom, Meredith, was killed by Badoon soldiers. She left behind an alien weapon that had belonged to the 10-year-old's father, whom he later learned was Prince J'Son of the Spartoi Empire. Peter realized that his destiny lay in space and, when he was old enough, he got a job as a mechanic at a NASA facility. He stole a Kree Warbird that the Avengers had given to NASA, then set out to roam the galaxy, calling himself Star-Lord.

> "Whaddya know? Star-Lord for the win."
>
> — STAR-LORD

Darkest Day

In order to defeat the Fallen One and save the lives of millions, Star-Lord was forced to sacrifice thousands of colonists on the mining outpost Avaleen-4. Devastated, and believing that he had lost touch with his humanity, Peter gave up being Star-Lord and turned himself over to the Nova Corps.

STAR-LORD

It takes a planet-sized ego to name yourself Star-Lord—and ego is something Peter Quill has in spades. Leader of the Guardians of the Galaxy (though Rocket Raccoon might dispute that), Star-Lord's incorrigible swagger is matched by his incredible courage, bravery, resourcefulness, and his unstinting devotion to his teammates.

This heat-dampening battle suit is of Kree origin and augments Star-Lord's abilities in outer space.

Peter Quill's face mask was fitted by the Kree. It protects from the vacuum of space, helps him to see better, and provides data analysis.

LORD ALMIGHTY

Though eager to embellish his past exploits, Star-Lord has more than earned his legendary status. The founder of the Guardians has led his team into —and out of—all kinds of perilous situations, overcoming cosmic threats and saving whole civilizations. He may be a reckless and cocky ladies' man, but his team knows, when their backs are against the wall, there is no one they can depend on more.

Titan Up

Languishing in space prison Kyln after causing thousands of deaths on Avaleen-4, Peter Quill met a figure who would come to loom large in his life: Thanos. He saw the power of the Mad Titan when Thanos helped to subdue a dangerous inmate. He realized then that, though dangerous and duplicitous, Thanos had his uses.

Star-Lord's Element Gun can fire all four elements: air, earth, water, and fire. He also likes to use two Kree sub-machine guns with more conventional ammunition.

DATA FILE

REAL NAME: Peter Jason Quill

OCCUPATION: Adventurer

BASE: Mobile; formerly Knowhere

HEIGHT: 6ft 2in

WEIGHT: 175 lbs

EYES: Blue

HAIR: Blond

FIRST APPEARANCE: *Marvel Preview* (Vol. 1) #4 (Jan. 1976)

DATA FILE

REAL NAME: Arthur Douglas

OCCUPATION: Destroyer

BASE: Mobile

HEIGHT: 6ft 4in

WEIGHT: 680 lbs

EYES: Red

HAIR: None

FIRST APPEARANCE: *Iron Man* (Vol. 1) #55 (Feb. 1973)

Drax wields a pair of knives in battle, but is also skilled in unarmed techniques, such as the martial art Dwi Theet.

Enemy Mine

Drax has fought Thanos many times, but the wily Titan has (almost) always evaded death. Once, on Earth, Drax joined forces with Iron Man to battle Thanos. On that occasion, the Mad Titan made his escape and left a booby-trapped android in his place. Another time, Drax believed he and Captain Marvel had destroyed his nemesis once and for all, but Thanos was saved by his own ship.

Born Again

Drax has gone through numerous changes since he was created. He was killed at the hands of his own daughter, Moondragon, when she became a power-crazed goddess, and was then reborn as a hulking simpleton. Later, after he was savagely beaten by his fellow inmates on board a crashed prison ship, his body regenerated (pictured) and his intellect returned.

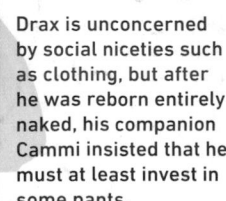

Drax is unconcerned by social niceties such as clothing, but after he was reborn entirely naked, his companion Cammi insisted that he must at least invest in some pants.

DESTROY ALL MONSTERS

His life's mission is to exterminate Thanos, yet Drax has found new purpose as a Guardian: defending the defenseless and fighting evil wherever it lurks. He is gruff and humorless, yet his courage and dedication have won him the love and respect of his teammates—especially Gamora. She loathes Thanos too, and acknowledges Drax as a great warrior.

Drax's green flesh was originally formed from Earth soil. His current body emerged from an earlier one that died.

ORIGIN

Ordinary human Arthur Douglas was driving across the Nevada Desert with his wife and daughter when their car was attacked by an alien ship. As Arthur lay dying, the last thing he saw was Thanos, who had targeted the car to keep his time on Earth a secret. Both Arthur and his wife died (their daughter was saved and taken to Titan, where she became Moondragon), but Arthur's soul was captured by Thanos' father, Mentor. He merged it with a new body to create Drax the Destroyer— the perfect weapon to destroy his son!

> "Thanos is my reason for being. His destruction is my destiny."
>
> DRAX THE DESTROYER

Road to Annihilation

Briefly marooned on Earth, Drax met Cammi, a human teenager from a broken home. Drax saw Cammi as a surrogate for his own daughter, and took her with him when he returned to space. The odd couple later teamed up with Richard Rider, the last of the Nova Corps, when Annihilus attacked the planet Xandar.

DRAX

Incredibly strong and incredibly angry, Drax was created solely to destroy Thanos of Titan. Having long shouldered this burden alone, Drax now shares it with the Guardians of the Galaxy. For Drax, the Guardians are friends, family, and fellow soldiers. For the Guardians, Drax is the team's solid bedrock: steadfast, sturdy, and as hard as anything.

THANOS

DATA FILE

REAL NAME: Thanos

OCCUPATION: Conqueror, avatar of Death

BASE: Titan

HEIGHT: 6ft 7in

WEIGHT: 985 lbs

EYES: Red

HAIR: None

FIRST APPEARANCE: *Iron Man* (Vol. 1) #55 (Feb. 1973)

In a galaxy where evil lurks around every corner, Thanos is the ultimate big bad. A thorn in the sides of Star-Lord, Drax (his sworn enemy), and Gamora (his adopted daughter) since before they became Guardians of the Galaxy, Thanos has an unquenchable thirst for power and is utterly devoted to his beloved Mistress Death.

There is enough power in Thanos' bare hands to repel an attack from the Hulk—and even to destroy entire planets.

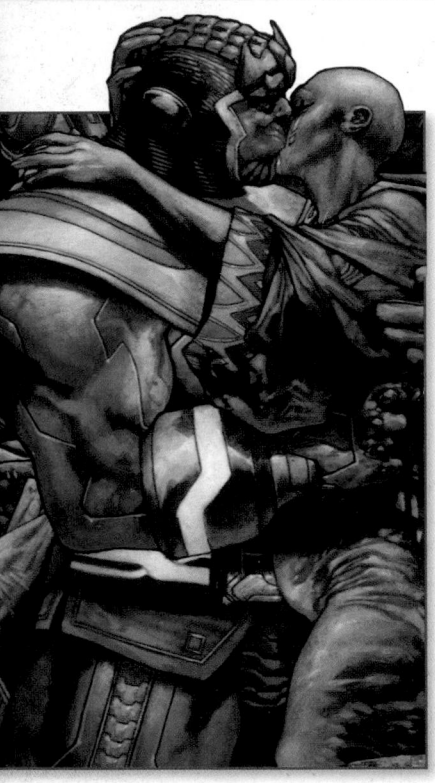

ORIGIN

The eldest son of Mentor, the leader of the Eternals of Titan, Thanos was always an outsider. Born with hide-like gray skin, as a boy he sought answers to explain why he was different. This led Thanos down a dark path paved by Mistress Death, who became his companion. Urged on by her, he began to dissect animals before turning his wrath on his fellow Eternals. In the first known murders on Titan, he killed two of his classmates and his own mother. He then fled Titan and began a reign of terror spanning the whole galaxy.

Unto Death

Mistress Death has held sway over Thanos ever since he was a boy. She first appeared to him as a nameless girl his own age, urging him on to ever-darker deeds before finally revealing her true identity when he was a teen. When Thanos became an adult, he offered Mistress Death a fitting tribute: the lives of thousands of his fellow Titans, whom he bombed from space.

> *"My every moment is spent in either dealing out death, or worshipping it!"*
>
> THANOS

ABSOLUTE POWER

A tyrant from the moon Titan, Thanos is driven by two impulses: the pursuit of power, and the desire to please his mistress —who is the personification of death. He has sought out objects of immense power in order to bend the universe to his will and bring about a union with Death. As a result, he is the Guardians' (and the galaxy's) greatest threat.

Thanos' great strength is matched only by his intellect. He is a genius in almost every field of scientific endeavor.

As well as having powerful psionic abilities, Thanos' own mind has proven to be impervious to most forms of psychic attack.

Infinity and Beyond

Thanos enjoyed his greatest triumph when he acquired all six Infinity Gems and created the incredibly powerful Infinity Gauntlet. With it, he wiped out half of all life in the universe as an offering to his mistress. This monstrous deed was eventually undone, and for a time Thanos lived quietly as a simple farmer, contemplating the lessons of his defeat.

Axis of Evil

When Annihilus, the ruler of the Negative Zone, launched an all-out attack on the galaxy, Thanos allied himself with the despot. However—as is usually the way with the Mad Titan—Thanos had his own reasons for doing so. In this instance it was simple curiosity at how Annihilus' invasion would affect the balance of power in the galaxy.

GAMORA

Trained in every form of armed and unarmed combat, Gamora is the most dangerous woman in the galaxy. A fearsome warrior who has spent much of her life as a mercenary, she has found a greater purpose with the Guardians, fighting injustice and protecting the weak. She has also found trust, loyalty, and friendship.

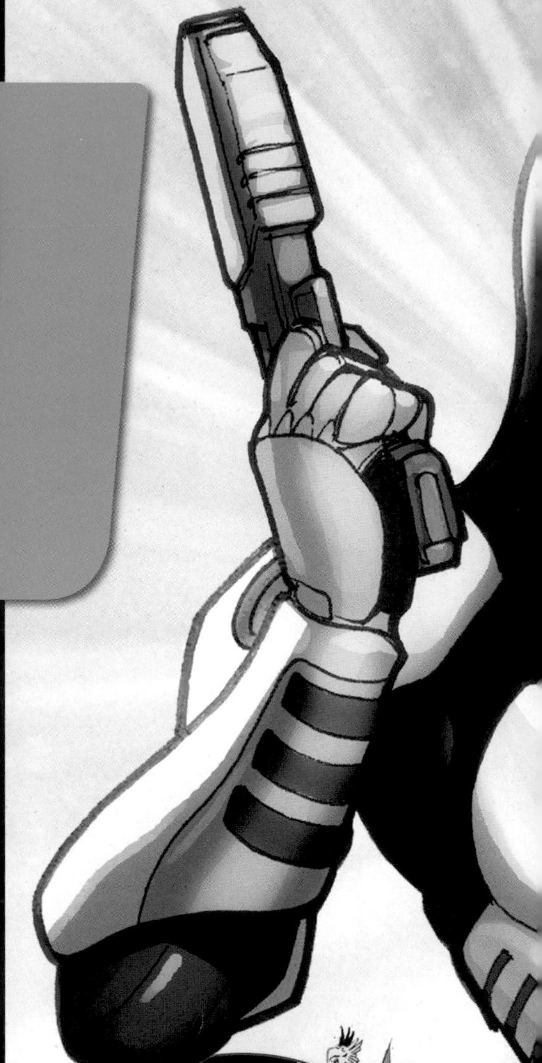

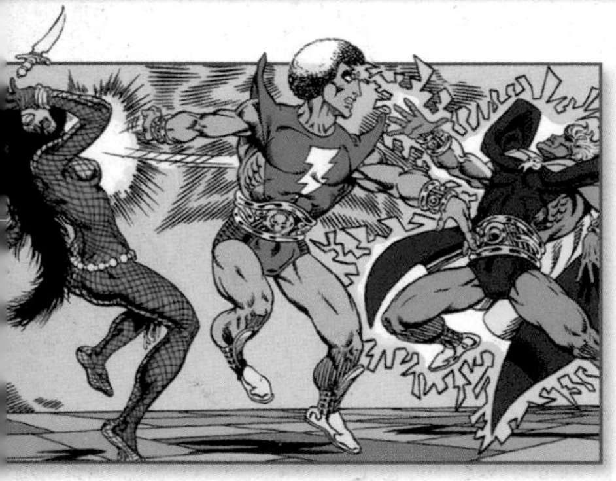

Lethal Weapon
Gamora was trained and physically augmented by Thanos with a very specific purpose in mind: to destroy the Magus, the evil future version of Adam Warlock. Fearing that the Magus would one day pose a threat to him, Thanos sent Gamora to ally with Adam Warlock and bring about the Magus' downfall.

*"Thanos is **not** my father!"*

GAMORA

ORIGIN

Orphaned at a young age when the rest of her people were slaughtered by the Universal Church of Truth, Gamora was adopted by Thanos, the Mad Titan. He trained her in all aspects of warfare, weaponry, and martial arts. He also altered her biological makeup, giving her enhanced strength, speed, stamina, and agility, as well as an accelerated ability to recover from injuries. When she learned that her adoptive father planned to extinguish every star in the universe, Gamora rebelled and struck out on her own—as a mercenary and adventurer.

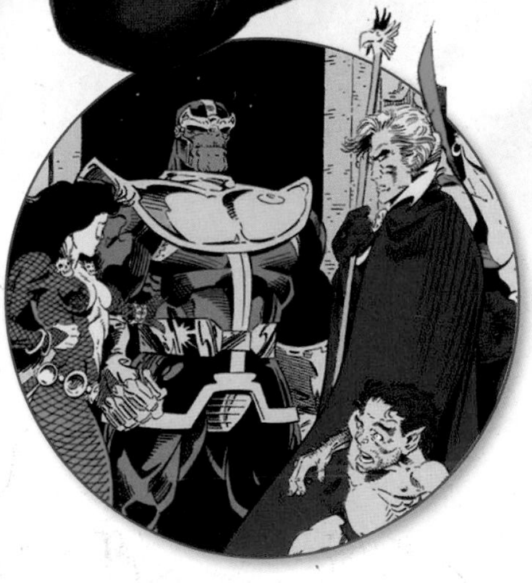

Allies to Infinity
The first time Gamora encountered her Guardians teammate-to-be Drax, she was still in thrall to Thanos. As a result, the Destroyer tried to kill her! Later, the two became allies in Adam Warlock's Infinity Watch team. It was here that the pair started to develop a deep mutual respect.

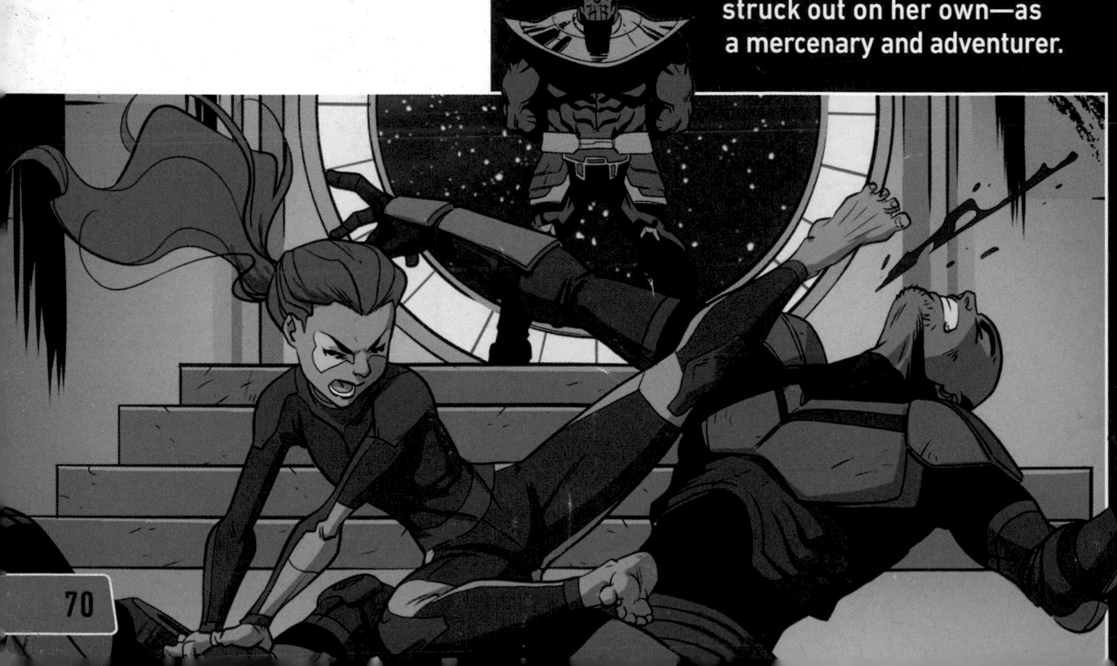

Gamora's strength has been augmented by Thanos, Adam Warlock, and the Black Vortex.

Guns are part of Gamora's extensive weaponry. She also has a sword called the Godslayer, capable of felling great beings.

FEMME FATALE

Brought up by Thanos to be a living weapon, Gamora is feared and respected in every star system. Her only goal was to sow mayhem across space—until she met the Guardians of the Galaxy. Before she joined Star-Lord's team, Gamora's only experience of family was Thanos—a cold, death-obsessed tyrant. The Guardians have become her surrogate family, giving her love, stability, and a life with meaning beyond plunder and conquest.

Gamora's body has cybernetic implants that give her enhanced strength, reflexes, and regenerative powers.

DATA FILE

REAL NAME: Gamora

OCCUPATION: Warrior, former assassin

BASE: Mobile

HEIGHT: 6ft

WEIGHT: 170 lbs

EYES: Green

HAIR: Black

FIRST APPEARANCE: *Strange Tales* (Vol. 1) #180 (Jun. 1975)

Gamora's Graces

When the Negative Zone tyrant Annihilus invaded the Guardians' galaxy, Gamora was on the backwater world of Godthab Omega. She had formed the Graces—a team of cosmically powered women—and was plundering the planet. When the Annihilation Wave armada arrived, many of the Graces were killed. Gamora swore vengeance against Annihilus and joined Drax and Star-Lord in the struggle against him.

MAJOR SPECIES OF THE GALAXY

The galaxy is littered with countless inhabited worlds, but it is the major species and their empires that have tended to shape galactic events. When these empires clash, the repercussions can be felt across space, and other species and individuals—including the Guardians of the Galaxy—are usually drawn into the fray.

SPARTOI

Human in appearance, the Spartoi are an aloof and often arrogant species. From their homeworld of Spartax they preside over an interplanetary empire made up of many other species. After J'Son (Star-Lord's father) became Emperor, the Spartoi assumed a more prominent role on the galactic stage, becoming major players in the Council of Galactic Empires. While Star-Lord has consistently shunned his royal birthright, his half-sister, Victoria, is a captain in the Spartax Royal Guard.

SHI'AR

Descended from birds, the Shi'ar have feathery crests and are naturally strong and swift. The Shi'ar Imperium is a vast, technologically advanced, largely benign empire, and the Shi'ar have played the role of peacemakers in a number of galactic conflicts. However, they are fearsome combatants when attacked—as in the Kree-Shi'ar War, when they used a galaxy-devastating Nega-Bomb. Their greatest warriors are the Shi'ar Imperial Guard—super-powered individuals led by Gladiator.

KREE

The ancient and noble Kree established their interstellar empire one million years ago. As technologically advanced warriors, they have frequently come into conflict with other empires—notably the Skrulls and the Shi'ar. They have done experiments on other species—creating evolutionary offshoots such as Earth's Inhumans—and dispatched heroes to other worlds, including Mar-Vell (Captain Marvel). The Kree are ruled by the Supreme Intelligence, a being composed of the brains of the greatest Kree, while the Accuser Corps—headed by Ronan—acts as their police force and militia.

SKRULLS

Devious and untrustworthy, the green-skinned Skrulls use their shape-shifting abilities in order to infiltrate unsuspecting societies and overthrow them from the inside. Theirs is the oldest empire known to exist, but the Skrulls were not always conquerors. Only after coming into contact with the Kree, which led to the massively devastating Kree-Skrull War, did they become so militarized. The Skrulls' greatest warrior is Kl'rt, the Super-Skrull, who was artificially augmented to have the same powers as Earth's Fantastic Four.

"No power on Earth can stop the Skrull invasion!"

SKRULLS

BROOD

Perhaps the most repellent of all galactic species, the Brood are aggressive, evil parasites, out to infest the galaxy. Their hierarchy is similar to insect societies, with workers commanded by Queens, and they lay their eggs in hosts who are then turned into further Brood. Their first major incursion came when they sought to oust Majestrix Lilandra of the Shi'ar in league with her sister, Deathbird. They have since made repeated attempts to infest Earth, as well as bedeviling the wider galaxy.

CHITAURI

Little is known about the Chitauri, except that they are fearsome and warlike. They made their first mark in the wider galaxy when they sent a massive attack fleet to Earth. On that occasion Nova put a stop to their plans to eliminate Earth and prevent its denizens from ever interfering in galactic events again. Since then, the Chitauri have repeatedly come into conflict with Nova and the Guardians of the Galaxy, allying themselves with any villain who will further their aims of conquest.

ANNIHILATION

Annihilus, the despotic insectoid ruler of the Negative Zone, launches an all-out assault on the galaxy with his horrific Annihilation Wave warships. To counter this threat, a group of Guardians-to-be will gather for the first time.

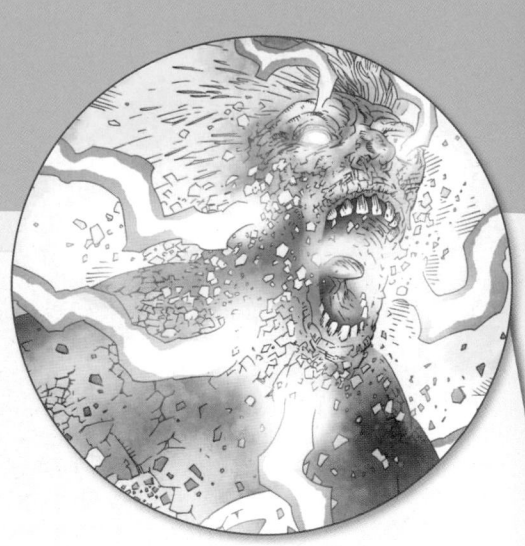

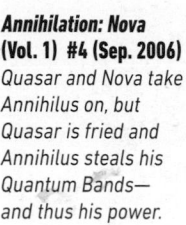

Annihilation: Nova (Vol. 1) #4 (Sep. 2006) Quasar and Nova take Annihilus on, but Quasar is fried and Annihilus steals his Quantum Bands— and thus his power.

WAVE OF ANNIHILATION

The Annihilation Wave fleet tears open a portal from the Negative Zone at the prison facility Kyln, destroying it. Their next target is Xandar, the base of the galactic police force the Nova Corps, who are in the middle of a briefing about the destruction of Kyln. The Nova Corps does its best to defend Xandar against the Annihilation Wave, but is wiped out to a man. The only survivor is Richard Rider of Earth.

Annihilation: Prologue (May 2006) Detainees newly arrived on Xandar, Drax the Destroyer and his Earth girl companion Cammi, steal a shuttle, hit the autopilot, and rocket to safety.

> "Annihilus is **the will and the way** and he will **not be denied**!"
>
> ANNIHILUS

Annihilation (Vol. 1) #2 (Nov. 2006) After enslaving Galactus and his herald the Silver Surfer, Annihilus turns the cosmically powered beings into weapons to use against the United Front.

A HERO FALLS

As the sole remaining Corps member, Richard Rider becomes Nova Prime: the repository for the Nova Force (the energy source that powers all members of the Corps). He, Drax, and Cammi encounter Wendell Vaughn (alias cosmic hero Quasar), who is overseeing a mass evacuation of the planet Nycos Aristedes. Before it's done, the Annihilation Wave arrives, then Annihilus himself. Nova barely escapes with his life; badly scarred, he is retrieved by Drax and Cammi.

VICTORY AND DEFEAT

Months later, a resistance to the Annihilation Wave, the United Front, has formed and established a beachhead on Daedalus 5. Commanded by Nova, and including Guardians-to-be Peter Quill, Drax, Gamora, and Phyla-Vell, the Front holds out against offensives by Annihilus' forces, including by his all-powerful Centurions. However, Annihilus has enslaved and weaponized the planet-devourer Galactus, against whose power the United Front stands no chance. As cosmic fire rains down on Daedalus 5, the resistance fleet flees for their lives.

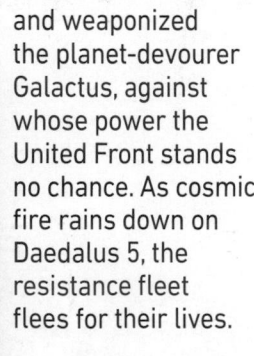

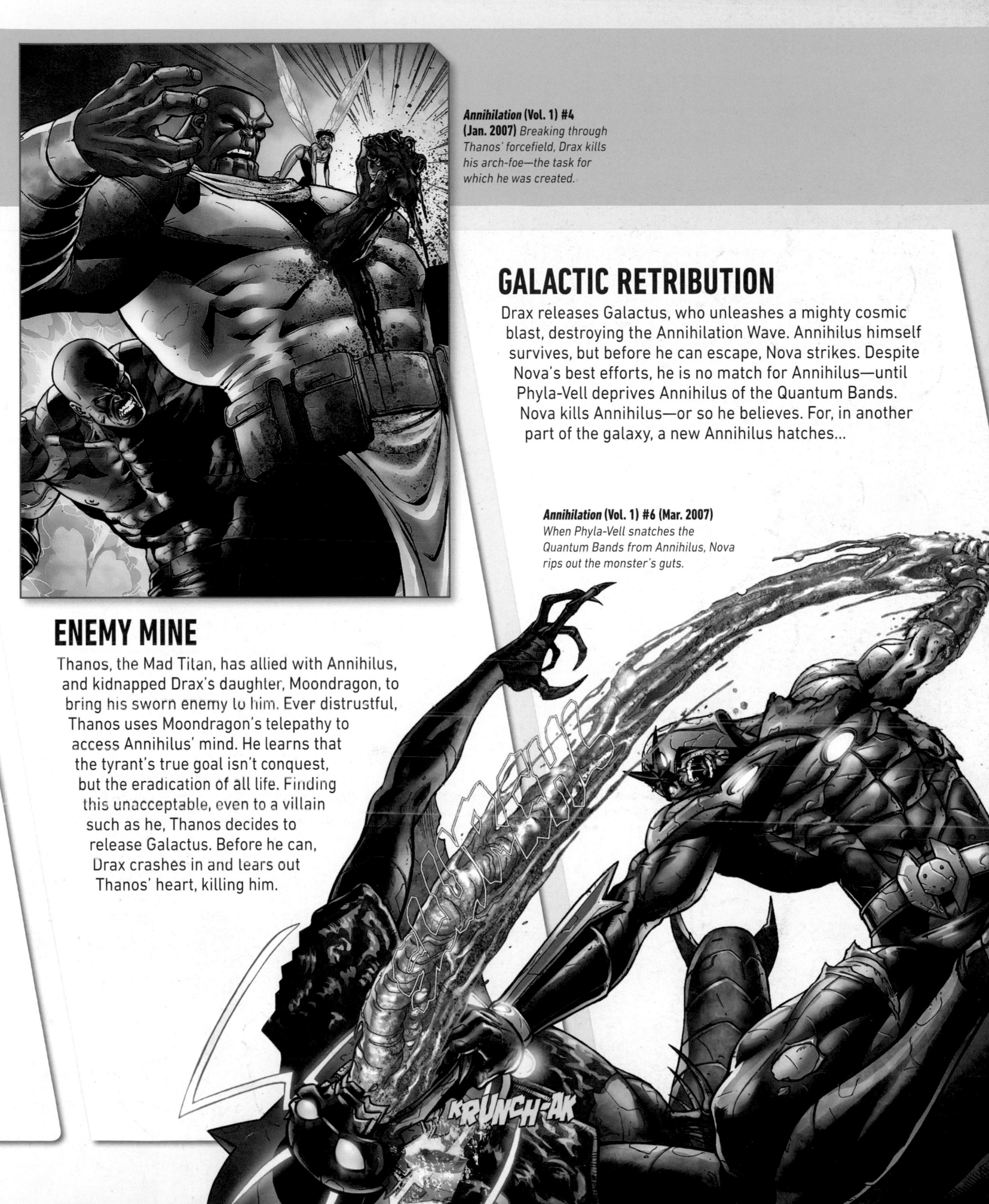

Annihilation (Vol. 1) #4
(Jan. 2007) *Breaking through
Thanos' forcefield, Drax kills
his arch-foe—the task for
which he was created.*

GALACTIC RETRIBUTION

Drax releases Galactus, who unleashes a mighty cosmic blast, destroying the Annihilation Wave. Annihilus himself survives, but before he can escape, Nova strikes. Despite Nova's best efforts, he is no match for Annihilus—until Phyla-Vell deprives Annihilus of the Quantum Bands. Nova kills Annihilus—or so he believes. For, in another part of the galaxy, a new Annihilus hatches...

Annihilation (Vol. 1) #6 (Mar. 2007)
*When Phyla-Vell snatches the
Quantum Bands from Annihilus, Nova
rips out the monster's guts.*

ENEMY MINE

Thanos, the Mad Titan, has allied with Annihilus, and kidnapped Drax's daughter, Moondragon, to bring his sworn enemy to him. Ever distrustful, Thanos uses Moondragon's telepathy to access Annihilus' mind. He learns that the tyrant's true goal isn't conquest, but the eradication of all life. Finding this unacceptable, even to a villain such as he, Thanos decides to release Galactus. Before he can, Drax crashes in and tears out Thanos' heart, killing him.

KRUNCH-AK

Nova's helmet gives access to the Xandarian Worldmind, a vast source of knowledge. When removed, the helmet becomes so pliable that it can be carried in a pocket.

Home from Home

After becoming Nova, Richard Rider initially confined himself to his homeworld, battling the super-villains that threatened Earth. But he eventually made his way to Xandar—homeworld of the Nova Corps—where he helped the Corps in their war with the Skrulls. In time Xandar would become a second home to Richard, and the Nova Corps his second family.

SUPER NOVA!

Richard Rider has never been a Guardian, but he was crucial to their formation. He marshaled resistance against the Negative Zone despot Annihilus—recruiting Star-Lord, Gamora, Drax, and Phyla-Vell—then gave Peter his backing and guidance when he proposed the Guardians. He has been a steadfast friend and ally to Peter and the other Guardians, offering his counsel and his power whenever they are needed.

Nova still wears the regulation Xandarian StarCorps uniform of the Nova Corps.

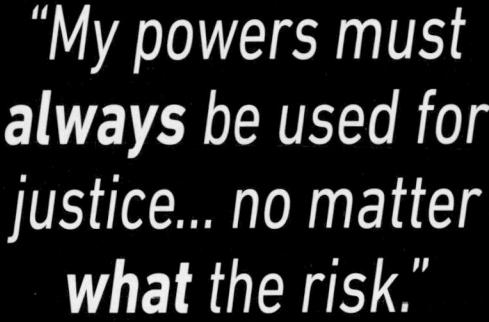

*"My powers must **always** be used for justice... no matter **what** the risk."*

NOVA

ORIGIN

Richard Rider was a regular teenager from New York, convinced he would never amount to much in life. But that all changed when the last surviving Centurion of the intergalactic police force the Nova Corps transferred his power to Richard, turning him into Nova, the Human Rocket! He discovered that he was now powered by the Nova Force, an energy that gave him superhuman strength and speed, invulnerability, and the ability to fly. In time, he would take his place as one of the Nova Corps and assume the mantle of Nova Prime.

Tough, flexible, and airtight (the mouth and eyes can both be sealed), Nova's uniform has built-in weapons and a life-support system.

Annihilated

Nova's darkest day came when Annihilus, the depraved ruler of the Negative Zone, launched a devastating invasion of the galaxy. Annihilus' unstoppable Annihilation Wave forces laid waste to the planet Xandar, wiping out almost the entire Nova Corps. Only Richard lived to fight another day, forming the United Front resistance to fight back against Annihilus.

New Warrior

Richard was still in high school when he became Nova, and possessing the Nova Force was a lot for him to handle. He joined the New Warriors—a super-team composed of young heroes—who helped ground him and give him focus. Among his teammates was Marvel Boy, aka Vance Astrovik—an alternative version of Guardian Major Victory.

NOVA

Powered by the Nova Force, an almost infinite source of energy, Nova is the galaxy's greatest cop. As a member of intergalactic enforcers the Nova Corps, his duty is to protect the galaxy from any and all threats. As a friend and ally of the Guardians, he is always willing to put his incredible power at their disposal—no matter the cost.

QUASAR
(WENDELL VAUGHN)

Armed with Quantum Bands—bracelets that give the wearer access to limitless energy—Wendell Vaughn is Quasar, Protector of the Universe. He has played decisive roles in countless cosmic conflicts, and his incredible power has helped to shape the Guardians of the Galaxy, both directly and indirectly.

*"My name is Wendell Vaughn... Quasar. I'm called the **Protector of the Universe**. Which is cool."*

QUASAR

Many Names, Many Roles

When he first gained his powers, Wendell went by the codename Marvel Boy. This became Marvel Man, and eventually Quasar. He fought bravely alongside heroes such as Captain America, Hulk, and the Falcon, and then joined experimental energy institute Project P.E.G.A.S.U.S. as head of security. Having putting paid to numerous threats on Earth, he finally decided to seek a greater purpose in space.

ORIGIN

Wendell Vaughn was a S.H.I.E.L.D. agent providing security at a top-secret institute established to study alien artifacts called the Quantum Bands. When forces from the villainous Advance Idea Mechanics (A.I.M.) attacked the base, Wendell put the bands upon his wrists and was instantly granted vast energy powers and cosmic knowledge. He crushed the A.I.M. strike, and was then trained by S.H.I.E.L.D. in the full use of his powers. First he became Earth's defender, then— as Quasar—the protector of the whole universe.

PROTECT AND SERVE

As Cosmic Protector, Quasar bears an awesome weight, yet he has risen to the challenge time and again—on his own or as a member of the Avengers. He has lent the Guardians his extraordinary energy powers, and been a resolute comrade during some of the team's most testing battles.

Quantum energy causes Quasar's naturally blue eyes to give off a golden glow.

The Quantum Bands are the source of all Quasar's powers. He learned they were made by the cosmic being Eon, to be worn by the Protector of the Universe.

DATA FILE

REAL NAME: Wendell Vaughn

OCCUPATION: Adventurer, Protector of the Universe

BASE: Mobile, formerly Project P.E.G.A.S.U.S.

HEIGHT: 5ft 10in

WEIGHT: 180 lbs

EYES: Blue

HAIR: Blond

FIRST APPEARANCE: (as Marvel Boy) *Captain America* (Vol. 1) #217 (Jan. 1978); (as Quasar) *Incredible Hulk* (Vol. 1) #234 (Apr. 1979)

Quantum Quest

After leaving Earth, Quasar investigated the origins of the Quantum Bands on Uranus. There, he met Deathurge, an entity who tried to convince him that he had gone there to die. He escaped Deathurge and encountered the cosmic being Eon, who bestowed the role of Cosmic Protector on him.

Two Against Annihilus

When Annihilus launched his invasion of the galaxy from the Negative Zone, Quasar joined forces with fellow cosmic hero Nova in an attempt to defeat the tyrant. The pair attacked Annihilus on his flagship, but were no match for his power. Annihilus grabbed Quasar and obliterated him, grabbing his Quantum Bands. This left the universe without its protector, for the moment, at least.

Quasar's Quantum armor was created using the Quantum Bands, which give the hero the ability to generate objects of any shape.

Phyla's blue eyes glow gold with Quantum energy. Even before she became Quasar, she had the power to absorb vast amounts of energy.

As Quasar, Phyla has based her costume on Wendell Vaughn's, with the addition of a hood.

Guardian Soulmates

Phyla-Vell met her lover Moondragon on Earth, through Moondragon's then-girlfriend (who was a friend of Phyla's brother, Genis-Vell). Moondragon was dismissive of Phyla at first, but after she broke up with her girlfriend, the pair realized they were attracted to each other. They decided to seek out adventure in space together.

FURY OF PHYLA

Having fought beside Star-Lord in the Annihilation War and the Phalanx invasion, Phyla-Vell was Peter Quill's first recruit to the Guardians. She went on to inherit an awesome responsibility from Wendell Vaughn, in the form of the power-giving Quantum Bands—a legacy she has striven to live up to as the new Quasar. Her hot-headedness has often gotten her into trouble, as when she relinquished the Bands and adopted a darker identity as Martyr. But though she is quick to anger, her fury can be effectively channeled, not least by her girlfriend, Moondragon.

Love Will Tear Us Apart

Phyla-Vell and Moondragon were torn from one another during the galactic war with Annihilus, evil ruler of the Negative Zone. Annihilus' ally, Thanos, kidnapped Moondragon in order to bait her father—his sworn enemy Drax. Phyla-Vell did her best to stop the Mad Titan, but he swatted her away with ease. He then ripped off one of Moondragon's ears, for Phyla to deliver to Drax as a message.

The Quantum Bands were partially corrupted through contact with Annihilus and threatened to overwhelm Phyla's mind for a time.

REAL NAME: Phyla-Vell

OCCUPATION: Adventurer

BASE: Mobile

HEIGHT: 5ft 9in

WEIGHT: 103 lbs

EYES: Blue

HAIR: White

FIRST APPEARANCE:
Captain Marvel (Vol. 5)
#16 (Jan. 2004)

ORIGIN

Phyla-Vell was brought into existence when her brother, Genis-Vell—the second Captain Marvel—had to reconstruct the universe after a catastrophe. This recreated universe was subtly different from its predecessor in various ways, and Phyla-Vell was one of those differences. As the artificially created daughter of Mar-Vell—the original Captain Marvel—Phyla-Vell possessed the ability to fly, superhuman strength, and powers of energy control. What she lacked was a purpose—until she met and fell in love with Moondragon, and the pair joined the fight against Annihilus in the Annihilation War.

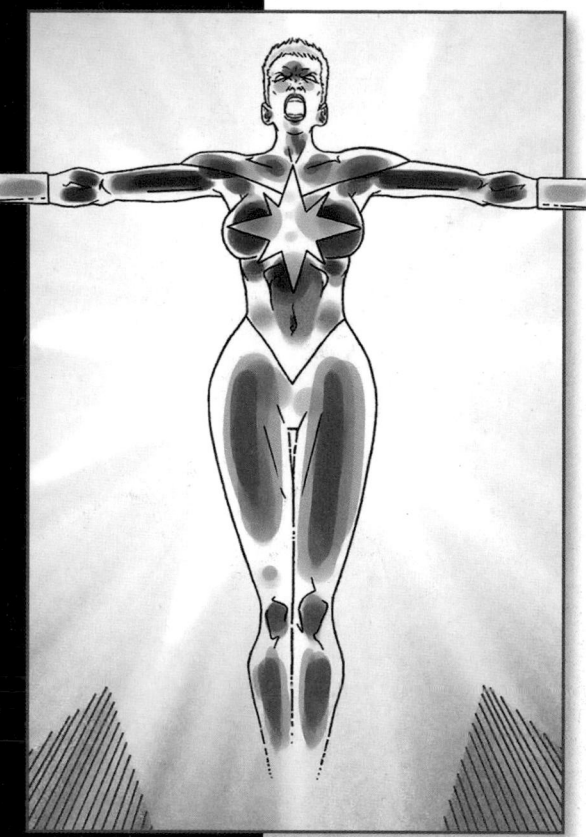

Quasar Reborn

After his Annihilation Wave forces invaded the galaxy from the Negative Zone, Annihilus killed cosmic hero Quasar (Wendell Vaughn) and stole his Quantum Bands, the source of all his power. Later, as the war with Annihilus' forces neared its climax, Nova (Richard Rider) and Phyla-Vell took on Annihilus himself. Phyla-Vell succeeded in wrenching the Bands from Annihilus' wrists, assuming the mantle of Quasar and blasting the monster with her newfound power.

> *"I carry the legacy of the **Quantum Bands**, retrieved from dread Annihilus **himself!**"*
>
> PHYLA-VELL

PHYLA-VELL

...warrior, what Phyla-Vell lacks in experience she makes up for... ...headstrong and reckless, she can be a wild card in battle, though... ...less also gives her the advantage of surprise. Phyla has used... ...as a Guardian, but whether wielding the Quantum Bands as... ...Quantum Sword as Martyr, she always has the backs of her team...

Heather Douglas was just a child, traveling across the Nevada Desert with her parents, when their family car was attacked by Thanos of Titan. Both her mother and father were killed in the resulting crash, but Heather was rescued by Thanos' father, Mentor. He took her to Titan, where she was raised by the Shao-Lom monks, who trained her mind and body in numerous disciplines: martial arts, athletics, science—even how to harness the power of telepathy. What they did not tell her was that her deceased father, Arthur Douglas, had been brought back to life by Mentor as a living weapon to be used against Thanos, and now went by the name of Drax the Destroyer!

Moondragon has complete control of her body, including her nervous system and pain receptors, thanks to years of training with Titan's Shao-Lom monks.

Tooth and Claw

An ancient demonic force, the Dragon of the Moon has long been a corrupting influence on the galaxy. The demon got its claws into Moondragon when she was in training with the Shao-Lom monks, feeding off her arrogance. However, she defeated the beast, taking the name Moondragon to celebrate her victory. Later, during the conflict with the Phalanx, it reasserted itself, turning her into an actual dragon.

> "I was trained in martial arts and telepathy by the adepts of **Titan**! I **can** handle myself!"
>
> MOONDRAGON

Family Reunion

Drax and Moondragon learned they were father and daughter when she joined forces with him, the Avengers, and Captain Marvel to fight Thanos. In battle, Thanos tormented Drax by restoring his memory of the night Thanos killed Arthur Douglas and his wife, revealing that Heather had survived to become Moondragon.

MOONDRAGON

Her body and mind trained to the peak of perfection, Moondragon is a formidable asset to the Guardians. A fearless warrior with mental powers to rival those of Mantis or Cosmo, her abilities sometimes lead to arrogance. However, this is tempered by her compassion for her teammates—not least Drax and Phyla-Vell.

Moondragon's psionic powers are among the most formidable in any galaxy, encompassing vast telepathic abilities and telekinesis.

A lifetime of combat has increased Moondragon's muscular power to near-superhuman levels.

DATA FILE

REAL NAME: Heather Douglas

OCCUPATION: Adventurer

BASE: Mobile

HEIGHT: 6ft

WEIGHT: 150 lbs

EYES: Blue

HAIR: Black (shaved bald)

FIRST APPEARANCE: *Iron Man* (Vol. 1) #54 (Jan. 1973)

TRAINING A DRAGON

Moondragon was well-versed in space adventure long before she became a Guardian of the Galaxy. The daughter of Drax the Destroyer, she grew up on Thanos' homeworld, Titan, then went on to be a member of both the Avengers and the Defenders. Therefore, when she joined the Guardians, she brought a lifetime's experience of cosmic-level threats to the team. She also brought welcome companionship for one member in particular: her girlfriend, Phyla-Vell.

Plaything of Thanos

Moondragon has sometimes joined her father, Drax, in his vendetta against Thanos, but she has also been used as a pawn in the struggle between the two enemies. After Thanos allied himself with Negative Zone ruler Annihilus, he kidnapped Moondragon so that Drax would seek him out. Thanos got his wish: Drax tracked him down and killed him right before Heather's eyes.

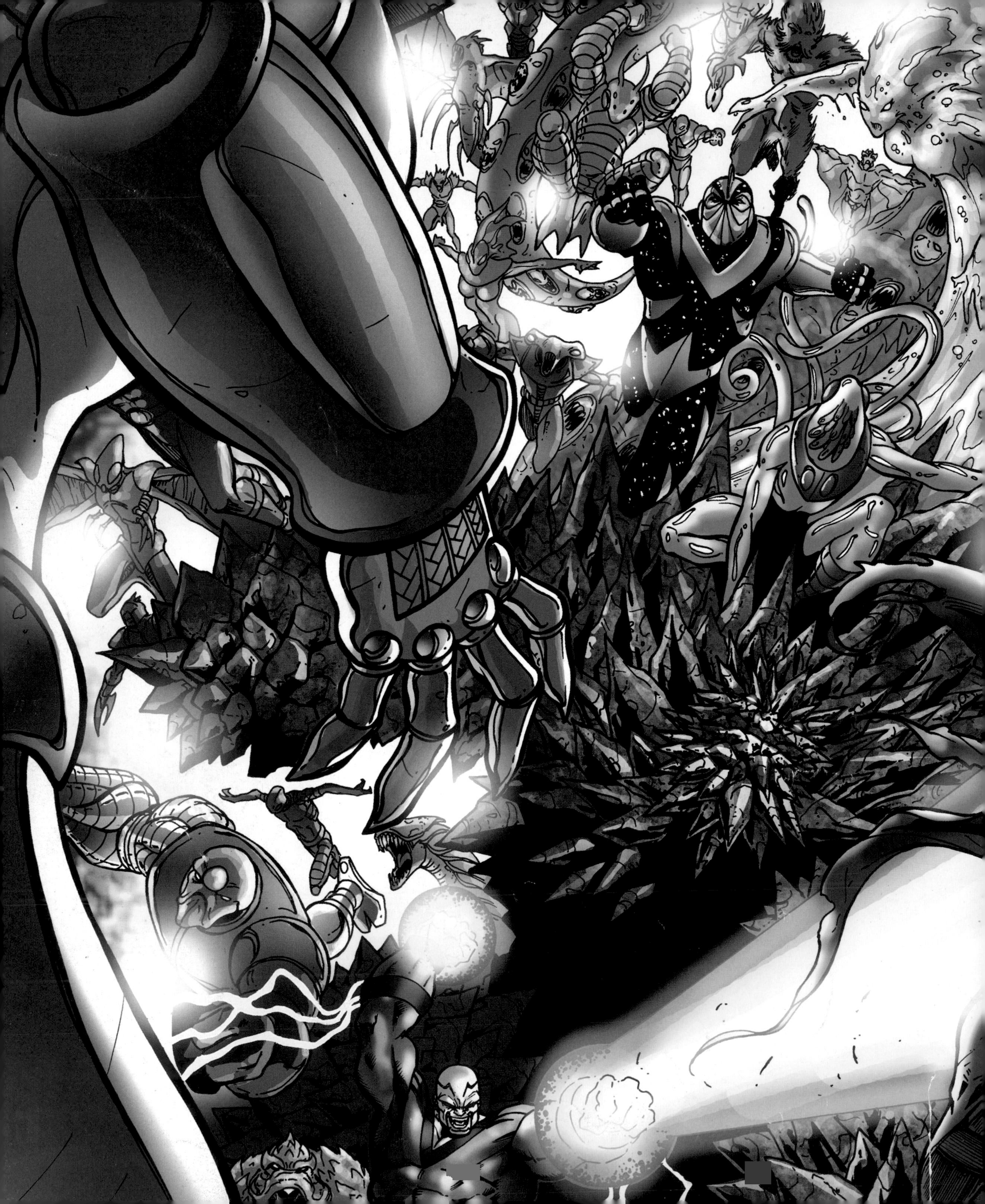

**ANNIHILATION (VOL. 1) #2
NOVEMBER 2006**

One of the fiercest battles of the Annihilation War took place on Daedalus 5, where the United Front had established a beachhead against Annihilus' forces. Peter Quill, Gamora, Nova, Ronan, and the rest of the United Front faced a furious assault by the Centurions—Annihilus' elite super-powered troops, commanded by the evil Ravenous.

KEY PLAYERS IN ANNIHILATION

A sprawling interstellar conflict, the Annihilation War sucked in many of the galaxy's major figures. As the devastating Annihilation Wave—an invasion fleet from the Negative Zone comprised of thousands of warships and legions of nightmarish troops—swept across the galaxy, few lives were left untouched.

ANNIHILUS

Ruler of the forbidding Negative Zone, the insectoid Annihilus is a power-mad despot. A perennial thorn in the sides of the Fantastic Four and a bitter rival of fellow Negative Zone tyrant Blastaar, Annihilus has tried to expand his territory many times, using the awesome power of the Cosmic Control Rod, an energy device of his own invention. He commanded a massive invasion fleet of monstrous creatures and warships known as the Annihilation Wave.

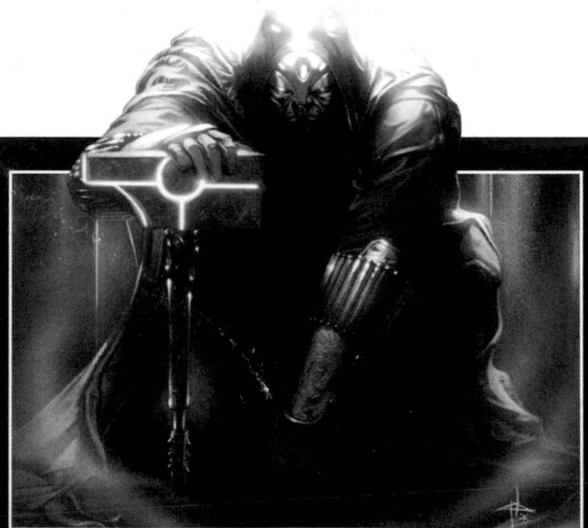

RONAN THE ACCUSER

The Accuser Corps are the judges, juries, and executioners for the Kree people, and Ronan is the greatest of them all. His commitment to the Kree is rivaled only by that of the Supreme Intelligence, from whom Ronan took over as ruler of the Kree. Noble but flawed, Ronan has been antagonist and ally to the forces of good, but in the Annihilation War, he pledged himself and the Kree to the United Front resistance.

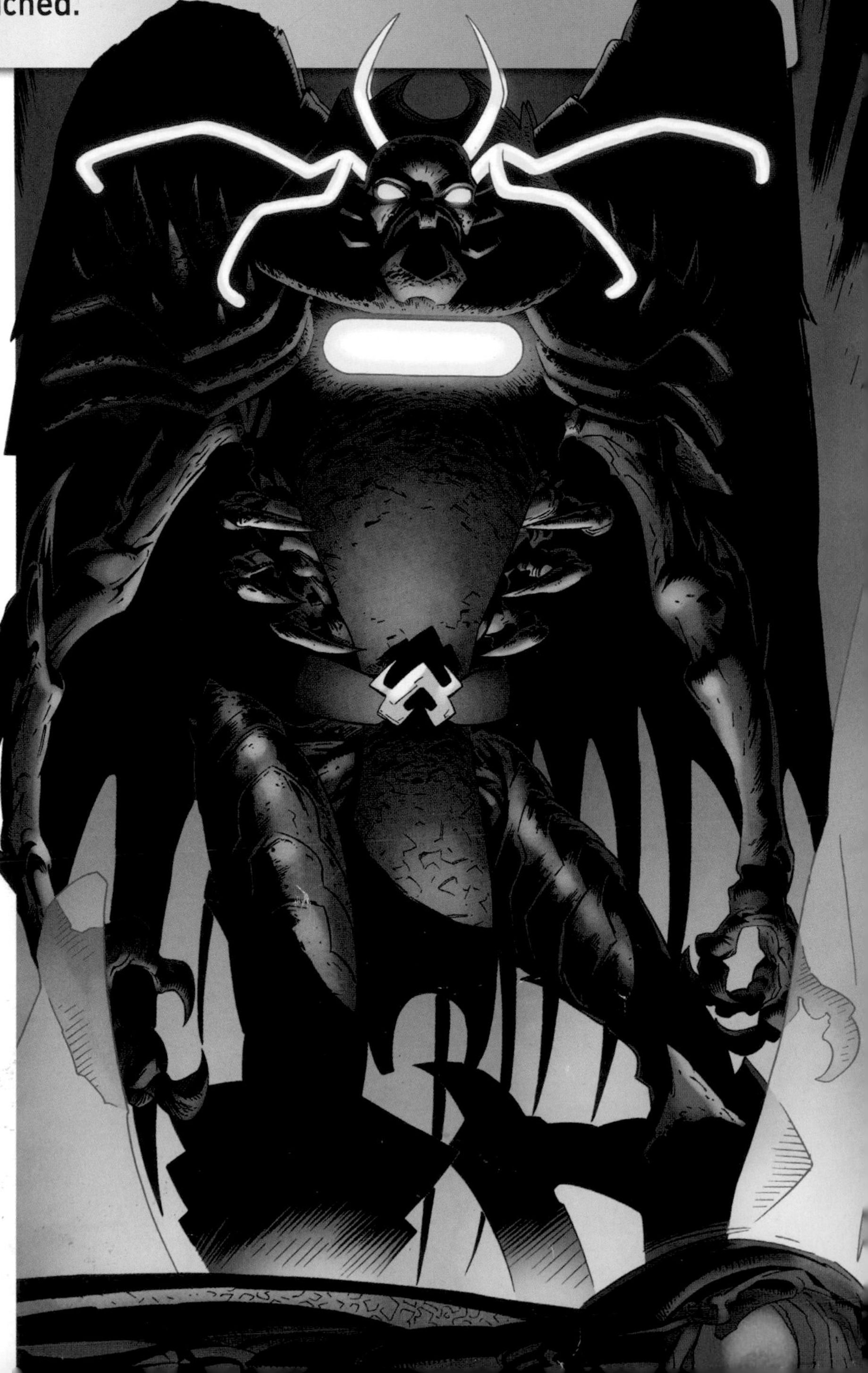

RAVENOUS

A senior commander in the Annihilation Wave, Ravenous was sent by his master to track down the Heralds of Galactus, so that Annihilus could add their power to his own. As the Annihilation Wave swept across the galaxy, Ravenous directed the fight against Nova, Peter Quill, Drax, Gamora, and the rest of the United Front resistance on the planet Daedalus 5. After the destruction of Annihilus, Ronan the Accuser made a pact with Ravenous, ceding swathes of the Kree Empire to him in order to keep the peace.

SUPER-SKRULL

Augmented with powers to match the Fantastic Four, Kl'rt the Super-Skrull is the Skrulls' greatest warrior. He has repeatedly fought the galaxy's heroes, but joined the war to defeat Annihilus when the Annihilation Wave hit the Skrull Empire. Kl'rt was seemingly killed after a mission to the Negative Zone, but when his body was rescued by sentient robot Praxagora, he returned to life.

TENEBROUS AND AEGIS

Tenebrous of the Darkness and Aegis, Lady of All Sorrows, were cosmic beings who warred with Galactus long ago. He imprisoned them, but they were released when the Annihilation Wave destroyed their jail. They struck a deal with Annihilus' ally Thanos, before capturing and enslaving Galactus, but were eventually destroyed by the Silver Surfer.

> ## "We seek Galactus. There are things... **unfinished** between us."
>
> AEGIS

EXTIRPIA

Claiming to be the most favored of Annihilus' three queens, Extirpia formed a hive-mind with Eradica and Extermina to help control the Annihilation Wave. She commanded the forces attacking Nova's United Front on Daedalus 5, until she was captured by Firelord. The buglike queen had the last laugh, however, telling her captors that Galactus had fallen to Tenebrous and Aegis.

PRAXAGORA

Praxagora is a sentient robot from the Negative Zone. The rest of her people were wiped out by Annihilus, and she was thrown in jail. She was freed by Kl'rt the Super-Skrull when he journeyed to the Negative Zone looking for a way to stop the Annihilation Wave. Finding that she had common cause with Kl'rt, Praxagora joined forces with the Super-Skrull, and the pair went on to become lovers during the war.

CENTURIONS

A team of super-powered beings from the Negative Zone, the Centurions were brought together by Annihilus. Led by their commander, Torrent, they helped overpower Nova and the United Front on the planet Daedalus 5.

GALACTUS AND HERALDS

Galactus the Eater-of-Worlds is an unfathomable force of nature. He and his Heralds—who seek planets to sate their master's hunger and act as portents of his arrival—often play a part in cosmic events, such as the Annihilation War.

FALLEN ONE

Galactus' first Herald, the Fallen One, was cast aside by his master after his sadistic nature became apparent. Fueled by Black Matter, he was determined to spread suffering and pain. He was hunted down by Star-Lord, but at the cost of thousands of lives. Later, having come under the influence of Thanos, the Fallen One encountered the ancient cosmic entities Tenebrous and Aegis. They used him to bring about a meeting with Thanos, before draining his power, killing him.

SILVER SURFER

Greatest of all the Heralds, the Silver Surfer was once Norrin Radd, denizen of the peaceful planet Zenn-La. When Galactus planned to destroy Zenn-La, Radd struck a bargain with the Devourer of Worlds: he would seek out other planets for Galactus to consume, in exchange for his own world's safety. Imbued with a portion of the Power Cosmic, he became the Silver Surfer, but rebelled when Galactus sought to devour Earth. He has since played a role in many cosmic events, such as the Annihilation War, when he sided with Galactus once more.

STARDUST

Stardust was Galactus' Herald when Annihilus launched the Annihilation Wave. She was sent to fetch the Silver Surfer, who became a Herald once more to better fight Annihilus. Stardust also joined the other Heralds in the Annihilation War, but fell trying to save the United Front from a weaponized Galactus. She later re-emerged, becoming Galactus' Herald once more.

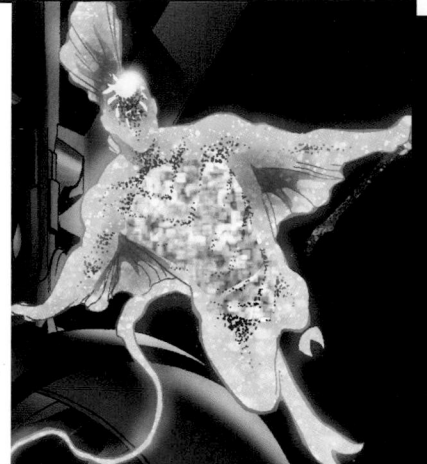

RED SHIFT

After the Fantastic Four and Silver Surfer stopped Galactus from devouring Earth, he tried again with Red Shift as his Herald. The Surfer defeated Red Shift, and the two later became allies in the fight against Annihilus. When Galactus was used by Annihilus to attack the United Front resistance, Red Shift tried to protect them, and was killed.

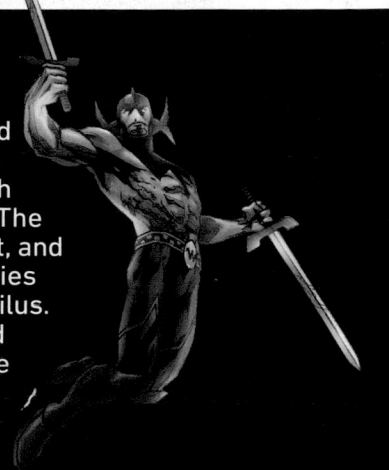

GALACTUS

Galactus was originally Galan, an explorer from the universe that existed before this one. The only survivor when his universe ended, he was reborn in the Big Bang as Galactus, Devourer of Worlds, wielder of the Power Cosmic. An agent of balance in the cosmos, Galactus is driven by a hunger that can only be sated by consuming planets. He tours the universe seeking worlds to devour, and uses his Heralds to locate more. This quest eventually brought him to Earth, where he was thwarted by Reed Richards and the Fantastic Four, and by his Herald, the Silver Surfer. During the conflict with Annihilus, Galactus was defeated by his ancient enemies Tenebrous and Aegis, and then turned into a living weapon by Annihilus. Eventually he was freed, and used the Power Cosmic to wipe out the Annihilation Wave.

AIR-WALKER

Gabriel Lan was a member of the Nova Corps who was abducted by Galactus and turned into the Herald Air-Walker. Galactus uploaded Air-Walker's consciousness to an android body, but then dispensed with his services. When Annihilus dispatched super-powered mercenary Ravenous to capture all of the Heralds, Air-Walker was badly hurt. He was rescued by the Silver Surfer, but he died not long after.

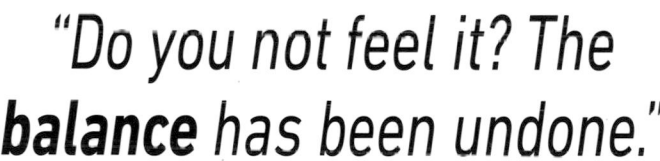

"Do you not feel it? The **balance** *has been undone."*

GALACTUS

FIRELORD

When Galactus transformed Gabriel Lan into Air-Walker, his fellow Nova Corps member Pyreus Kril sought out the Devourer of Worlds, who turned him into Firelord. He was part of the United Front resistance during the Annihilation War, and hunted for Annihilus' super Centurions in its aftermath, destroying some and tasking others with repairing the damage done by the war.

TERRAX

Tyros was a dictator who was chosen by Galactus to become a Herald. He was transformed by the Power Cosmic into Terrax the Tamer, and embraced his role with enthusiasm. Later, as the Annihilation Wave swept through the galaxy, Terrax was taken prisoner by the agents of Ravenous. Annihilus had plans to tap the Herald's cosmic powers, but when Nova defeated Annihilus, Terrax promptly escaped. To reassert his status, he then fought and defeated the dictator Randau the Space Parasite. Instead of freeing the world Randau had subjugated, however, Terrax utterly destroyed it, deeming it weak.

Made of Stone

Rocket's nose for trouble led him to the planet Dandesh Four. Here, he stumbled upon a colony of plant people the D'Bari hiding out from the Skrulls. Angry at being uncovered, the colonists attacked Rocket and used their petrification tech to turn him into a stone statue, but he was found and freed by a passing She-Hulk.

ORIGIN

Genetically enhanced to be keeper of the Loonies—the insane humanoid inmates of the quarantined colony Halfworld—Rocket Raccoon went on to become protector of the entire Keystone Quadrant. When war erupted between two factions of Halfworld's intelligent animals, Rocket helped find a cure for the Loonies and forged an alliance with them that brought peace to the planet. Thereafter, Rocket set out for the stars to seek his destiny on a series of adventures and honing his combat skills that would lead to him becoming a Guardian of the Galaxy.

"Frutackin' flarcknards from Glornu!"

ROCKET RACCOON

Small Soldier

After straying into a Kree restricted zone by accident (or so he claimed), Rocket was drafted into Star-Lord's team of expendable prisoners sent to fight techno-organic conquerors the Phalanx. He quickly formed a bond with another conscript—Groot—who proved handy in transporting Rocket's heavy ordnance.

This handheld missile launcher is Rocket's first choice of ordnance, though he is master of all military hardware, from handguns to ship-to-ship missiles.

ROCKET RACCOON

Fearless, ferocious, and fiercely loyal to his friends, Rocket is the Guardians' diminutive, furry, wisecracking military genius. He's as sharp with his tongue as he is handy with a gun. His strategic smarts have proved decisive against foes, while his devotion to his teammates has bound the group together.

Thanks to his raccoon physiology, Rocket has a heightened sense of hearing. He also has superior eyesight and sense of smell.

Rocket's arms are strong for a raccoon, but he often enlists Groot's aid in carrying all his heavy weaponry.

FURIOUS FURBALL

Rocket Raccoon has earned a deserved reputation as a fearsome warrior. A brilliant tactician with an aptitude for heavy weaponry, Rocket draws much of his martial ability from his heightened animal instincts. However, as unpredictably bloodthirsty as he is in battle, he remains a steadfast ally to his fellow Guardians, not least his firm friend, the *Flora colossus* Groot.

Little and Large

Rocket got a glimpse of life beyond his home planet when the Hulk accidentally arrived on Halfworld. The Jade Giant was initially baffled by the pint-sized talking animal. However, the pair formed an unlikely alliance against nefarious mole Judson Jakes and his cyborg Killer Clowns, with the Hulk's brawn complementing Rocket's military mind.

GROOT

Of all the Guardians of the Galaxy, Groot is perhaps the strangest. Essentially a living tree, when he speaks all most people hear is "I am Groot"—apart from his best buddy Rocket Raccoon, who understands him perfectly. He has become an indispensable part of the team—trusted, dependable, courageous in battle.

Groot can turn his hands into blades. His ability to morph his own structure is an extension of his power to control all other plant matter.

X-Offender

After leaving Planet X, Groot journeyed to Earth. Young and impulsive, he made out he was the King of Planet X, and that he intended to take an Earth town back to his homeworld! The townspeople he met fended him off with fire and covered him with termites, causing him to rue his foolish actions.

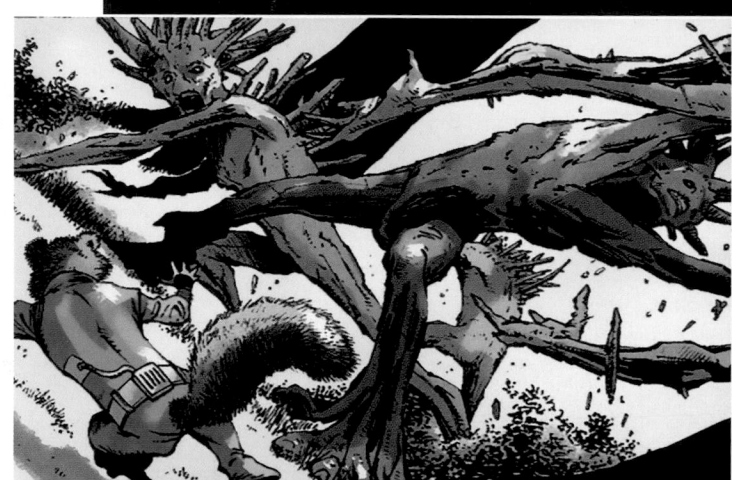

ORIGIN

Born and raised on Planet X, Groot spent his early years absorbing the knowledge and teachings of the Arbor Masters, the custodians of the Branch Worlds. When he was just a sapling, he liked to visit the herbaceous habitats, where maintenance mammals and other fauna tended to the needs of the biome. One day, he chanced upon some of his fellow *Flora colossi* in the habitats, tormenting small mammals. Angered by their behavior, Groot got into a fight and destroyed the tormentors. As a punishment, the Arbor Masters exiled him. He was put on a ship at the Planet X spaceport, and sent away from home.

"I am Groot!"

GROOT

Creature Commando

While hiding out on Earth, Groot was found and captured by the Howling Commandos, a S.H.I.E.L.D. squad composed of the Living Mummy, Vampire by Night, and a variety of other unusual monsters. Confined to a cell, Groot reflected upon his aggressive actions when he arrived on Earth. He turned over a new leaf and became a member of the Howling Commandos, joining their battle against a nefarious sorcerer.

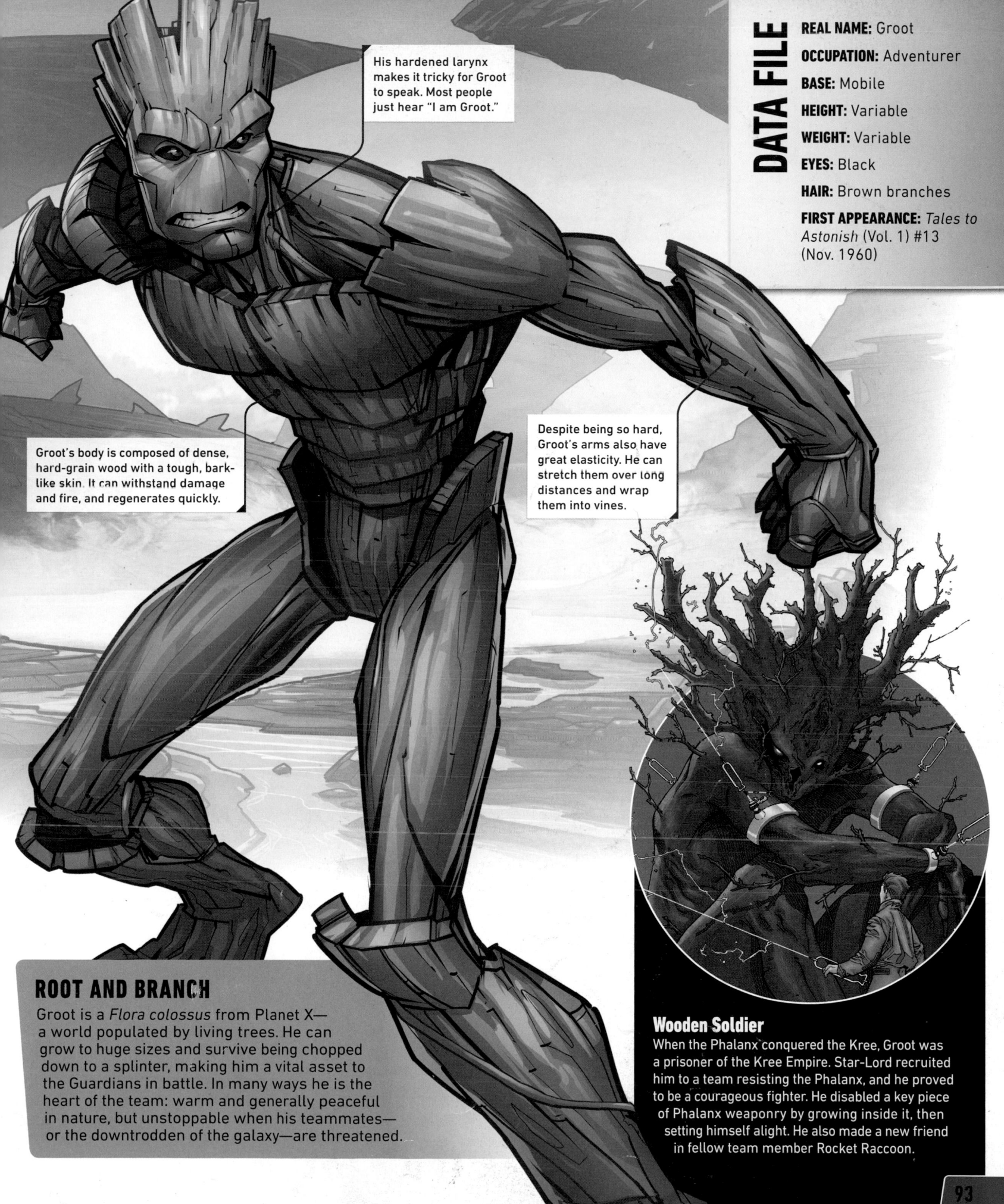

REAL NAME: Groot

OCCUPATION: Adventurer

BASE: Mobile

HEIGHT: Variable

WEIGHT: Variable

EYES: Black

HAIR: Brown branches

FIRST APPEARANCE: *Tales to Astonish* (Vol. 1) #13 (Nov. 1960)

His hardened larynx makes it tricky for Groot to speak. Most people just hear "I am Groot."

Groot's body is composed of dense, hard-grain wood with a tough, bark-like skin. It can withstand damage and fire, and regenerates quickly.

Despite being so hard, Groot's arms also have great elasticity. He can stretch them over long distances and wrap them into vines.

ROOT AND BRANCH

Groot is a *Flora colossus* from Planet X— a world populated by living trees. He can grow to huge sizes and survive being chopped down to a splinter, making him a vital asset to the Guardians in battle. In many ways he is the heart of the team: warm and generally peaceful in nature, but unstoppable when his teammates— or the downtrodden of the galaxy—are threatened.

Wooden Soldier

When the Phalanx conquered the Kree, Groot was a prisoner of the Kree Empire. Star-Lord recruited him to a team resisting the Phalanx, and he proved to be a courageous fighter. He disabled a key piece of Phalanx weaponry by growing inside it, then setting himself alight. He also made a new friend in fellow team member Rocket Raccoon.

ANNIHILATION: CONQUEST

The war with Annihilus has been won, and Peter Quill is making sure the galaxy is ready for future threats. To that end, he has convinced the Kree to grant access to their defense systems, so that the Galadorian Spaceknights can enhance them.

SAVIOR OF THE KREE

On the fringes of Kree space, Phyla-Vell—alias Quasar—and her lover Moondragon, are attacked by a Phalanx-infected Kree Sentry. They defeat it in time to witness a signal coming from Hala that creates an energy barrier around the entire Kree Empire, sealing everyone and everything in. Phyla-Vell receives a telepathic message from the Kree Supreme Intelligence, telling her to find the being who can help save the Kree. After a long quest—during which Moondragon is transformed into an actual dragon—the pair find a cocoon, from which emerges legendary cosmic hero Adam Warlock!

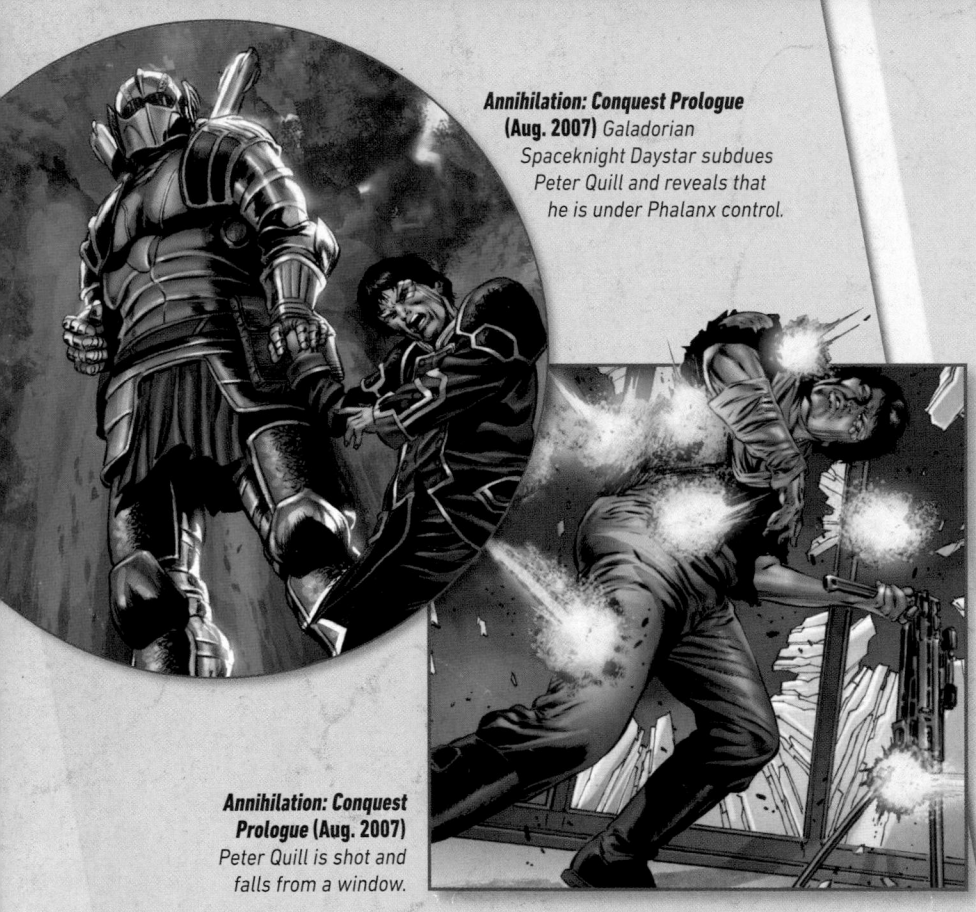

Annihilation: Conquest Prologue (Aug. 2007) *Galadorian Spaceknight Daystar subdues Peter Quill and reveals that he is under Phalanx control.*

Annihilation: Conquest Prologue (Aug. 2007) *Peter Quill is shot and falls from a window.*

Annihilation: Conquest #1 (Jan. 2008) *Phalanx troops including Korath and Xemnu surround Quasar, Adam Warlock, and Moondragon—in her new dragon form.*

ENEMY WITHIN

As soon as the Galadorian software is uploaded to the Kree defense net, the Kree's robotic sentries begin to attack their masters. The cyborg Spaceknights have been infected by the Phalanx—an aggressive techno-organic species of conquerors! As the malware spreads across the Kree homeworld of Hala, Quill tries to organize a fightback, but even the Kree troops become infected. Peter is shot, and plummets from a window, seemingly to his death. Hala now belongs to the Phalanx!

Annihilation: Conquest #3 (Mar. 2008) Star-Lord finds himself at the mercy of Ultron.

Annihilation: Conquest #6 (Jun. 2008) Adam Warlock and the similarly named techno-organic being Warlock join forces against the Phalanx threat.

STAR-LORD RETURNS

Saved from death by the Kree resistance, Peter Quill reclaims the mantle he had given up: Star-Lord. He takes charge of a team of convicts—including future Guardians Rocket Raccoon, Groot, Mantis, and Bug—and sets out to destroy a key Phalanx facility. When they encounter the Phalanx's megalomaniacal leader, the android Ultron, Peter is captured and tortured.

> *"Kree space is ours. **You are ours**. There is nowhere to run."*
>
> THE PHALANX

SLAVES OF THE PHALANX

Richard Rider—aka Nova, last of the Nova Corps—receives a barrage of emergency signals from the Kree Empire. He heads to Hala, where he is infected with the Phalanx virus by his former ally and lover Gamora. As agents of the Phalanx, they capture another old ally, Drax, and infect him, too. Eventually, Nova starts to resist, and journeys to the Phalanx planet—Kvch—where techno-organic beings Tyro and Warlock cure the trio.

Annihilation: Conquest #6 (Jun. 2008) Gamora, Nova, and Drax with the techno-organic beings Tyro and Warlock.

SHOWDOWN ON HALA

At the edge of Kree space, Phyla-Vell, Moondragon, and Adam Warlock are attacked by Ultron and the Phalanx. Moondragon is killed, but Quasar and Adam defeat the Phalanx and head for Hala. They arrive shortly before Nova, Gamora, and Drax. Along with a freed Star-Lord and his team, plus a force commanded by Kree leader Ronan the Accuser, they take the fight to Ultron. The battle is epic, but when Quasar and Adam combine their power, Ultron falls—and the Phalanx with him.

Annihilation: Conquest #6 (Jun. 2008) Quasar faces Ultron in the final battle on Hala.

ANNIHILATION: CONQUEST STARLORD

GIFFEN
GREEN II
OLAZABA
FAIRBAIRN

MARVEL
LIMITED SERIES
1 of 4

SEPTEMBER 2007

ANNIHILATION: CONQUEST—
STAR-LORD #1

PETER QUILL LEADS A SQUAD OF EXPENDABLE CONVICTS TO TAKE THE FIGHT TO THE PHALANX.

Techno-organic invaders the Phalanx have taken control of the Kree homeworld Hala, and now have their sights on the rest of the Kree Empire. Peter Quill unwittingly helped the conquerors by letting the Phalanx-infected Spaceknights gain access to Hala's security net. Peter barely escaped with his life—now he must make amends.

MAIN CHARACTERS
Peter Quill—Star-Lord

SUPPORTING CHARACTERS
Kree Captain Chan-Dar •
Kree Admiral Galen-Kor
• Rocket Raccoon • Groot •
Mantis • Bug • Deathcry
• Captain Universe—Gabe
Vargas • Fallen One

MAIN LOCATIONS
Aladon Prime—Kree
Fringe System

1 In a Kree hospital, Peter awaits surgery to repair his battered body and remove his cybernetic implants. At first, the surgeon is reluctant to treat him, arguing that Peter was to blame for the fall of Hala. Chan-Dar retorts that Peter helped stop the Annihilation Wave; fell defending Hala; and is now needed again.

2 Lying on the surgeon's table, Peter reflects on his career as Star-Lord: a life spent zipping around the cosmos righting wrongs and fighting monsters. He recalls the time he sacrificed thousands of lives to defeat the Fallen One. In the aftermath of that decision, he rejected the name and role of Star-Lord, and ran away from his humanity by getting cybernetic implants.

3 As soon as he recovers, Peter is briefed by Kree Admiral Galen-Kor, who tells him he has been healed to lead an expendable team of prisoners in an assault on the Phalanx's infiltration system, to stop them infecting the entire galaxy. Among the team of conscripts are Rocket Raccoon, Groot, Bug, and Mantis.

> "The problem with **having a past**, Mr. Quill, is that sooner or later it will **catch up** with you..."
>
> KREE CAPTAIN CHAN-DAR

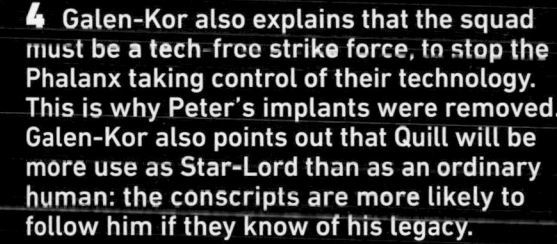

4 Galen-Kor also explains that the squad must be a tech-free strike force, to stop the Phalanx taking control of their technology. This is why Peter's implants were removed. Galen-Kor also points out that Quill will be more use as Star-Lord than as an ordinary human: the conscripts are more likely to follow him if they know of his legacy.

5 Outfitted with uniforms that dampen their heat signatures, and equipped with rudimentary firearms, the team prepares for the off. They will be inserted into Hala's capital, and from there must fight their way to the facility where the Phalanx are building viral bombs for infecting the whole galaxy—and blow it up!

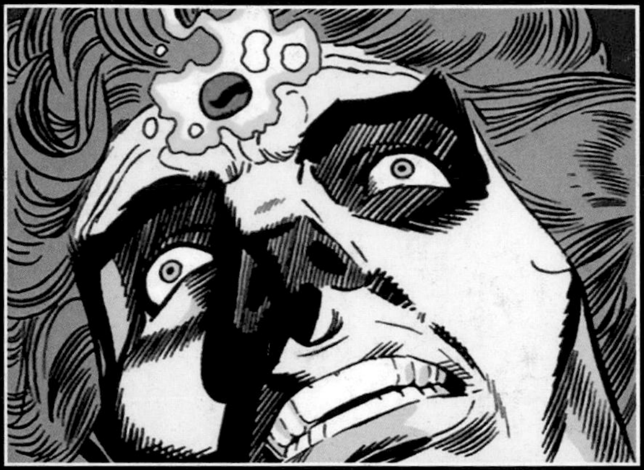

Soul Power

The High Evolutionary taught Adam an appreciation of—and a compassion for—life in all its forms. He also gave him the powerful Soul Gem, one of the reality-warping Infinity Gems. Adam formed the Infinity Watch to guard the Gems from those who sought to abuse them, such as Thanos. Its members included the Guardians-to-be Drax, Gamora, and Moondragon.

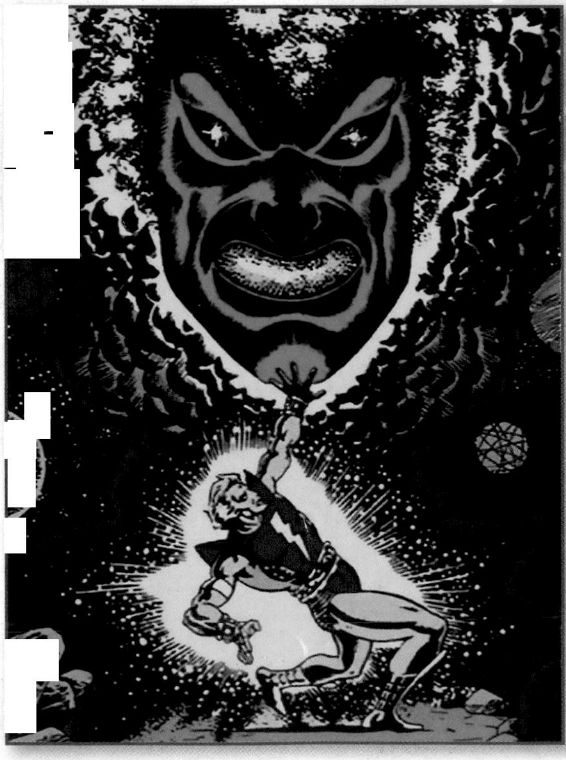

The Dark Half

In the course of his cosmic travels, Adam came into conflict with the aggressively expansionist Universal Church of Truth and their god, the evil Magus. Horrified to learn that the Magus was a corrupted version of himself from the future, Adam successfully altered his own timeline. Though he saved himself from becoming the Magus, the dark power within him remains a risk.

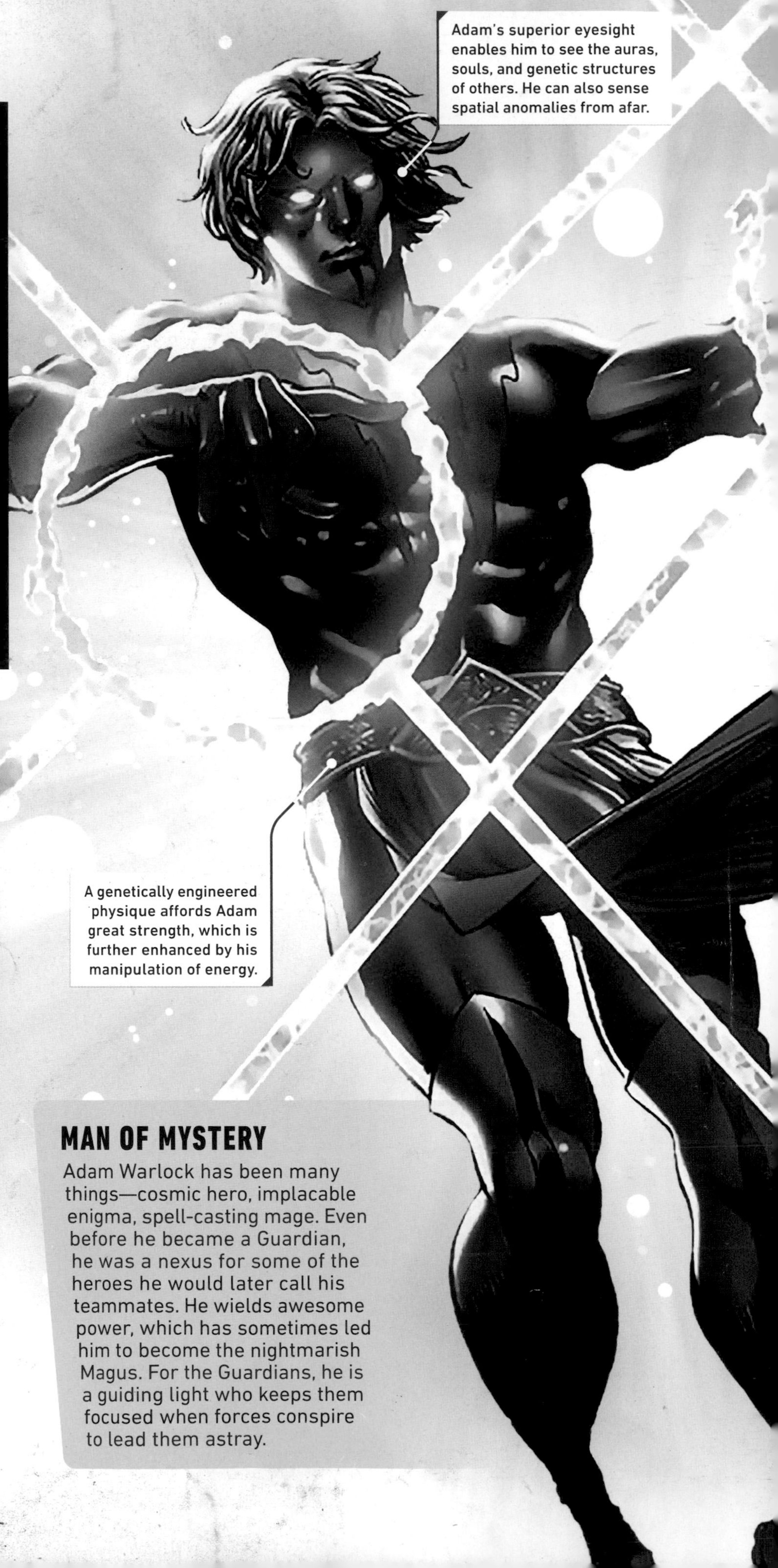
Adam's superior eyesight enables him to see the auras, souls, and genetic structures of others. He can also sense spatial anomalies from afar.
A genetically engineered physique affords Adam great strength, which is further enhanced by his manipulation of energy.

MAN OF MYSTERY

Adam Warlock has been many things—cosmic hero, implacable enigma, spell-casting mage. Even before he became a Guardian, he was a nexus for some of the heroes he would later call his teammates. He wields awesome power, which has sometimes led him to become the nightmarish Magus. For the Guardians, he is a guiding light who keeps them focused when forces conspire to lead them astray.

> ## "We've got to keep the galaxy stable. *It's become too fragile.*"
> — Adam Warlock

ORIGIN

The being known only as "Him" was created by a group of Earth scientists who sought to bring forth the perfect human. Gestated in a cocoon, he was "born" fully grown and invested with incredible strength, psychic powers, and near invulnerability. He sought his destiny among the stars, where he met genetic manipulator the High Evolutionary, who gave him the name "Warlock." On Counter-Earth—the mirror world created by the High Evolutionary—Adam learned that, though there was evil in the galaxy, there was also goodness, and that one man was enough to make a difference in the cosmos.

Adam Warlock's ability to manipulate energy extends to projecting powerful cosmic blasts from his hands.

Warlock Reborn

Originally born from a cocoon, Adam sometimes returns to one in order to regenerate. When the techno-organic species the Phalanx conquered the Kree, he emerged from hibernation equipped with a whole new set of powers, including the ability to use quantum magic, teleport, and raise force fields.

ADAM WARLOCK

Adam Warlock is the Guardians' golden-skinned warrior sorcerer. A riddle wrapped in a mystery, he is an artificially created man who has dedicated his existence to saving lives and protecting the galaxy. When dark forces threaten to tear the fabric of space asunder, Adam Warlock will move heaven and earth to keep our universe secure.

DATA FILE

REAL NAME: Adam Warlock

OCCUPATION: Sorcerer, galactic protector

BASE: Knowhere

HEIGHT: 6ft 2in

WEIGHT: 240 lbs

EYES: White

HAIR: Golden

FIRST APPEARANCE: (as "Him") *Fantastic Four* (Vol. 1) #66 (Sep. 1967); (as Warlock) *Marvel Premiere* (Vol. 1) #1 (Apr. 1972)

MANTIS

Serene and mysterious, Mantis is the Guardians' resident psychic and counselor. Based mostly on the Guardians' HQ, Knowhere, she also accompanies the team on missions from time to time. That's when she gets to show off her full range of skills, which include unparalleled martial arts prowess and powerful telepathy.

Antennae help Mantis sense the feelings of others and communicate telepathically.

> "Yes, I **know** what you're thinking. No, **really**."
>
> MANTIS

Celestial Avenger

Before she became a Guardian, Mantis was an Avenger. It was during her time with that team that she first encountered her future Guardians teammates Moondragon and Drax. It was not a friendly first meeting with the Destroyer, however. Drax had broken into the Avengers Mansion seeking aid in his hunt for Thanos and wound up in an altercation with Mantis, Black Panther, and Swordsman.

ORIGIN

As a young child, Mantis was left by her father (the villain Libra), with a sect of the Kree called the Priests of Pama. At their monastery in the Vietnamese jungle, the priests taught her martial arts skills and trained her mind to bring about powers of telepathy. They worshipped her, believing that she would one day become a being they called the Celestial Madonna. After she left the monastery, Mantis joined the Avengers for a time, before leaving Earth to seek her destiny among the stars.

Mantis' arms are lethal. As well as being trained in martial arts, she can sense and target her enemies' weakest pressure points.

Through meditation, Mantis uses her brain to consciously control functions that are more usually automatic, such as her heartbeat and blood flow.

DATA FILE

REAL NAME: Unknown

OCCUPATION: Celestial Madonna

BASE: Knowhere

HEIGHT: 5ft 6in

WEIGHT: 115 lbs

EYES: Green

HAIR: Black

FIRST APPEARANCE: *The Avengers* (Vol. 1) #112 (Jun. 1973)

Madonna vs. Madman

After her time with the Avengers, Mantis traveled the galaxy in search of enlightenment. Instead, she found violence and madness, often caused by Thanos. Fearing that, as the Celestial Madonna, Mantis was a threat to him, the Mad Titan pursued her across time and space. In battle, Mantis' will proved stronger than that of Thanos, and she prevailed.

MIND POWER

Mantis is a trusted advisor and guide to the Guardians, offering empathic counsel after mentally scarring missions. At one with the universe, she can be maddeningly cryptic, but her ability to glimpse the future makes her one of the key Guardians—as do her telepathy and hand-to-hand combat skills.

Kung-Fu Fighter

Mantis proved her combat effectiveness as part of the team Star-Lord assembled to fight the Phalanx invasion. With her precognition and telepathy skills, she was able to anticipate her enemies' moves before felling them with her martial arts. She became a trusted adviser and confidante for Peter Quill, a role she would continue to fulfill as a Guardian.

SHHHK-KKT

THE PHALANX AND ULTRON

Barely recovered from the Annihilation War, the galaxy was shaken by another devastating conflict. Armed with a virus that could infect both technology and organic matter, the cybernetic Phalanx conquered the Kree homeworld, Hala, before spreading across the Kree Empire.

"I am the Phalanx. And the Phalanx is me."

ULTRON

THE PHALANX

Techno-organic in nature, the Phalanx have existed in various forms. An offshoot of the cybernetic race the Technarchy, the first recorded instance of the Phalanx was on Earth, when a group of mutant-hating humans infected themselves with the Technarchy's transmode virus. Later, another version of the Phalanx used their virus to infect the Shi'ar Empire. The Phalanx that conquered the Kree Empire were yet another variety, this one corrupted by and modeled on their master, Ultron. After conquering the Kree homeworld of Hala by gaining control of its security net, this strain of Phalanx built a Babel Spire on the planet—a transmitter designed to spread the species.

CHIEF SUBJUGATOR

The Phalanx's Chief Subjugator was charged with selecting and capturing those individuals the Phalanx wanted to add to their collective—beings with special abilities or particular usefulness. Once chosen, these Selects—as the Phalanx termed them—were made into agents of the Phalanx, subject to their will, but allowed to retain some of their original personalities. The reasoning was that this would make the Selects independent enough to perform effectively on their own instincts, while also keeping them loyal to their Phalanx masters.

SELECT GAMORA

As the Phalanx spread outward from Hala across the Kree Empire, Gamora found herself in their path. One of the first super-powered individuals to be captured and turned into a Select, she was tasked with eliminating Nova as a threat to the Phalanx, or processing him for Selection. After she turned her former lover and Annihilation War ally into a Select, the pair set out to locate another former ally, Drax, and turned him into a Select as well.

ULTRON

Created by Hank Pym—alias Ant Man/Goliath from the Avengers—Ultron is a deranged sentient robot hell-bent on conquest. His schemes have plagued the Avengers for years, with each new encounter resulting in Ultron's defeat or even his destruction. Yet he always returns, his consciousness transferred to a new, improved robot body. To stop this cycle, Ultron's consciousness was finally consigned to deep space, where il was retrieved by the Phalanx. Rather than submit to the cybernetic species, however, Ultron seized control of the Phalanx. He moulded them in his own likeness and gave them new direction and devastating purpose.

SELECT NOVA

After responding to distress calls from Hala, Nova fought off the techno-organic virus, only to be transformed into a Select by Gamora. Together, they hunted down Drax and delivered him for Selection, but in time Nova was able to rid himself of the virus once and for all, and escaped Hala. He, in turn, was pursued by Gamora and Drax, but lured them to a place where they too could be freed from the Phalanx's influence.

SELECT RONAN

Ronan the Accuser, leader of the Kree, succumbed to the Phalanx after Hala, the Kree homeworld, fell. The Phalanx used his innate talents as a master interrogator to question prisoners, but Ronan fought against his programming, refusing to accept final Selection. Eventually Ronan was released from the Phalanx's influence by a rebel force that included his Annihilation War allies Praxagora and Super-Skrull.

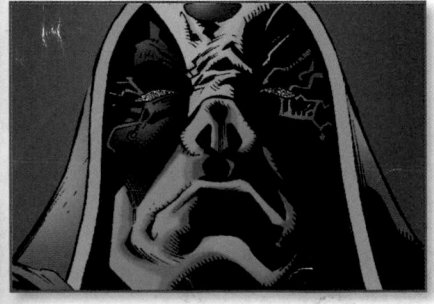

SELECT BLASTAAR

The Negative Zone villain Blastaar fought a war of resistance against the Phalanx, commanding a troop of Kree soldiers on Hala. But the Phalanx captured him and turned him into a Select. His last act as a resistance fighter was to transmit vital schematics for the Phalanx's Babel Spire to Star-Lord and his team. Once transformed, however, Blastaar captured Star-Lord and killed team member Gabe Vargas.

SELECT SUPER-ADAPTOID

Created on Earth by the criminal scientists A.I.M. (Advanced Idea Mechanics), the Super-Adaptoid was an android that could mimic the abilities of any super-powered being. It left Earth and joined the Phalanx, finding new purpose as a Select. Moondragon and Phyla-Vell fought the android while they searched for Adam Warlock, and Phyla-Vell eventually slew it with her Quantum Sword.

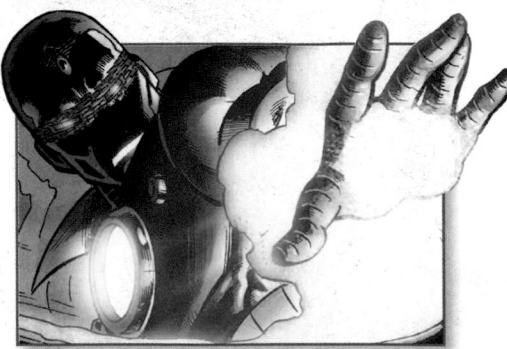

> The kinetic energy he generates from his hands not only allows Blastaar to strike opponents from afar, but also to propel himself through the air.

> "I fear nothing!! I can be stopped by no one! I am a law unto myself!! I am supreme!! I am Blastaar!!"
>
> BLASTAAR

Double Negatives

Blastaar's chief rival in the Negative Zone is Annihilus, another tyrant with a thirst for power. At first the villains worked together to conquer the Zone, but they soon betrayed one another. Later, Blastaar tried to enlist the aid of Annihilus when invading Earth, only to end up fighting him for supremacy.

Blastaar Unbound

Blastaar is driven by an urge to conquer, as he demonstrated not long after he escaped the Negative Zone for the first time. Allying himself with the super villain Sandman, he launched an attack on New York, as the first stage in his plan to rule Earth. Even the combined might of the Fantastic Four could barely slow him down, until Mister Fantastic succeeded in fitting a specially designed helmet onto Blastaar's head, which stopped him blasting energy bolts from his hands.

ORIGIN

On the planet Baluur in the Negative Zone, Blastaar ruled his fellow Baluurians with an iron first. Eventually Blastaar's people rebelled and overthrew their tyrannical monarch, but they were unable to slay him because he was so powerful. Instead, they sedated him, encased him in a containment suit, and exiled him in space. When Blastaar woke, he blasted himself free and made his escape from the Negative Zone by using the Fantastic Four's dimensional portal. He then launched a reign of terror on Earth—the first of many rampages across the galaxy.

BLASTAAR

One of the Guardians' most destructive foes, Blastaar is a power-hungry despot from the Negative Zone. Unpredictable and literally explosive—he can blast energy at his opponents—he is willing to collaborate with the Guardians when it suits his own aims, though these temporary and uneasy alliances are entirely lacking in trust.

Blastaar's thick, gray hide can withstand enormous variations in temperature and pressure, and even missile strikes!

Friend or Foe?

When it serves his own ends, Blastaar has been known to side with the forces of good. He was willing to fight his old enemy Annihilus in the Annihilation War, and joined forces with Star-Lord's assault team in the battle against the Phalanx. However, he ended up as a slave of the Phalanx, capturing Star-Lord and killing a member of his team.

VOLATILE VILLAIN

Time and again, Blastaar has turned up in the Guardians' lives—especially that of Star-Lord. Initially, he was an ally in the fight against Annihilus' Annihilation Wave, but later encounters have proved far more antagonistic. With a hunger for power that knows no end—and mighty energy-blasting powers—Blastaar is an opponent to be reckoned with, as the Guardians have learned to their cost.

Powerful musculature and superhuman stamina enable Blastaar to run at incredible speeds without fatigue for several days.

DATA FILE

REAL NAME: Blastaar

OCCUPATION: Outlaw, despot, would-be conqueror

BASE: Baluur

HEIGHT: 6ft 6in

WEIGHT: 520 lbs

EYES: Gray

HAIR: Gray

FIRST APPEARANCE: *Fantastic Four* (Vol. 1) #62 (May 1967)

Forged in the fire of Annihilation and Annihilation: Conquest, a maverick team of present-day Guardians of the Galaxy debuted in their own title in 2008. The new series starred an innovative mix of intergalactic misfits and outsiders: Star-Lord, Drax the Destroyer, Gamora, Rocket Raccoon, Groot, Adam Warlock, and Phyla-Vell.

GUARDIANS OF THE MODERN ERA

GUARDIANS OF THE GALAXY (VOL. 2) #2 (AUG. 2008)
Discovering Major Victory from the 31st-century Guardians in a block of ice, the new Guardians decide to name themselves after his team!

GUARDIANS OF THE GALAXY (VOL. 2) #15 (AUG. 2009)
The War of Kings goes into overdrive, as the Guardians desperately defend their HQ, Knowhere, from the Shi'ar, the Kree, and the Inhumans.

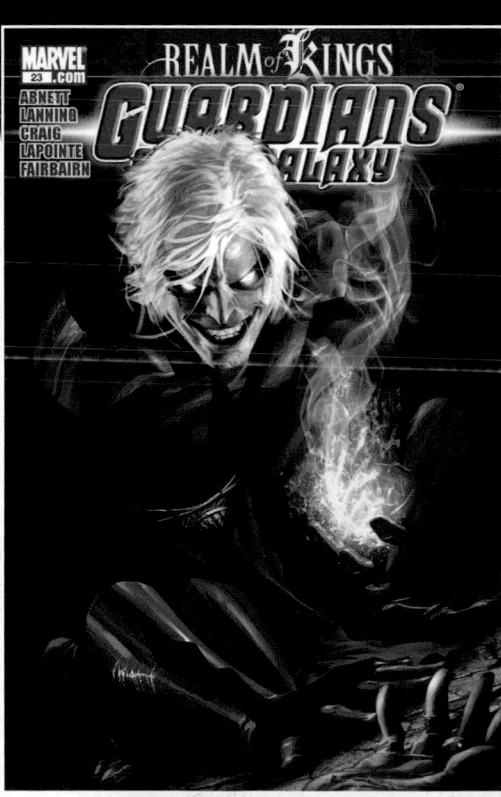

GUARDIANS OF THE GALAXY
(VOL. 2) #23 (APR. 2010)
The Magus—a future Adam Warlock—kidnaps half the Guardians, triggering events that will tear the team apart.

THANOS IMPERATIVE: IGNITION
(VOL. 1) #1 (JUL. 2010)
Thanos has returned—but he might just be the galaxy's only hope, as the Magus unleashes an undead invasion from another dimension!

MAY 2008

MAIN CHARACTERS
Peter Quill—Star-Lord • Rocket Raccoon • Groot • Adam Warlock • Phyla-Vell—Quasar • Drax • Gamora

SUPPORTING CHARACTERS
Richard Rider—Nova • Cosmo • Mantis • Matriarch of the Universal Church of Truth

MAIN LOCATIONS
Hala—the Kree homeworld • Knowhere—the Guardians' interdimensional base • Universal Church of Truth Templeship *Tancred*

GUARDIANS OF THE GALAXY (Vol. 2) #1

FORWARD-THINKING PETER QUILL RECRUITS A NEW TEAM TO PROTECT THE GALAXY.

Two conflicts have devastated the galaxy. First the Annihilation Wave, then the Phalanx conquest of the Kree. Peter Quill, alias Star-Lord, knows the galaxy will not survive another assault. It needs increased protection. With the help of his ally Nova (Richard Rider) and his first recruit, Quasar (Phyla-Vell), he sets about assembling a brand new force.

1 Star-Lord seeks out Rocket Raccoon and Groot, with whom he fought the Phalanx. He explains that he needs Rocket's military smarts, and the pair agree to team up with him once again. Rocket even comes up with a few team names, including "Ass-Kickers of the Fantastic" and "Rocket Raccoon and His Human Hangers-On." Neither one is met with enthusiasm.

2 Drax broods beside the grave of his daughter, Moondragon. Her lover, Phyla-Vell, arrives to tell him that she has an offer that could give him a new purpose. When he points out that he is a liability—a killer who is not fit for company—Phyla counters that they will see how long they can put up with him.

3 When Gamora is visited by her occasional lover Nova, she thinks at first that he's intent on rekindling their romance. She reacts angrily when she learns that he's recruiting for Star-Lord's new team. However, Nova's argument that joining would help her sense of self-worth sways her, and the two make up (and out).

> ## "I'm suggesting **an ass-kicking force**. Tough, elite, ready to deploy the instant **anything** flies toward the fan."
>
> PETER QUILL

4 The unnamed team is completed by the addition of Adam Warlock, who is alarmed at the weakened condition of the fabric of space-time. The squad's first assignment bears out Adam's fears, as a Universal Church of Truth Templeship breaches a fissure in the fabric of space, causing an extra-dimensional monstrosity to be unleashed.

5 After exploding the Universal Church of Truth ship to seal the fissure, the team return to their new base, Knowhere. Almost as soon as they arrive, however, Adam Warlock detects another fissure in space. Waiting to be found there, on a frozen asteroid, is a figure encased in ice holding Captain America's shield...

COSMO

He might look like a regular dog (albeit one wearing a spacesuit), but Cosmo is no ordinary canine. This remnant from the Russian space program is a telepath who "speaks" with a Russian accent and emits telekinetic blasts. He is a faithful friend to the Guardians, joining them on missions and guarding their base Knowhere.

Cosmo's telepathic powers make his brown eyes glow electric blue and enable him to control minds and create illusions.

Passports to Peril

Cosmo has given the Guardians access to many of Knowhere's technological wonders, such as passport bracelets. These wrist-mounted devices allow the user to teleport anywhere within any universe. When Nova first came to Knowhere, he was on the run from the Phalanx-infected Drax and Gamora, so Cosmo gave him a passport bracelet to help his flight from his pursuers.

> "No more **Mr. Nice Dog**. Now Cosmo will hurt **everyone**."
>
> COSMO

Mind Over Monsters

When Cosmo first encountered Nova, the space dog showed off the full extent of his telekinetic powers. With Knowhere under sustained attack by Abyss—an evil sorcerer who was turning the station's inhabitants into zombies—Cosmo unleashed a mighty psionic pulse. This blasted the monsters away, leaving only the thoroughly impressed Corpsman.

ORIGIN

In the early days of Earth's space program, the human race used dogs and chimps as test subjects—launching them into orbit and beyond. One such animal was Cosmo, a dog who was sent into Earth's orbit by the Soviet Union. However, Cosmo's rocket drifted into deep space, where he mutated, gaining human-level intelligence, powers of telepathy and telekinetic skills. In time, he found his way to Knowhere— the bizarre space station inside a giant severed head—and won the position of station security chief. There he met Nova, last of the Nova Corps, and the pair became friends when they teamed up to keep the station safe. This eventually led him to cross paths with Drax, Gamora, and the other Guardians.

FRIEND AND GUARDIAN

Far more than just man's best friend, Cosmo is responsible for the safety of many species in his capacity as Knowhere's chief of security. To the Guardians, he is a cherished and trusted team member, who affords access to vital facilities such as teleport bracelets, and who even joins them on the occasional mission.

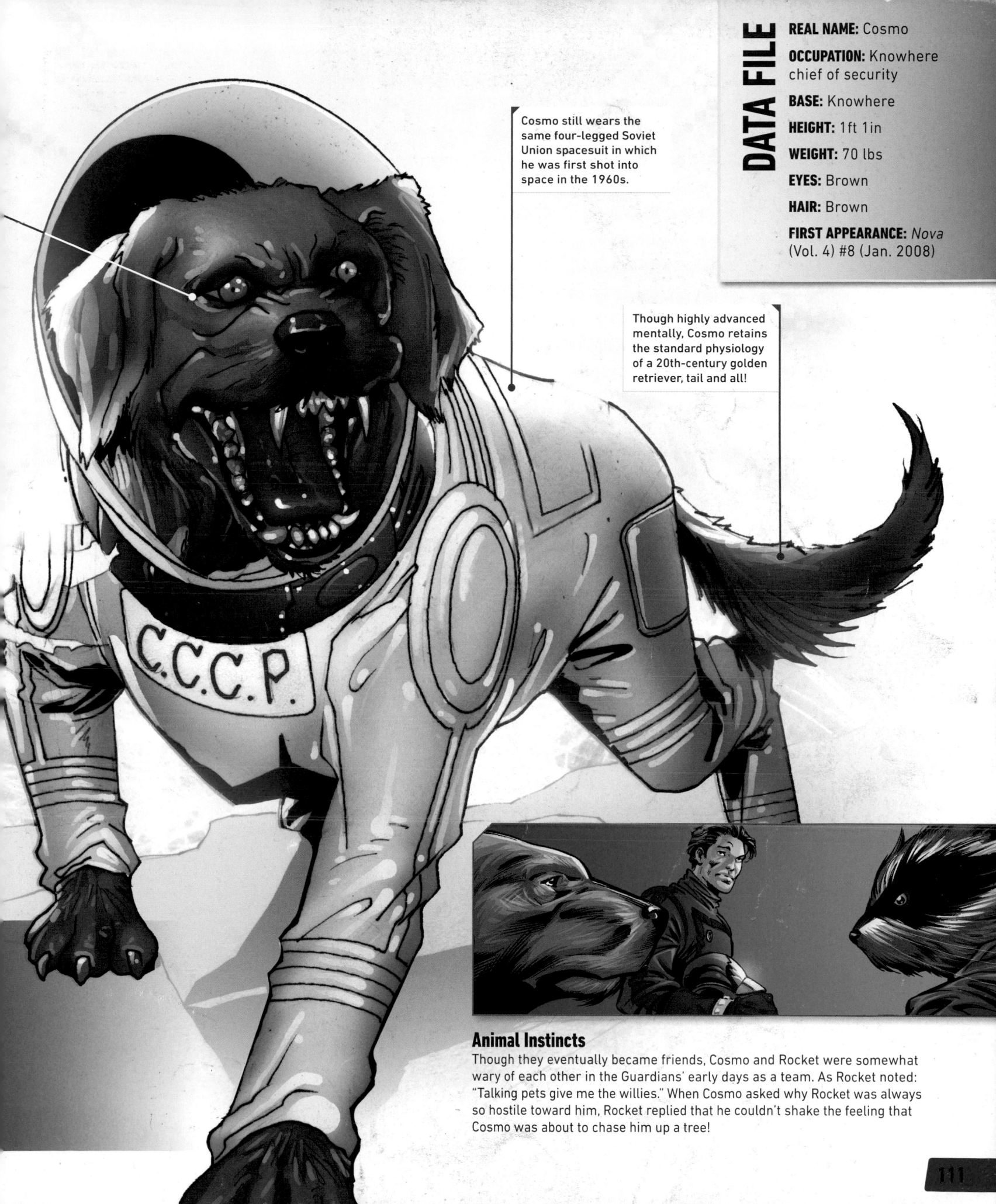

REAL NAME: Cosmo

OCCUPATION: Knowhere chief of security

BASE: Knowhere

HEIGHT: 1ft 1in

WEIGHT: 70 lbs

EYES: Brown

HAIR: Brown

FIRST APPEARANCE: *Nova* (Vol. 4) #8 (Jan. 2008)

Cosmo still wears the same four-legged Soviet Union spacesuit in which he was first shot into space in the 1960s.

Though highly advanced mentally, Cosmo retains the standard physiology of a 20th-century golden retriever, tail and all!

C.C.C.P.

Animal Instincts

Though they eventually became friends, Cosmo and Rocket were somewhat wary of each other in the Guardians' early days as a team. As Rocket noted: "Talking pets give me the willies." When Cosmo asked why Rocket was always so hostile toward him, Rocket replied that he couldn't shake the feeling that Cosmo was about to chase him up a tree!

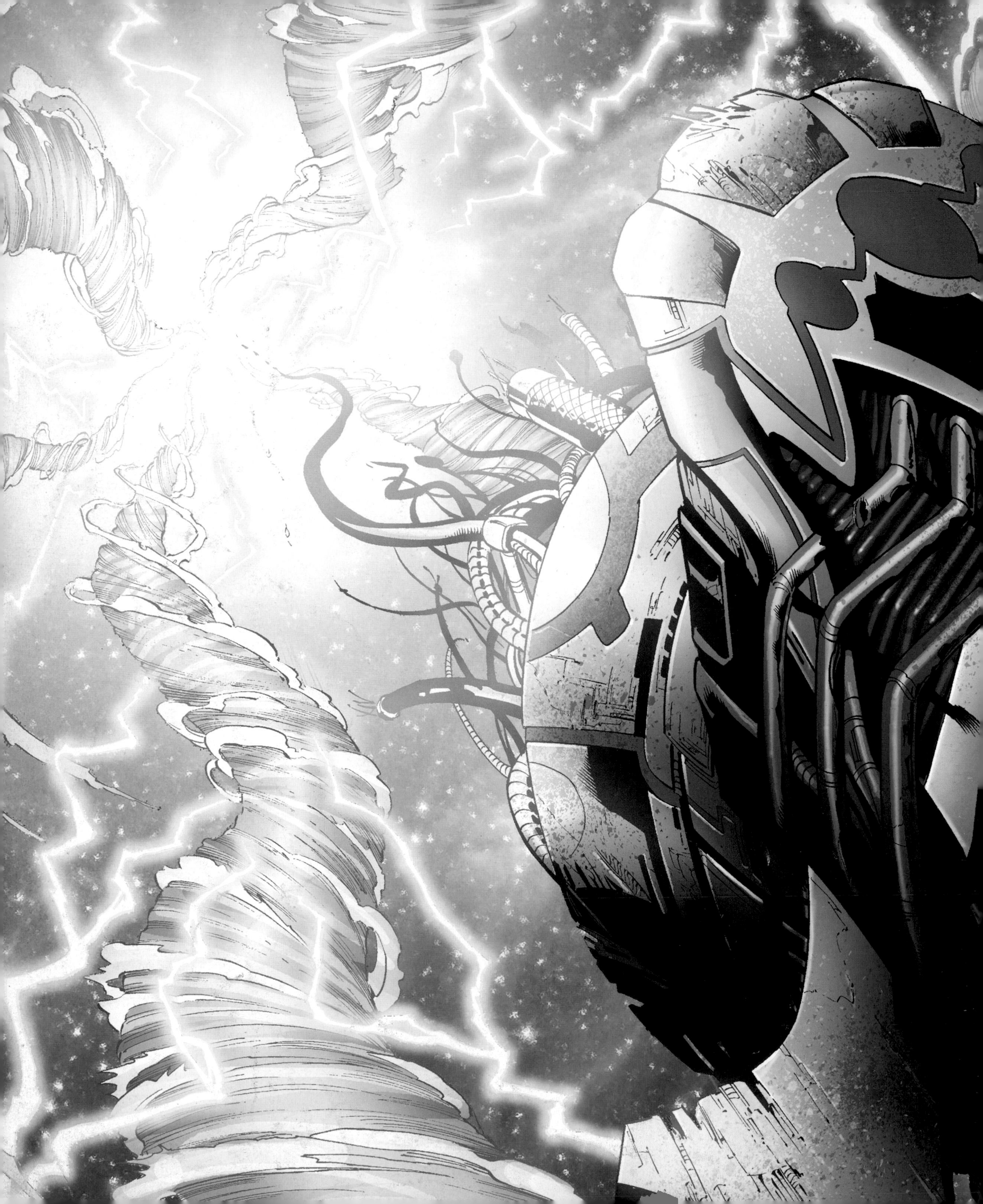

NOVA (VOL. 4) #8
JANUARY 2008

Knowhere is the Guardians' base—a space station constructed inside the gigantic severed head of a Celestial (an ancient cosmic being). Situated at an interdimensional nexus, it was discovered by Nova while on the run from the Phalanx. Later, Knowhere's chief of security, Cosmo, invited the Guardians to make the station their HQ.

THE LUMINALS

A rival team to the Guardians, the Luminals are the protectors of their homeworld Xarth Three, and their base, the pan-dimensional nexus Knowhere. When the Guardians made Knowhere their base, too, the teams began a rivalry that sometimes turned into violence.

"What in the name of **Xarth...?!**"

CYNOSURE

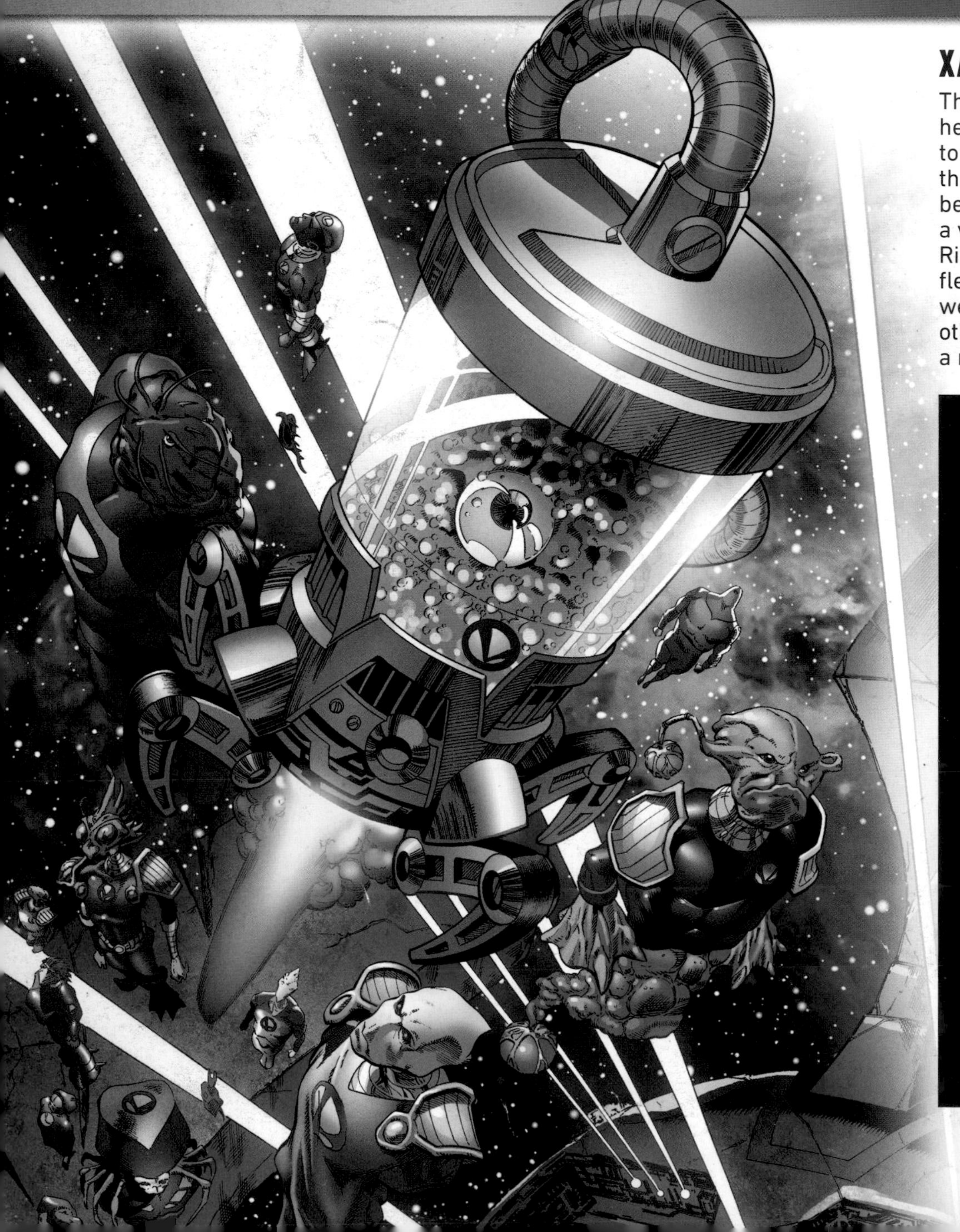

XARTH'S FINEST

The Luminals are a team of peace-keeping heroes from Xarth Three, roughly equivalent to Earth's Avengers. Based out of Knowhere, they are led by Cynosure—a hereditary title bestowed upon the team's leader—and take a variety of shapes and forms. Nova (Richard Rider) met them when he came to Knowhere fleeing the Phalanx. At that time the Luminals were led by Saen Sendak, but he and several other Luminals were killed when they took on a nightmarish entity known as Abyss.

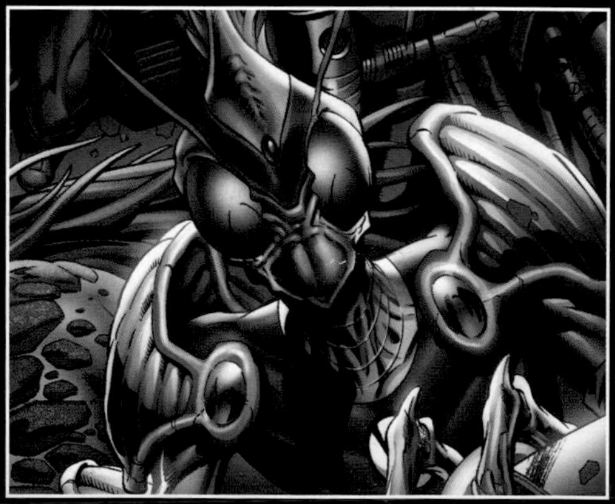

IMPACT

An expert hand-to-hand fighter, Impact is a Dwi Theet master of six martial arts. He, Massdriver, and Brightstorm were deputized to hunt down Drax after the Guardian went rogue hunting for Skulls on Knowhere. Drax tricked Impact into striking Brightstorm, shattering his ribs, before Impact turned on the Destroyer and sent him flying. However, Drax, also a Dwi Theet master, finally prevailed.

MASSDRIVER

The team's powerhouse, Massdriver is a heavyweight fighter who could go ten rounds with Terrax and not break a sweat. Joining Impact and Brightstorm in their clash with Drax during the Skrull Secret Invasion, she more than matched the Destroyer for brute strength, but was eventually bested when he dislocated her arms. She was later infected by a demonic entity after a Luminal expedition into the dimensional rift leading to the Cancerverse. The entity sent her on a berserker rampage before bursting out of her body, killing her in the process.

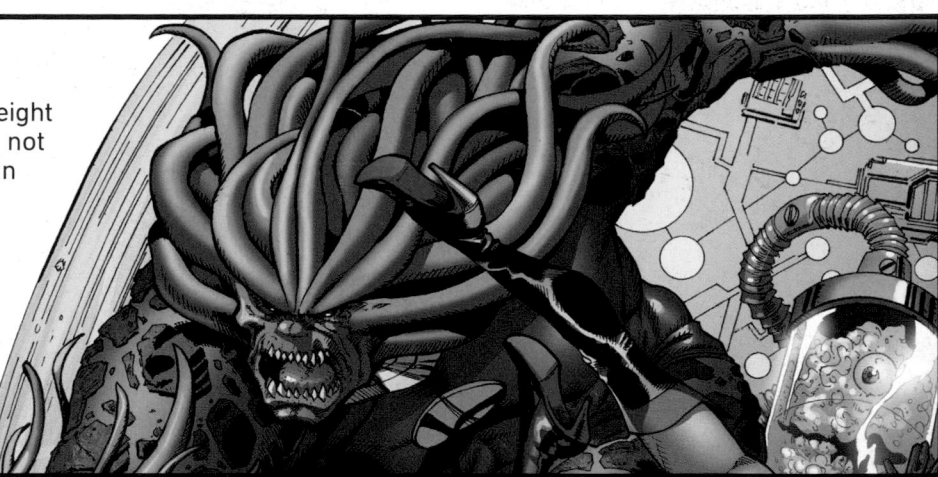

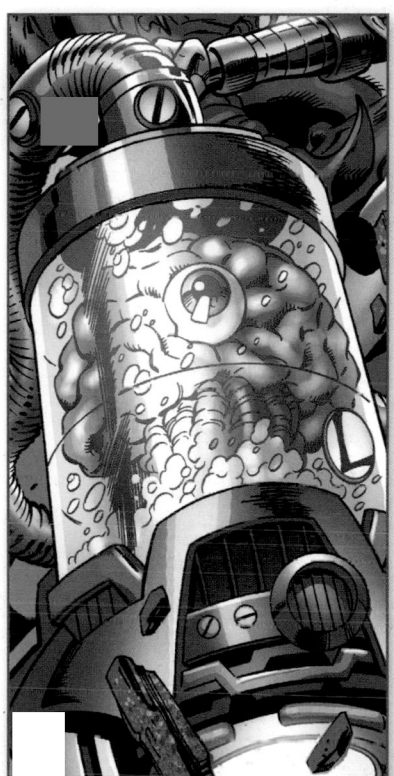

JARHEAD

A giant brain in a weaponized life-support unit on robot legs, Jarhead is the strangest of all the Luminals. Unfailingly loyal to Cynosure, he was at her side when the Luminals located the Skrull cell on Knowhere during the Secret Invasion, and he has been known to speak for her in negotiations—being somewhat more diplomatic than Cynosure herself. He was at the forefront of the Luminals response when the Universal Church of Truth abducted both Cynosure and Moondragon and took them to Sacrosanct, the Church's home planet. Jarhead and his fellow Luminals teamed up with the Guardians to launch an all-out assault, teleporting the whole of Knowhere to Sacrosanct. As they began the attack, Jarhead ordered his teammates to "pick your targets and mash them!"

CYNOSURE (LENA SENDAK)

Lena Sendak inherited the role of Cynosure, leader of the Xarthian Luminals, from her brother Saen. He was killed battling Abyss' undead army alongside Nova when he first came to Knowhere. As Cynosure, Lena liaises with Cosmo, Knowhere's canine chief of security, and with Knowhere's Administrative Council. She took a disliking to Star-Lord and the Guardians as soon as they started using Knowhere as their base. She saw them as a bunch of vigilantes who had set up on the station without permission. The bad feeling was mutual, but after the two teams joined forces to defeat the Universal Church of Truth, Lena and Star-Lord gained a new respect for one another.

BRIGHTSTORM

The Luminals' energy caster is able to emit powerful photonic blasts from the orbs at the end of his antennae. When Impact, Massdriver, and Brightstorm were assigned to locate Drax, Brightstorm was the first to be attacked by the Destroyer, who identified him as the greatest danger of the three. Knowing that Brightstorm was made of tough stuff, Drax hit him with a spasm-inducing nerve punch. This made his opponent emit photonic blasts uncontrollably, briefly taking out Massdriver.

THE UNIVERSAL CHURCH OF TRUTH

Led from their homeworld of Sacrosanct by the manipulative Matriarch, the Universal Church of Truth has long been an oppressive force in the galaxy. The present-day Guardians of the Galaxy went up against them on their very first mission as a team.

MATRIARCH

Supreme leader of the Universal Church of Truth, the Matriarch is devoted to the expansion of the Church and the eradication of all unbelievers and heretics. She guarded a mysterious cocoon that she believed would one day disgorge the Church's god, the Magus. When she discovered that Adam Warlock, who was destined to become the Magus, had joined the Guardians, she sent her Cardinals to locate and interrogate them. In time, the Magus took control of Adam, and the Matriarch placed the Church at his disposal.

*"I want you to **worship** me. I want you to **follow** me."*

THE MAGUS

THE MAGUS

A corrupt version of Adam Warlock from an alternative future, the Magus was the leader and deity of the Universal Church of Truth when Adam first encountered him. Adam was able to alter his own future timeline to wipe the Magus from existence, but he later did battle with another version of the Magus for control of the Infinity Gauntlet. Later still, Adam used the mystical energy of the Magus to forestall an invasion from the twisted Cancerverse, enabling his potential future self to take control of both him and the Universal Church. The Magus then kidnapped half of the Guardians and allied himself with the Cancerverse's ruler, Lord Mar-Vell.

THE BLACK KNIGHTS

The Universal Church's foot soldiers and shock troops, the Black Knights, have faith-enhanced physiques, armor-plating, and weaponry that discharges bolts of belief energy. Legend has it they can take down a planet in hours. They first fought the Guardians when Phyla-Vell led an assault on the Church homeworld, Sacrosanct. Later, the Black Knights battled the short-lived successors to the Guardians, the Annihilators, on Earth. Though the Knights came off worst in that clash, they did trick the Avengers into thinking the Annihilators were invading Earth.

RAKER AND THE CARDINALS

Led by the ruthless and devout Raker, the Cardinals are the senior officials and elite force of the Universal Church of Truth. They were sent by the Matriarch to find Star-Lord's newly formed Guardians after the team destroyed a Templeship on their very first mission, in order to seal a rift in space. Attacking the Guardians in the Binary Stasis Twelve Dyson Sphere, Raker was on track to get the better of them—until his Cardinals were swallowed up by an out-of-control mutant biomass! Raker subsequently boarded Knowhere—base of the Guardians—and took Moondragon hostage in the belief that she would give birth to the Church's new messiah. Drax killed Raker when the Guardians came to rescue Moondragon.

THE FAITHFUL

To the Universal Church of Truth, lowly worshippers are mere cannon fodder— a resource to be exploited as required. Take, for example, the Faith Generators: the engines at the heart of the Church's Templeships. These are powered by the prayers of the Church faithful—whose entire bodies become part of the ships' engineering. The Magus used the faith of these and other believers to tear open a dimensional portal to the Cancerverse. This destroyed countless Templeships and even entire Church worlds located at the mouth of the interdimensional fissure.

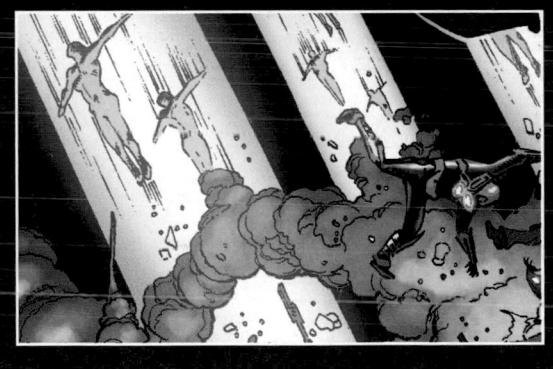

THANOS

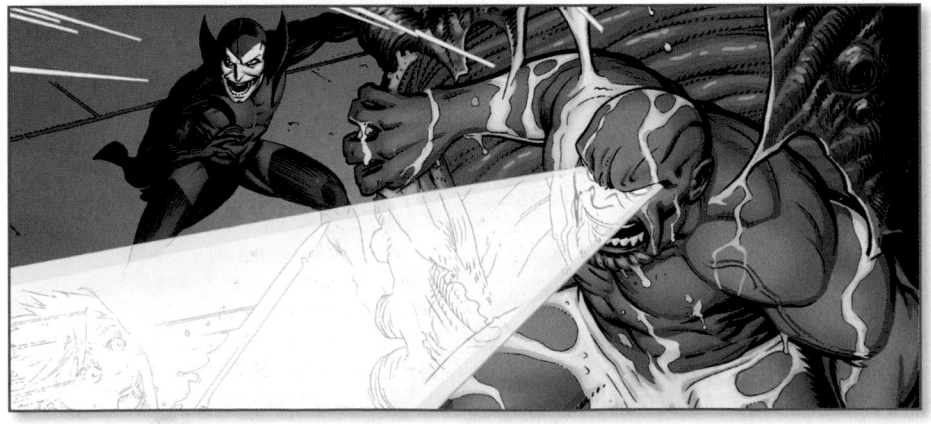

The Matriarch believed the cocoon she had been protecting would bring forth the reincarnation of the Magus. Phyla-Vell, on the other hand, thought it would reveal a renewed Adam Warlock, freed from the influence of the Magus. Phyla-Vell was appalled when the cocoon actually turned out to hold Thanos, who emerged and promptly killed her. Adam had placed the Mad Titan's dead body in the regenerative cocoon after he was killed in the Annihilation War. His hope was that Thanos might one day be able to counter the Magus if Adam's dark alternative self ever re-emerged.

SECRET INVASION

In an attempt to claim the Earth for themselves, the shape-shifting Skrulls have secretly taken the place of many of the planet's heroes. Events on Earth can seem distant to the Guardians, but could there also be imposters in their midst on Knowhere?

THE ONLY GOOD SKRULL...

On Knowhere, Star-Lord and Cosmo are about to check the station's teleport system when Mantis rushes up with a psychic warning not to go any further. Moments later, an explosion rips through the station, blowing all three off their feet. They escape with minor injuries, but 38 of Knowhere's inhabitants are killed. As the Guardians wonder whether the blast was brought about by accident or design, three of the victims are discovered to be other than they seemed. They are Skrulls!

Guardians of the Galaxy (Vol. 2) #4 (Aug. 2008) Star-Lord, Mantis, and Cosmo are caught in an explosion on Knowhere.

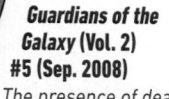

Guardians of the Galaxy (Vol. 2) #5 (Sep. 2008) The presence of dead Skrulls on Knowhere raises the possibility of there being live ones, too!

TRUST NO ONE

Though able to assume any form, Skrulls revert to their true appearance upon death. Rocket points out that there could be other imposters on Knowhere—and maybe even some of the Guardians are Skrulls! Neither Mantis nor Cosmo sense any Skrulls telepathically, but they might be shielded. An argument ensues, as mistrust and paranoia take hold of the recently formed team.

ALL IN THE MIND

Unnoticed, Drax slips away to hunt for Skrulls. He overhears Star-Lord and Mantis discussing a secret: when the team formed, Star-Lord had Mantis alter their thoughts to make them commit to the team. Later, Phyla-Vell finds Drax setting psychic mines throughout Knowhere. When she challenges him, he sets off the mines, causing station-wide brain death!

Guardians of the Galaxy (Vol. 2) #6 (Oct. 2008) Phyla-Vell clashes with Drax as he hunts for Skrulls.

SKRULL'S BEST FRIEND

The effect of the psychic mines is only temporary, allowing Drax to trace the Skrulls. He and Phyla rush to their location, where they discover five young Skrulls—and Cosmo! Drax attacks, but the space dog telepathically stops him in his tracks. Cosmo explains that he has been protecting the adolescent Skrulls, who are peaceful and do not pose a threat. The rest of the Guardians arrive, followed by another team of Skrull-hunters: the Luminals. In the tumult, one of the Skrulls is shot.

> "**Skrulls**. Every time they make a move, **this** is what happens. Mistrust. Fear. **Paranoia**."
>
> ADAM WARLOCK

Guardians of the Galaxy (Vol. 2) #5 (Sep. 2008)
Cosmo's eyes glow with telepathic energy as he prepares to defend a group of young Skrulls.

Guardians of the Galaxy (Vol. 6) #4 (Oct. 2008) Rocket takes Groot with him as he walks out on Star-Lord and the Guardians disband.

SECRETS AND LIES

A furious Cosmo floors everyone present with a massive telekinetic blast. Once everyone has regained their senses—including the wounded Skrull, who is recovering in the medical bay—Star-Lord declares the crisis over. However, Drax has told the other Guardians about the conversation he overheard between Mantis and Star-Lord. Angry, hurt, and betrayed, the Guardians all go their separate ways. As he carries Groot out of the room, Rocket takes a look back over his shoulder and tells Star-Lord the team is finished.

JACK FLAG

While most of the Guardians are old hands at space adventuring, Jack Flag is a relative newbie. A decidedly down-to-Earth hero, he has brought his skills as an urban brawler to bear on galactic-sized foes. Quick-witted and super-strong, when fists start to fly, he is the equal of any Guardian.

Exposure to the Hyde Formula has improved Jack's musculature and skeleton, affording him superhuman strength.

ORIGIN

When his parents lost all their money in a property scam, Jack Harrison put on a mask and costume inspired by Captain America and became Jack Flag. Armed with his "Boom Box"—a weapon disguised as a ghetto blaster—Jack infiltrated the evil Serpent Society, the perpetrators of the scam. As a test of loyalty, Jack was made to battle the villain Mister Hyde. During this fight, Jack was bathed in the chemicals that gave Hyde his strength and, as a result, gained his own superhuman abilities. He then began a crime-busting career, in which he often teamed up with his idol, Captain America.

Last Stand

Jack's career as a crimefighter on Earth was derailed when the U.S. Government introduced its Superhuman Registration Act. Having refused to surrender his anonymity by registering, Jack was hunted down by a team of government-sponsored super villains called the Thunderbolts. Though Jack fought bravely, his battle with the Thunderbolts left him paralyzed from the waist down, seemingly with no hope of ever walking again.

"Strictly blue collar superheroics. I hate cosmic stuff."

JACK FLAG

FLYING FLAG

The last place Jack Flag expected to wind up was in space. Yet, despite his professed skepticism for cosmic shenanigans, he soon got into the swing of being a Guardian and became a valued member of the team. His superhuman strength and his quick thinking have often proved crucial, while his doubts about life in space help keep the other Guardians grounded.

Jack's spine was badly damaged by Bullseye from the Thunderbolts, but was later repaired by alien doctors.

DATA FILE

REAL NAME: Jack Harrison

OCCUPATION: Adventurer

BASE: Knowhere

HEIGHT: 6ft 1in

WEIGHT: 210 lbs

EYES: Blue

HAIR: Red, white, and blue (naturally brown)

FIRST APPEARANCE: *Captain America* (Vol. 1) #434 (Dec. 1994)

Jailbird Jack

After his arrest for defying the Superhuman Registration Act, Jack was sent to Prison 42, a jail in the Negative Zone especially for unregistered superhumans. He was found by Star-Lord, who also wound up in the facility, and the two men formed an alliance. United against the villains in the jail, Jack and Peter soon became friends.

Jack's simple mask is based on a flag, while the rest of his outfit takes its cues from Captain America's patriotic stars and stripes design.

Jack's Back

Jack Flag was rescued from Prison 42 by the Guardians when they broke in searching for Star-Lord. The doctors on Knowhere—base of the Guardians— were able to fix Jack's back in no time, enabling him to walk again. Though not overly enamored of cosmic adventuring, Jack decided to hang with the Guardians— at least for a while.

INTERDIMENSIONAL RESCUE

Having only just formed, the Guardians have been torn apart. Star-Lord has been frozen out after the rest of the team found out that he tricked them into joining. A partial team has reformed around Rocket, while Drax and Phyla-Vell are both going it alone.

IN THE ZONE

With the Guardians in pieces, Star-Lord heads to Hala, the Kree homeworld, to warn them of possible Skrull infiltration. On Hala, he is attacked by the Kree ruler, Ronan the Accuser, who still blames Star-Lord for the Phalanx invasion. Ronan banishes him to the Negative Zone, where he is met by the last person he wants to see: his old enemy—or old ally, depending on the day of the week—Blastaar.

Guardians of the Galaxy (Vol. 2) #9 (Mar. 2009) Star-Lord goes stark naked on his arrival at Prison 42.

Guardians of the Galaxy (Vol. 2) #7 (Jan. 2009 Minions tend to Blastaar in the Negative Zone.

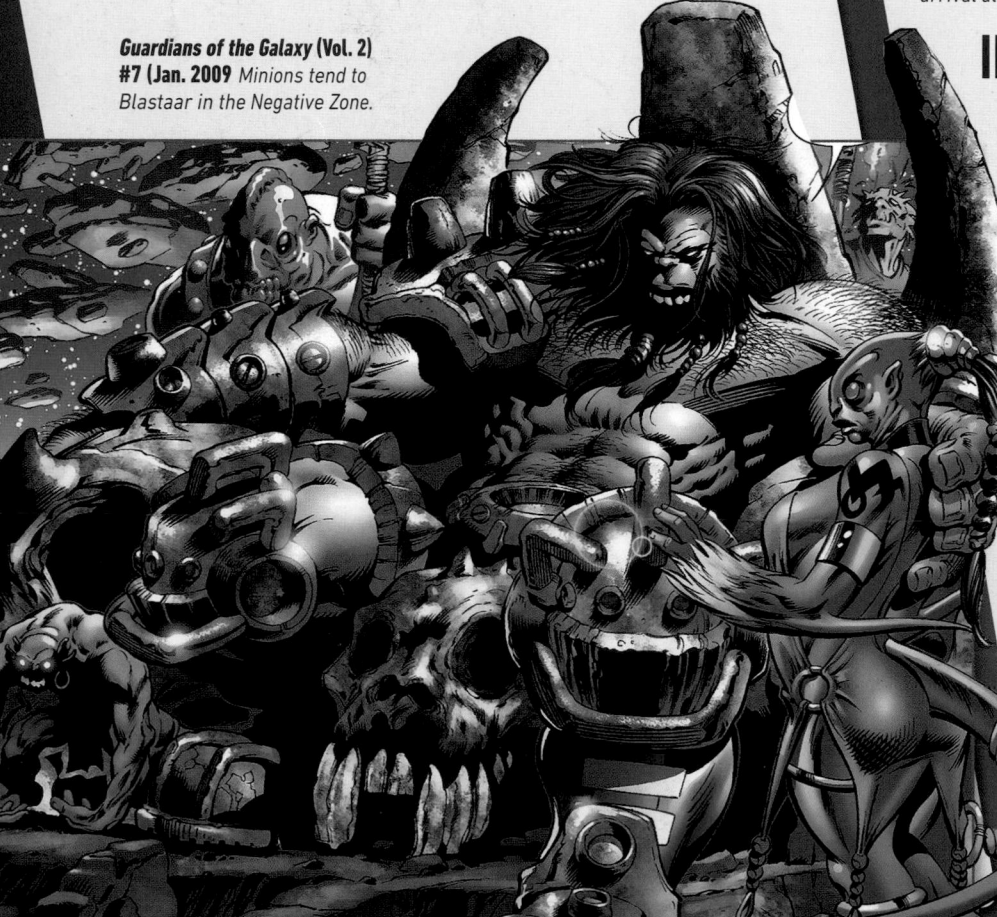

ILLEGAL ENTRY

Blastaar has a job for Star-Lord. Inside Prison 42—the Negative Zone maximum security jail for Earth's super-powered criminals—there is a portal to Earth, and Blastaar wants to use it to invade the planet. Stripping Star-Lord naked so that he presents no threat, Blastaar sends him to the prison to work on his behalf. In jail, Star-Lord meets Jack Flag, a wrongly imprisoned Earth hero. The prison's Super Villains have been trying to open the portal themselves, but Star-Lord and Jack agree that neither they nor Blastaar should be allowed to do so—even if it means fighting them all.

*"The Guardians' concept has **blown up** on the launch pad!"*

STAR-LORD

Guardians of the Galaxy (Vol. 2) #10 (Apr. 2009) Star-Lord and Jack Flag are glad to see Groot, Rocket, Major Victory, and other Guardians in the midst of battle.

GUARDIANS REUNITED

Learning of Star-Lord's banishment, the other Guardians teleport into the Negative Zone—only to arrive right in the middle of Blastaar's personal army! They fight their way into Prison 42 and find Star-Lord and Jack, then teleport back to Knowhere together, leaving Blastaar fuming. Star-Lord sends a message to the Fantastic Four's Mister Fantastic on Earth, warning him not to open the portal. Then the Guardians welcome Star-Lord back to the fold—and Jack to the team.

BEYOND THE VEIL

As the other Guardians are reunited, Drax and Phyla-Vell are on a mission of their own. Moondragon, Drax's daughter and Phyla's lover, is dead, but her adoptive father, Mentor of Titan, says her soul could be saved—if Drax and Phyla die, too! The pair willingly fall at his hands, then awake in limbo, a dimension between life and death. Here they are attacked by the late Captain Marvel and death-worshipper Maelstrom!

Guardians of the Galaxy (Vol. 2) #11 (May 2009) Drax strikes back as Phyla-Vell comes under attack from the undead ghost of Captain Marvel in limbo!

Guardians of the Galaxy (Vol. 2) #12 (Jun. 2009) Wendell Vaughn and Drax look on with surprise as a new-look Phyla-Vell rescues Moondragon.

DRAGON SLAYER

Drax and Phyla-Vell learn that Moondragon is trapped inside the demonic Dragon of the Moon. Maelstrom gains Phyla's Quasar powers by stealing her Quantum Bands and then feeds her to the Dragon—but is then surprised by the arrival of the original Quasar, Wendell Vaughn. He was drawn to limbo by the Bands, which he takes from Maelstrom. He then turns to the Dragon, only to see Phyla slice her way out of it with Moondragon in her arms! Phyla (now calling herself Martyr), Moondragon, and Drax are resurrected by Mentor, and warmly reunited.

INHUMANS

Genetically engineered long ago by the Kree, the Inhumans are a super-powered offshoot of the human race. Based in their city of Attilan (with smaller colonies elsewhere), they have traditionally been secretive and guarded, but have recently assumed a more prominent position on the galactic stage as rulers of the Kree—sparking the War of Kings with the Shi'ar...

BLACK BOLT

King of the Inhumans, Black Bolt is a resolute defender of his people, devoted to their wellbeing and their survival above all other concerns. In common with all Inhumans, Black Bolt has gone through Terrigenesis—exposure to the Terrigen Mists—in order to bring out his own particular powers and abilities. In Black Bolt's case, this process—which can also cause radical changes in appearance—conferred great strength, stamina, and endurance, as well as a hugely powerful voice. Just one word from Black Bolt can level mountains! As a result, he largely maintains a regal silence. In recent times, Black Bolt has led the Inhumans into the Kree Empire, seizing control from Ronan the Accuser and installing himself and the Inhuman Royal Family as the new rulers of the Kree.

MEDUSA

Medusa is Queen of the Inhumans and the wife of Black Bolt. The Terrigen Mists gave her the ability to control the movement of her long hair, which is incredibly strong and elastic. Through her long association with Black Bolt, she has become adept at reading his body language, allowing her to convey his silent directives. In an attempt to halt the war between the Shi'ar and the combined forces of the Inhumans and the Kree, Star-Lord led a team to see Black Bolt in Attilan. When he asked Black Bolt to stop the fighting, Medusa replied with a curt, "No."

CRYSTAL

The younger sister of Medusa, Crystal is the Inhuman Royal Princess. Terrigenesis gave her the ability to psionically control the elements—water, fire, earth, and air. To cement the union between the Inhumans and the Kree, she was betrothed to Ronan the Accuser. When Black Bolt and Medusa refused the Guardians' plea to end the war with the Shi'ar, their meeting almost became a fight, until Crystal used her powers to call a halt. Phyla-Vell then grabbed her and held a blade to her throat in an attempt to force an agreement.

KARNAK

Unlike most other Inhumans, Karnak did not undergo Terrigenesis. Instead he was sent to a monastery, where he was trained in martial arts and a wide range of mental disciplines. As a result, he has become one of the greatest hand-to-hand combatants the galaxy has ever seen—able to detect stress points and other weaknesses in his opponents and target them to devastating effect. Karnak did battle with Mantis after Phyla-Vell took Crystal hostage and the Inhumans pursued the Guardians to Knowhere. After complimenting Mantis on her combat skills, he noted that he would find the weakness in her technique. In the event, she bested him before he got the chance.

GORGON

Personal bodyguard to Black Bolt, Gorgon possesses great strength and powerful bull-like legs and hooves, which he uses to create earthquake-like shockwaves. Quick to anger, he flew into a rage when Guardian Bug told Medusa that she had beautiful eyes. In order to restrain him, Medusa had to grab hold of Gorgon with her hair.

MAXIMUS

Black Bolt's brother, Maximus the Mad, is an unhinged super-genius, forever plotting to overthrow his king. Despite this, he often advises Black Bolt, especially on scientific matters. At the close of the War of Kings, when the Guardians and the Inhumans joined forces, Maximus showed that he could understand the usually impenetrable Groot.

LOCKJAW

An oversized bulldog-like creature, Lockjaw is not merely the Inhuman Royal Family's faithful companion. He possesses his own super-power (some say as a result of exposure to the Terrigen Mists): the ability to teleport himself and others. When Phyla-Vell kidnapped Crystal during the War of Kings, it was Lockjaw who teleported Black Bolt and co. to Knowhere in order to retrieve her.

THE STARJAMMERS

A band of interstellar pirates and brigands, the Starjammers are also legendary adventurers and freedom fighters, battling to rid the galaxy of Shi'ar oppression. They were first encountered by the Guardians during the War of Kings between the Kree, led by the Inhumans, and the Shi'ar, led by the villainous Vulcan.

HAVOK

A mutant and a former member of the X-Men, Havok is Alex Summers, brother of Scott Summers (Cyclops) and Gabriel Summers (Vulcan). Like his brothers, Havok has extraordinary power as a result of mutation—in his case the ability to generate destructive plasma blasts. After a long career with the X-Men and its sister team X-Factor, Havok took over command of the Starjammers when his father, Corsair, was killed by Vulcan, who had assumed control of the Shi'ar Imperium. As leader, Havok led the Starjammers on a mission to rescue the deposed Shi'ar Majestrix Lilandra, who had been imprisoned by Vulcan.

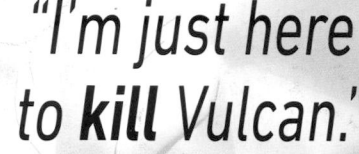

"I'm just here to kill Vulcan."

HAVOK

POLARIS

Polaris is Lorna Dane, Havok's longtime on-off lover. A mutant with magnetic powers, Polaris served with the mutant teams X-Men and X-Factor before she joined Havoc and other X-Men on a mission to battle Vulcan in Shi'ar space. She and Havok rekindled their rocky romance when they helped to form the Starjammers, and she played a key role in rescuing deposed Shi'ar Majestrix Lilandra.

CORSAIR

Corsair is Christopher Summers, father of Havok, Cyclops, and their villainous brother, Vulcan, the Shi'ar Emperor. Corsair formed the original Starjammers after he and his wife Katherine were abducted by the Shi'ar. Katherine was killed and Christopher was sent to a mining camp, where he met Raza, Hepzibah, and Ch'od. The four escaped the camp and stole a ship, naming themselves the Starjammers (after their stolen vessel). Vulcan later seemed to murder his father, but somehow Corsair survived.

CH'OD

A Saurid from the planet Timor, Ch'od can breathe on land as well as underwater. Powerfully built and standing almost nine feet tall, he is an imposing individual with superhuman strength, Fortunately, however, he is generally genial in nature. He was a slave on a mining colony when he first met Corsair, becoming a founder member of the Starjammers and a mainstay of the team thereafter.

KORVUS

A powerful Shi'ar warrior who wields the Blade of the Phoenix, Korvus was sent to stop the X-Men when they headed to Shi'ar space to battle with the newly crowned Emperor Vulcan. When he tracked them down, his mind accidentally became linked with that of Marvel Girl and he allied with the X-Men against Vulcan. After Corsair was killed, he joined the Starjammers alongside Marvel Girl.

MARVEL GIRL

Earth mutant Rachel Summers is the daughter of an alternative future Cyclops and Jean Grey, alias Phoenix. Propelled to the past from an apocalyptic future where mutant-hunting Sentinel robots ruled the United States, she joined the X-Men and sister team Excalibur as Marvel Girl. She was one of the X-Men who took on Vulcan, after which she joined the Starjammers.

RAZA

The last of his species, Raza Longknife is a cyborg—part flesh and blood, part machine. He was imprisoned in the Shi'ar slave pits alongside Corsair, Hepzibah, and Ch'od, escaping with them to form the Starjammers. When Corsair's villainous son Vulcan took control of the Shi'ar Imperium, Raza took on Vulcan's Imperial Guard. They linked him with an alien symbiote, which caused him to become an unwilling addition to their own ranks for a time.

HEPZIBAH

A skunk-like Mephitisoid, Hepzibah met Corsair, Ch'od, and Raza when they were imprisoned together as slaves. Her superhuman reflexes and agility served her well when she became a founder member of the Starjammers, and in time she and Corsair also became lovers. She was devastated when he was killed by Vulcan.

WAR OF KINGS

Millennia ago, the Kree engineered an offshoot of mankind: the Inhumans. Now, Black Bolt, King of the Inhumans, has replaced Ronan the Accuser as ruler of the Kree. To cement the union of the two species, the Inhuman Crystal is set to marry Ronan.

War of Kings (Vol. 1) #1 (Mar. 2009) *When Vulcan's Imperial Guard crashes the wedding of the Inhuman Crystal and the former Kree leader Ronan the Accuser, Black Bolt exchanges blows with the Imperial Guardsman Gladiator.*

KINGS LANDING

Vulcan—an Earth mutant and brother of X-Men Cyclops and Havok—has become ruler of the Shi'ar after deposing Majestrix Lilandra. Hell-bent on expanding his empire, he launches a crippling assault on the Kree homeworld, Hala. In the middle of Crystal and Ronan's wedding, his troops seize Lilandra, who has sought refuge on Hala, leaving the planet in ruins—and the Inhumans out for revenge.

WARLOCK'S WAR

Vulcan's use of devastating Nega-Bombs spurs two teams of Guardians to seek peace between the Shi'ar and the Inhumans. While teleporting, Adam Warlock becomes separated from his team, and finds himself alone on the Shi'ar flagship. He is attacked by Vulcan, and retreats after a vicious battle that causes him to become evermore malevolent and Magus-like.

Guardians of the Galaxy (Vol. 2) #15 (Jun. 2009) *Vulcan, the Earth-mutant Emperor of the Shi'ar, rains fire down on Adam Warlock, forcing the Guardian to unleash the inner darkness that threatens to overwhelm him.*

Guardians of the Galaxy (Vol. 2) #13 (Apr. 2009) *Havok leads the Guardian-augmented Starjammers into battle against Majestrix Lilandra's Shi'ar captors.*

> *"The fragile fabric of space/time **will not withstand** such pernicious abuse."*
>
> ADAM WARLOCK

MISSION POSSIBLE

Adrift in space after being repelled by Shi'ar teleport shields, the rest of Adam's team are picked up by the Starjammers—a team led by Havok to rescue Lilandra and restore her to the Shi'ar throne. Rocket, Drax, Major Victory, and Groot join forces with Havok and board the ship carrying Lilandra. They are surprised when one of Vulcan's Imperial Guard, Gladiator, switches sides and swears his allegiance to Lilandra!

BATTLE ROYAL

The Inhumans and the Shi'ar both teleport to Adam's location at the same time, having tracked his retreat. As they battle, Rocket and his team return, and learn that Lilandra has been assassinated. This comes as a blow to Black Bolt, who decides to end the war with an incredibly powerful T-Bomb. Vulcan tackles him, leading to a bloody brawl that causes the bomb to detonate. The blast tears the fabric of space itself, opening a door to the nightmarish Cancerverse...

Accidental hostage

While one team of Guardians tackled the Shi'ar, Star-Lord led his team to talk peace with the Inhumans. With Black Bolt unwilling to cease hostilities, Phyla-Vell took matters into her own hands and seized Crystal. Star-Lord teleported his team out—but Phyla kept hold of the Inhuman, effectively taking her hostage! (*Guardians of the Galaxy* (Vol. 2) #15 (Jun. 2009))

War of Kings (Vol. 1) #6 (Aug. 2009) *The Inhuman and Shi'ar leaders fight as a devastating T-Bomb comes closer to exploding.*

GUARDIANS SQUARED

Almost from the beginning, the present-day Guardians of the Galaxy have found their lives intertwined with the 31st-century Guardians. An encounter with a Guardian of the future gave the Guardians of today their name, and the teams' paths have crossed again and again ever since.

DATE WITH DESTINY

On only their second mission together, Star-Lord, Warlock, Quasar, Gamora, Drax, and Rocket discovered what appeared to be a chunk of Avengers Mansion floating in space. When the ice melted, a disoriented figure emerged, clutching Captain America's shield. It was Vance Astrovik, alias Major Victory, of the 31st-century Guardians of the Galaxy—and thus the modern-day Guardians named themselves.

Guardians of the Galaxy
(Vol. 2) #2 (Aug. 2008)

FUTURE SHOCK

Now a member of the modern-day Guardians, Major Victory found himself repeatedly attacked by time-traveling alternate versions of his 31st-century Guardians teammate Starhawk. An error in the timestream was unraveling the future, causing all potential 31st centuries to be destroyed over and over again. Starhawk had traced the error to the present day and located the source of the destruction: Major Victory, the man out of time.

Guardians of the Galaxy (Vol. 2) #3 (Sep. 2008)

BLAST FROM THE PAST

With 31st-century space and time collapsing due to a fault in the past, Starhawk took the Guardians of today to 3009. They learned that almost all of reality had been destroyed. All that remained were the 31st-century Guardians, their enemies the Badoon, and a chunk of Earth with Avengers Mansion on it. Guardians present and future joined forces to battle the Badoon and save the last vestiges of the universe.

Guardians of the Galaxy (Vol. 2)
#16 (Sep. 2009)

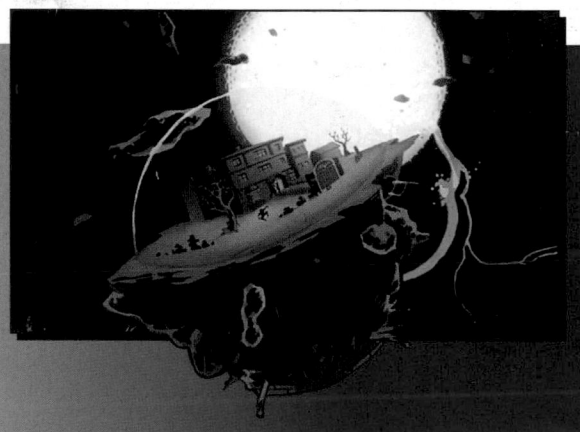

FIGHT FOR THE FUTURE

Propelled to an alternate Earth of 3009, the present-day Guardians fought alongside the 31st-century Guardians. Their opponents: giant Martian Tripods, who had overrun Earth and enslaved much of humanity. Suffering the effects of time dislocation—including Star-Lord being a pensioner—the present-day Guardians met the leader of the 31st-century Guardians: legendary Martian-slayer Killraven.

Guardians of the Galaxy (Vol. 2) #18 (Nov. 2009)

TOMORROW PEOPLE

Landing in New York in the past, the Guardians of 3014 and their ally Star-Lord—a distant descendant of Peter Quill— encountered the 21st-century Guardians, who were investigating the trans-temporal disturbance caused by the arrival of the future Guardians' ship. Together, the two teams identified the problem: sentient robotic conquerors the Stark, whom the 31st-century Guardians had unwittingly brought with them!

Guardians 3000 #7 (Apr. 2015)

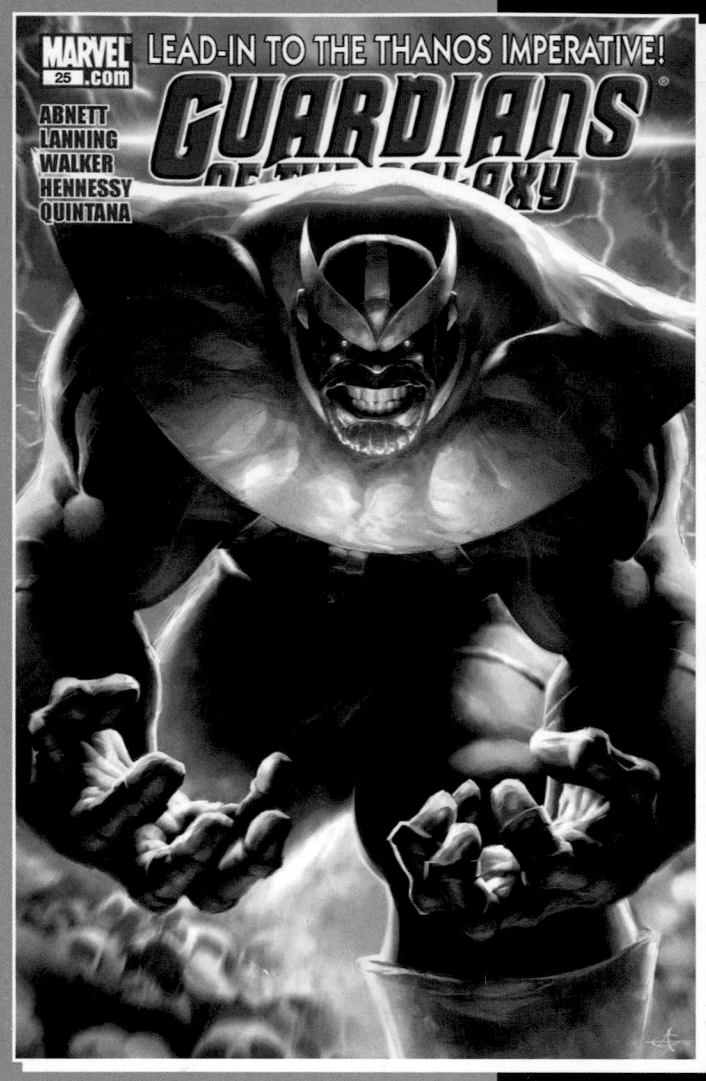

MARVEL 25 .com
LEAD-IN TO THE THANOS IMPERATIVE!
GUARDIANS OF THE GALAXY
ABNETT
LANNING
WALKER
HENNESSY
QUINTANA

GUARDIANS OF THE GALAXY (Vol. 2) #25

THE REBIRTH OF THANOS SPELLS THE BEGINNING OF THE END FOR THE GUARDIANS.

Thanos has been reborn, and he's mad as hell. The Mad Titan has emerged from the cocoon in which he has been growing in a mindless rage. Having killed Phyla-Vell, he is now rampaging across Sacrosanct, homeworld of the Universal Church of Truth, who nurtured Thanos' cocoon believing it contained their god, the Magus.

JUNE 2010

MAIN CHARACTERS
Peter Quill—Star-Lord • Drax • Moondragon • Groot • Gamora • Rocket Raccoon • Mantis • Bug • Jack Flag • Major Victory • Thanos

SUPPORTING CHARACTERS
Starhawk • Vance Astro • Charlie-27 • Martinex • Yondu • Nikki • Firelord • Killraven

MAIN LOCATIONS
Sacrosanct • Chamber of the Council of the Guardians of All Galaxies

1 In the year 3010, a Council of the Guardians of All Galaxies convenes, with representatives of the Guardians from all possible futures. It is the Council's belief that it has saved every future after it corrected a mistake in the past, centered on the time-displaced Guardian Major Victory. However, it now seems the Council is gravely mistaken.

2 In the 21st century, the present-day Guardians head for Sacrosanct. Moondragon has received a psychic flash from Phyla-Vell suggesting that someone that they thought dead is alive. Expecting to find the Magus, they're met instead by a scene of utter destruction—and at its center is Thanos!

> *"The only ones who stand between the galaxy and **ultimate annihilation** are Peter Quill and his original **Guardians of the Galaxy**."*
>
> Starhawk

3 The Guardians pile onto Thanos, but not even Drax can stop him. When Mantis and Cosmo fail in their telekinetic efforts to shut down his mind, Star-Lord uses the damaged Cosmic Cube he's been keeping in reserve. It has barely enough power for one blast, but it's enough, and Thanos falls.

4 With Thanos taken prisoner, the Guardians raise a toast to fallen comrades. Rocket asks Star-Lord whether he regrets forming the team, given the high price paid. He replies that they beat Thanos—and who knows what they will do tomorrow?

5 Back in the 31st century, the Council is keeping its eye on events as they unfold in the 21st. Starhawk declares that the rebirth of Thanos is the mistake they have been trying to correct, and that history is about to go into shock. The fate of the future will be decided by the 21st-century Guardians... along with Thanos the Mad Titan!

THE THANOS IMPERATIVE

The War of Kings tore a "Fault" in space that leads into the twisted Cancerverse. In this corrupt reality, nothing dies and familiar heroes are reimagined as villains. The Lord of the Cancerverse has seen the Fault, and views it as a route to conquest...

The Thanos Imperative #2 (Sep. 2010) Even Galactus and an alliance of other incredibly powerful cosmic entities could not defeat the deathless forces of the Cancerverse.

INTO THE CANCERVERSE

Star-Lord theorizes that the only way to beat the Cancerverse is to bring back death to the realm—and the Guardians just happen to hold Thanos, the servant of Mistress Death, as a captive. Overriding Drax and Moondragon's objections, the Guardians and Thanos transport to the Cancerverse. There, they face the Revengers—twisted versions of the Avengers—led by Lord Mar-Vell, counterpart to the deceased Kree hero Captain Marvel.

> "I'll kill your whole universe, and **I will not stop** until every last soul is extinct!"
>
> Thanos

The Thanos Imperative #5 (Dec. 2010) Mar-Vell corrupted the heroes of his reality as part of his bid to cheat death, creating the terrifying Revengers.

OUT OF THE FAULT

The Magus—the dark version of Adam Warlock—has allied with the Cancerverse. He uses his magic to gather dozens of worlds at the Fault, then detonates them, tearing it even wider. Monsters and warships burst through, and heroes such as Nova and the resurrected Quasar (Wendell Vaughn), plus the Inhumans and the Shi'ar, try to contain the threat. Knowing that this alliance will only delay the Cancerverse invaders, the Silver Surfer marshals his own force, made up of Galactus, the Celestials, and other cosmic beings.

The Thanos Imperative #4 (Nov. 2010) After years of conflict, Drax and Thanos finally succeed in killing each other—but death has no meaning in the Cancerverse.

THE COST OF VICTORY

Allowing himself to be captured, Thanos gets close enough to Mar-Vell for Mistress Death to claim him. With Mar-Vell's passing, the Fault seals and the Cancerverse itself begins to die. Thanos begs his mistress to end his life, too, but she refuses and he goes insane. Star-Lord and Nova are forced to stay in the Cancerverse to keep Thanos from a murderous rampage, while—back in their own universe—the rest of the Guardians mourn their losses, erecting statues to Star-Lord, Nova, Drax, and other fallen heroes.

The Thanos Imperative #6 (Jan. 2011) Believed dead or trapped forever in a universe that no longer connects to their own, Star-Lord and Nova are commemorated in stone.

BACK FROM THE DEAD

In the Cancerverse, Drax seizes the opportunity to kill his mortal enemy and slaps an antimatter bomb onto Thanos, who is instantly disintegrated. Star-Lord is furious, as without Thanos the plan has no hope, but Drax is unrepentant. However, Thanos is swiftly resurrected. He then kills Drax, who stays dead. Though it is seemingly impossible to die from other means in this universe, as the representative of Death herself, Thanos' touch is fatal.

Lord of the Cancerverse

The Cancerverse was created when the Captain Marvel from another reality was dying of cancer. Granted new powers by cosmic beings known as the Many-Angled Ones, Lord Mar-Vell banished death, but this let the Many-Angled Ones into his universe, corrupting everything in it, and leaving him as the lord of this twisted new realm.

THE ANNIHILATORS

With Star-Lord and Nova lost in the Cancerverse, the Guardians of the Galaxy ceased to exist as a team. But the galaxy still needed protection, and a new team of cosmic heavy-hitters formed in the Guardians' wake...

> "We will simply be **the last resort.**"
>
> SILVER SURFER

BIG GUNS

Shortly before he was trapped in the Cancerverse with Nova, Star-Lord told Cosmo that the galaxy no longer had a need for Guardians. Instead, what it needed now was big guns, bad-asses, annihilators. So that was what Cosmo set about assembling, recruiting Quasar (Wendell Vaughn), Ronan the Accuser, the Silver Surfer, Beta Ray Bill, and Gladiator (leader of the Shi'ar). Any doubts as to the power of this new team were dispelled when they traveled to Earth to locate a Universal Church of Truth cell. Tricked into a fight with the Avengers, the Annihilators proved more than a match for the Earth's mightiest heroes, before the two teams joined forces and turned their firepower on the Universal Church instead.

IKON

No sooner had the Annihilators come together than they were contacted by Ikon, a Galadorian Spaceknight. She told them that she had been selected by her people to join the Annihilators—but that the team was destined to be a failure because it was far too powerful. However, she was proven wrong. On a subsequent mission, with Ikon among their number, the Annihilators demonstrated that they had more than muscle alone when they brokered a peace between the Galadorians and their long-standing enemies, the shape-shifting Dire Wraiths.

GLADIATOR

A Strontian born under Shi'ar rule, Gladiator possesses all the superhuman powers that are common to his species. Commander of the Shi'ar's elite Imperial Guard, he became leader of the Shi'ar Imperium after the evil Vulcan was defeated. Gladiator was keen that the Annihilators should not be a permanent team, but that did not reflect any lack of commitment on his part. When the Annihilators fought the Universal Church of Truth and a resurrected Magus on Earth, Gladiator let himself be infected by the Magus' consciousness so that he—and the Magus—could be killed. In the event, Gladiator survived, but his bravery seriously impressed his teammates.

BETA RAY BILL

A physically augmented member of the Korbinite species, Beta Ray Bill originally came to prominence when he took the place of Thor for a time. He wielded the mystical hammer Mjolnir before gaining his own Asgardian weapon, Stormbringer. Of all the galactic heroes Cosmo visited on his recruitment drive, Bill was the most reluctant. Busy helping with the effort to rebuild Navis Koana Five, following the war with the Cancerverse, he repeatedly told Cosmo that he wasn't interested. Cosmo convinced him that people didn't just need houses to live in, but also the security to protect those houses.

*"I will **not** see millions slaughtered."*

GLADIATOR

ROCKET & GROOT: BEST BUDDIES

From their first encounter, Rocket Raccoon and Groot have been almost inseparable. Thrown together in war, the pair became firm friends—a relationship cemented by Rocket often being the only one who can understand what Groot is saying. They continue to buddy up to this day, both as Guardians and away from the team.

BROTHERS IN ARMS

Rocket and Groot were both prisoners of the Kree when the Phalanx conquered the Kree Empire. The pair were conscripted into a squad commanded by Star-Lord, with a mission to sabotage Phalanx installations on Hala, the Kree homeworld. In training, they formed a strong bond. Groot served as transport for Rocket's heavy ordnance, while Rocket acted as a wisecracking, slightly irritating foil for the forbidding *Flora colossus*.

Annihilation: Conquest—Starlord (Vol. 1) #1 (Sep. 2007)

I SPIT ON YOUR GROOT

When Groot was overwhelmed by the Phalanx, Rocket thought he had lost his buddy. Rocket was delighted when Groot reappeared—in somewhat diminished form. Now barely a sapling, Groot was forced to hitch a ride on Rocket's shoulder—a complete reversal of their former arrangement. To add to the indignity, when Groot pointed out that he needed moisture to grow, Rocket spat on him!

Annihilation: Conquest—Starlord (Vol. 1) #3 (Nov. 2007)

RESCUE FROM PLANET X

After Star-Lord's disappearance in the Cancerverse, the Guardians split up for a time. Rocket took a job in an office mail room, where he came across a package containing a piece of sentient wood. Believing it came from Groot's homeworld, he took it back to Planet X, where he learned that Groot had been imprisoned for posing as king of the planet. Rocket located Groot on the Isle of Punishment and blasted his buddy free. The reunited friends embraced warmly.

Annihilators (Vol. 1) #1 (May 2011)

RETURN TO HALFWORLD

Rocket and Groot were forced to take on clown assassins and killer rabbits after paying a visit to Halfworld, the asylum planet where Rocket once worked as a warden. After bringing the mayhem to an end, Rocket vowed that—with the Guardians out of action—he and Groot alone would dedicate themselves to saving the universe!

Annihilators (Vol. 1) #3 (Jul. 2011)

TROLLING AROUND

Waking up on a backwater world, Groot discovered that Rocket had vanished—but had carved a map to follow in Groot's bark! Groot searched the cosmos until he heard about a dictator in the Yon Quadrant named Lord Rakzoon who ruled with a furry fist. Traveling to the Yon Quadrant, Groot was captured and brought before "Rakzoon," who pretended not to know Groot. Eventually, Rocket broke down and admitted the whole thing had been a prank!

Rocket Raccoon and Groot (Vol. 1) #1–3 (Mar.–May 2016)

Relaunched into a new series in 2013 under the guiding hand of writer Brian Michael Bendis, the Guardians of the Galaxy got mobile again, setting forth on a new starship. They also added some Earth heroes to the team—Iron Man, Agent Venom, Captain Marvel, and Kitty Pryde—and one goddess, in the shape of Asgardian warrior Angela.

GUARDIANS ON THE RUN

GUARDIANS OF THE GALAXY (VOL. 3) #0.1 (APR. 2013)
Star-Lord's origins are explored, including the romance between J'Son of Spartax and Meredith Quill, Peter's boyhood on Earth, and the death of Meredith.

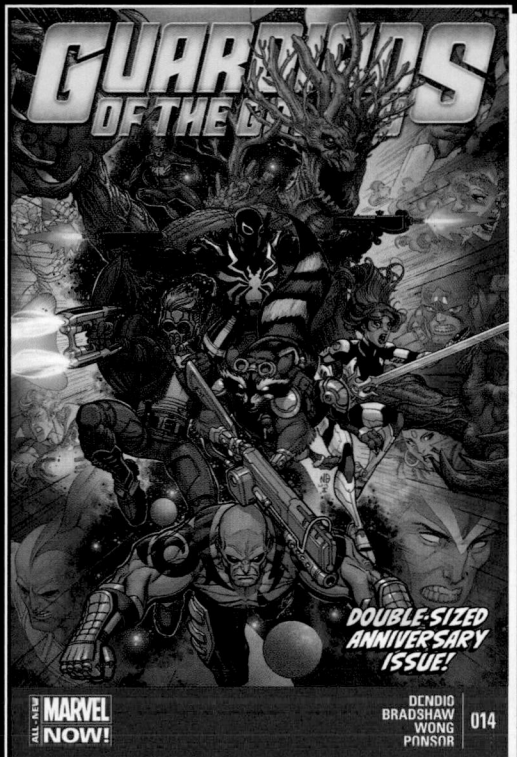

GUARDIANS OF THE GALAXY (VOL. 3) #14 (JUN. 2014)
The Guardians celebrate 100 issues of their own title by being torn apart by J'Son and the Spartoi. Groot's secret origin is also revealed.

LEGENDARY STAR-LORD (VOL. 1) #1 (SEP. 2014)
Confirming his legendary status (in his own mind), Peter Quill gets his very own series, and meets his half-sister, Victoria.

GUARDIANS OF THE GALAXY ANNUAL (VOL. 3) #1 (FEB. 2015)
For the first time in 20 years, a team of Guardians get their very own Annual, as they encounter a S.H.I.E.L.D. Helicarrier in deep space.

GUARDIANS OF THE GALAXY #1

BENDIS • MCNIVEN MARVEL NOW! DELL • PONSOR

JOIN THE REVOLUTION | 001

MAY 2013

MAIN CHARACTERS
Peter Quill—Star-Lord •
Gamora • Rocket Raccoon •
Drax • Groot • Iron Man

SUPPORTING CHARACTERS
J'Son of Spartax • Badoon •
Galactic Council

MAIN LOCATIONS
Unnamed bar on unnamed
planet • Space, in the vicinity
of Earth • London

GUARDIANS OF THE GALAXY (Vol. 3) #1

THE GUARDIANS ARE TOGETHER AGAIN—AND THERE'S A STARK NEW ADDITION TO THE TEAM.

Though widely believed to have perished fighting
Thanos in the Cancerverse, Peter Quill is alive
and well and once more leading the Guardians
of the Galaxy. At least, some of the time... Right
now, he's in a bar hitting on a gorgeous Kree.
The last thing he needs, then, is for his father
to walk through the door.

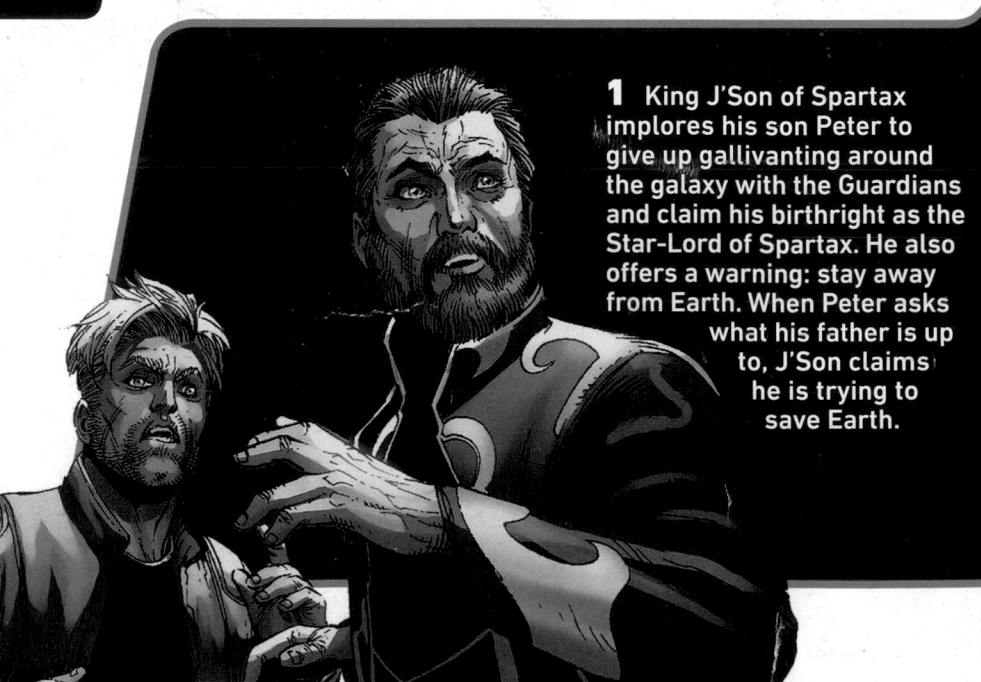

1 King J'Son of Spartax
implores his son Peter to
give up gallivanting around
the galaxy with the Guardians
and claim his birthright as the
Star-Lord of Spartax. He also
offers a warning: stay away
from Earth. When Peter asks
what his father is up
to, J'Son claims
he is trying to
save Earth.

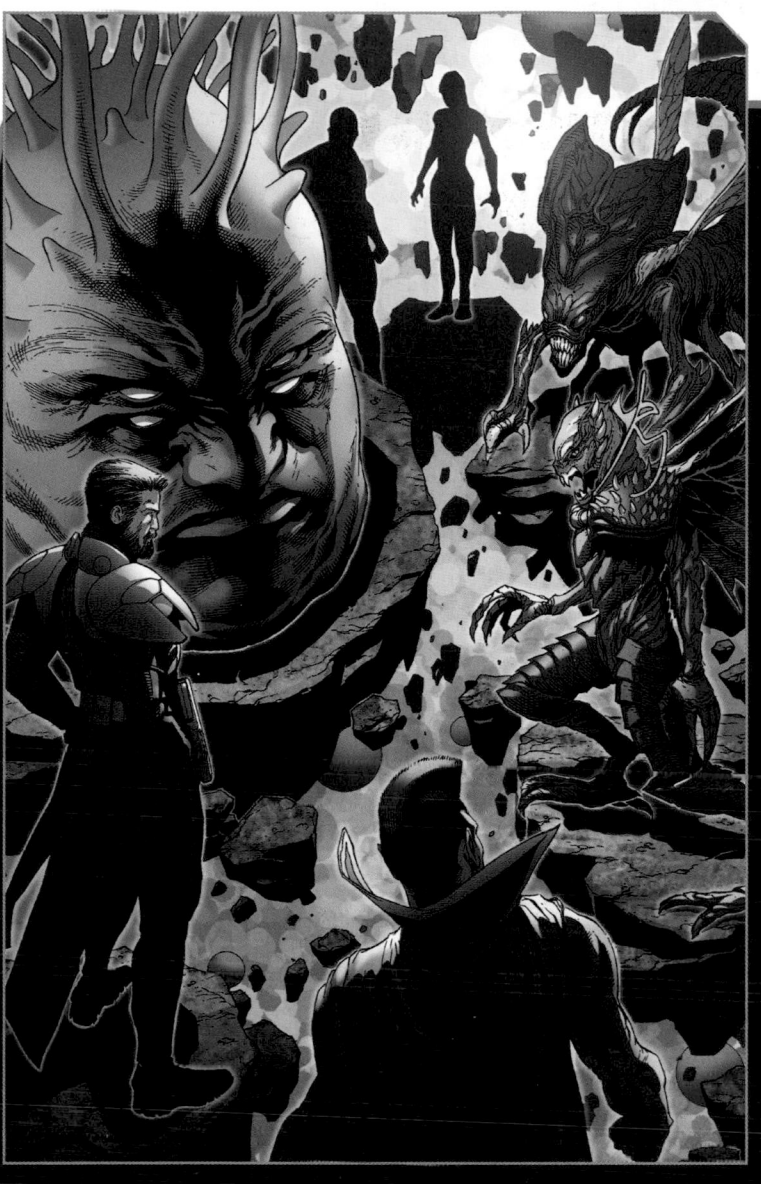

2 J'Son explains that the Galactic Council (made up of the Spartoi, the Shi'ar, the Kree Supreme Intelligence, the Brood, and others) has declared Earth off-limits for extraterrestrials. It reasons that Earth must be left alone if it is ever to become part of galactic civilization. Peter's angry response to this—and to claiming his birthright—is not what J'Son wants to hear.

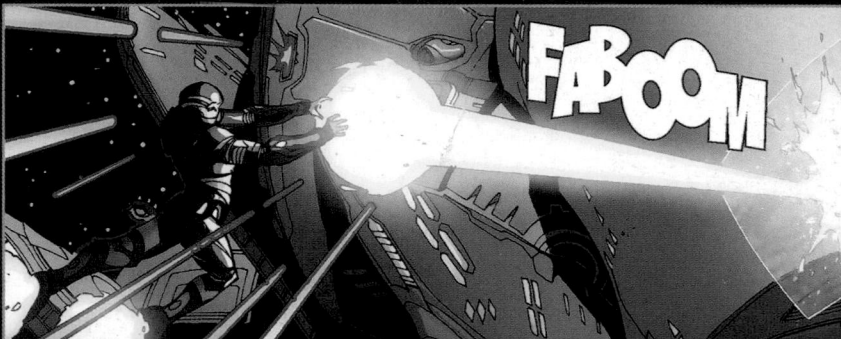

3 In space, not far from Earth, Tony Stark is taking the opportunity to get away from it all in a specially designed Iron Man suit. His intention is to take the Guardians up on their offer to join them, but instead he finds himself under attack from a Badoon warship.

> *"I hate to say this, Quill, I really do... but I think your father **set you up**."*
>
> GAMORA

4 Iron Man is surprised when the Guardians appear and join the fray—but not as surprised as the Badoon, who are mystified as to how the Guardians knew where to find them. On the verge of defeat, the Badoon self-destruct their main ship and send a smaller vessel toward Earth.

5 As the Badoon attack Earth, Star-Lord wonders why J'Son would leave it undefended. Gamora reasons that J'Son must have known Earth would come under attack, and that Peter and the Guardians would protect it. In other words: If J'Son can't have Peter, he and Earth can go to hell. Not to mention that J'Son also expected to profit from the planet's collapse.

J'Son bears the weight of imperial rule on his shoulders, albeit made more comfortable by the finest tailoring!

ORIGIN

When Prince J'Son of Spartax's spaceship crash-landed on Earth, he was pulled from the cockpit by Meredith Quill. She allowed J'Son to stay with her while he regained his health and repaired his ship. The pair began a relationship, but as soon as his ship was fixed, J'Son left. He was unaware that Meredith later gave birth to their son, Peter, or that Peter was orphaned when Meredith died in a Badoon attack. When J'Son became ruler of the Spartoi, word reached him of the adult Peter's exploits, and the new king set his sights on his son as a potential successor to his throne.

> ### "I am your father **and** your king!"
>
> J'SON TO STAR-LORD

J'SON OF SPARTAX

Proud and noble, J'Son is the ruler of the Spartoi Empire. He is also Star-Lord's father—though in little more than name, as he was unaware of Peter Quill's existence until his son was a grown man. That hasn't stopped J'Son doing all he can to get Star-Lord to accept his royal birthright— even if it means killing the Guardians of the Galaxy!

J'Son's military bearing is testament to his time as a soldier—a period that formed part of his traditional upbringing.

DATA FILE

REAL NAME: J'Son

OCCUPATION: Emperor of the Spartoi Empire

BASE: Mobile, Spartax

HEIGHT: Unknown

WEIGHT: Unknown

EYES: Blue

HAIR: Brown

FIRST APPEARANCE: *Guardians of the Galaxy* (Vol. 3) #0.1 (Apr. 2013)

OF ROYAL BLOOD

Born into royalty, J'Son is used to getting his own way—which is why his failure to bring Star-Lord into the fold frustrates him so. He has lied, schemed, and used every means at his disposal—from the Royal Guard to cutthroat mercenaries—to bring his son to heel. Yet each time Peter and the Guardians have prevailed in the face of his schemes, leaving J'Son more bitter than ever.

Father's Day

J'Son was instrumental in forming the Council of Galactic Empires, which counts Gladiator of the Shi'ar, the Kree Supreme Intelligence, and the Brood Queen among its diverse members. He manipulated the council into declaring Earth out-of-bounds to off-worlders, then got word to the Badoon that the planet was unprotected. J'Son knew that his son and the Guardians would rush to Earth's aid, making themselves galactic criminals and giving J'Son an excuse to place Star-Lord under arrest and gain control over him.

A Sharp Character

J'Son was eventually deposed as Emperor of Spartax when Star-Lord broadcast the truth of his duplicitous dealings to the entire empire. Outraged at his treatment, J'Son sought revenge on the Spartoi and his son. He took on a new identity— Mister Knife— and hired a team of mercenaries known as the Slaughter Squad. He then set out to locate an artifact of terrible power: the Black Vortex!

Son of J'Son

J'Son has tried to get Star-Lord to accept his birthright as Spartoi royalty many times. However, Peter has never forgiven his father for abandoning him and his mother— nor for her untimely death. Their encounters have been angry and confrontational, as J'Son has repeatedly attempted to trick and ensnare his estranged offspring.

GUARDIANS AND AVENGERS

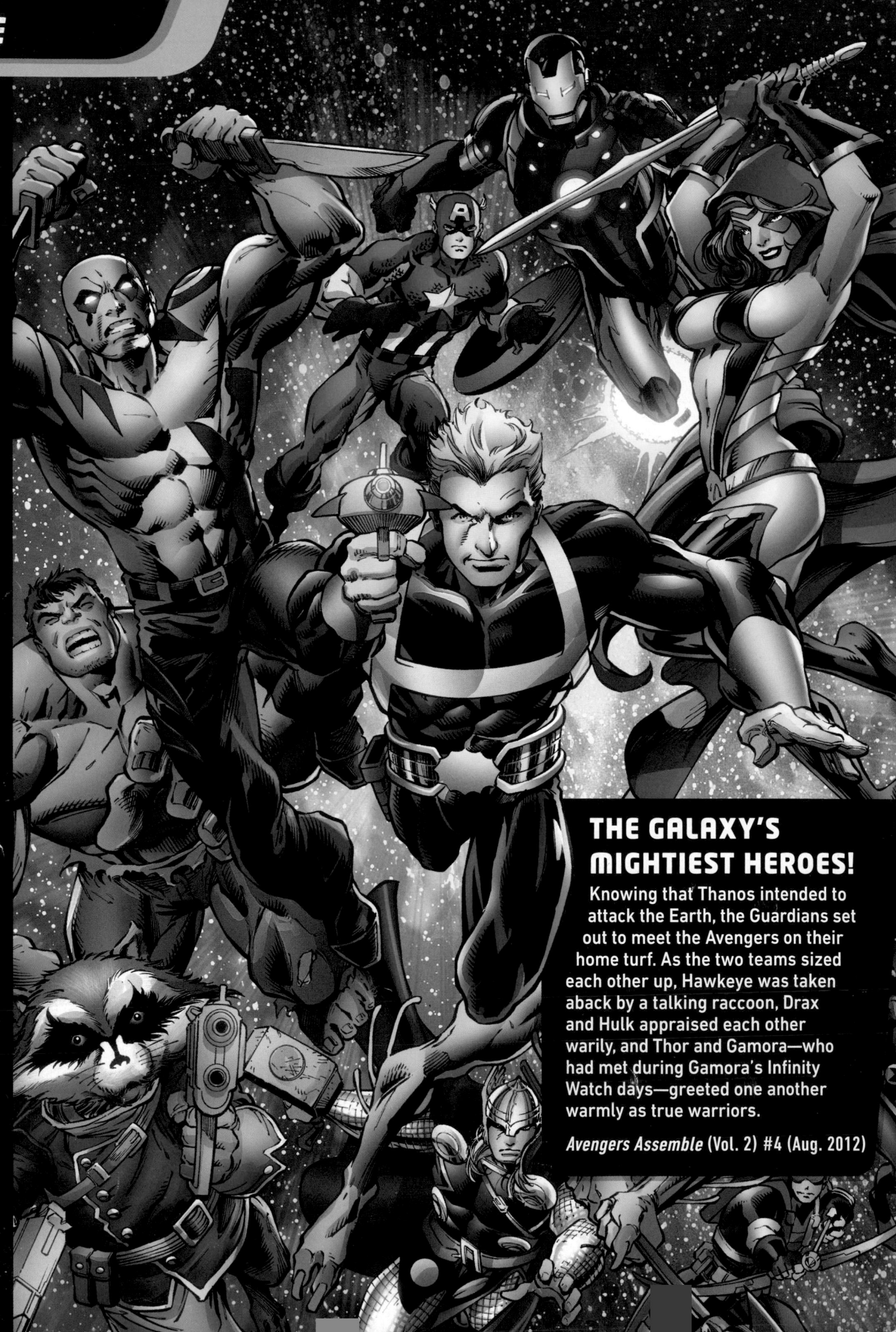

THE GALAXY'S MIGHTIEST HEROES!

Knowing that Thanos intended to attack the Earth, the Guardians set out to meet the Avengers on their home turf. As the two teams sized each other up, Hawkeye was taken aback by a talking raccoon, Drax and Hulk appraised each other warily, and Thor and Gamora—who had met during Gamora's Infinity Watch days—greeted one another warmly as true warriors.

Avengers Assemble (Vol. 2) #4 (Aug. 2012)

It took a while for word of the Guardians to reach Earth. Reed Richards of the Fantastic Four got an inkling when Star-Lord sent him a warning about Blastaar's plan to escape the Negative Zone. But when the Guardians finally met the Avengers, Earth's heroes really got to know the galaxy's protectors.

ALLIED AGAINST A GOD

When Thanos stole a powerful Cosmic Cube, the Guardians of the Galaxy and the Avengers teamed up to oppose the vast, godlike being he became. Thor used a device obtained from the cosmic being known as the Collector to bring the Mad Titan back down to size, after which the combined might of the Guardians and the Avengers was enough to defeat him. The battle won, Iron Man admitted that he envied the Guardians' freedom, so Star-Lord invited him to join them.

Avengers Assemble (Vol. 2) #7 (Nov. 2012)

AT WORLD'S END

The Guardians fought alongside the Avengers when an event known as an Incursion saw New York under attack from the heroes of an alternative Earth. Drax and Rocket Raccoon came to the aid of the Avengers' Captain Marvel by turning their fire on her opponent —the Iron Man from the other Earth. As the wider conflict raged and hero battled hero, Drax and Rocket agreed that they both hated Earth.

Secret Wars (Vol. 1) #1 (Jul. 2015)

HEROES ASSEMBLE

When the Guardians tracked a warship full of Chitauri warriors to Earth, a new team of Avengers was waiting to lend a hand. Rocket Raccoon and Spider-Woman got off on the wrong foot when she confessed that the idea of a talking raccoon freaked her out, and he criticized her costume. Cannonball admitted that Drax scared him, though Sunspot said he liked the gung-ho Destroyer.

Guardians of the Galaxy Team-Up (Vol. 1) #1 (May 2015)

OFF-WORLD AVENGERS

When Gamora was abducted on the orders of her enemy Kindun, the Guardians enlisted the Avengers' help to find her. The Avengers' teleporter, Manifold, transported both teams to Kindun's planet, where the combined firepower of Groot, Hyperion, Drax, Star Brand, Rocket, and Spider-Woman brought Kindun and his world to their knees.

Guardians of the Galaxy Team-Up (Vol. 1) #2 (May 2015)

147

ANGELA

Born in Asgard and raised in Heven, Angela is a God who became an Angel. The daughter of Asgardian All-Father Odin, she was taken from him as a baby, and grew up to become one of the finest hunters Heven has ever seen. Those talents have proven invaluable to the Guardians—as have Angela's godlike strength and hefty sword.

With her right hand, Angela wields Xiphos, a double-edged one-handed short sword also known as the Sword of Stars. This leaves her other hand free to use one of the axes referred to as the Blades of Ichor.

Heven Sent

Angela had a happy life in Heven, dedicating herself to the vocation at which she excelled: hunting. It was on a hunt that she was pulled through a dimensional tear into the Guardians' galaxy. Standing upon the vast severed head of the monstrous troll she had just slain, a bewildered Angela stared down on a world she had heard about only in fables—Earth!

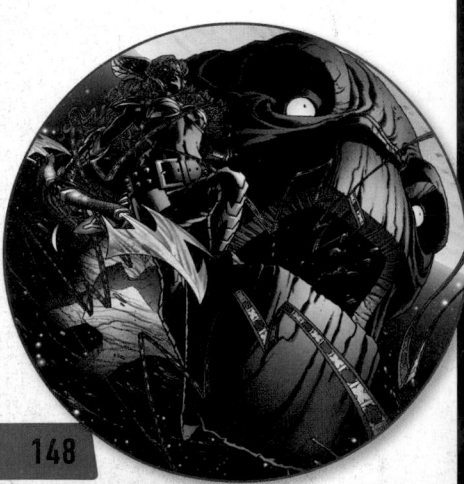

ORIGIN

Long ago, war broke out between the Angels of Heven and the Gods of Asgard. With battle raging, the Queen of Heven kidnapped the baby daughter of Odin— All-Father of the Asgardians—to force him to end the war. When Odin refused, the Queen killed the baby girl—or so it appeared. In fact the child survived, and was raised as an Angel under the name Angela. She grew to become one of Heven's greatest hunters—until the day when she was swallowed by a great light and torn from Heven.

*"This galaxy of yours is **full of madness**, Mister Quill."*

ANGELA

DATA FILE

REAL NAME: Aldrif Odinsdottir (raised as Angela)

OCCUPATION: Hunter

BASE: Mobile; formerly Heven

HEIGHT: 6ft 2in

WEIGHT: 480 lbs

EYES: White

HAIR: Red

FIRST APPEARANCE: *Age of Ultron* (Vol. 1) #10 (Aug. 2013)

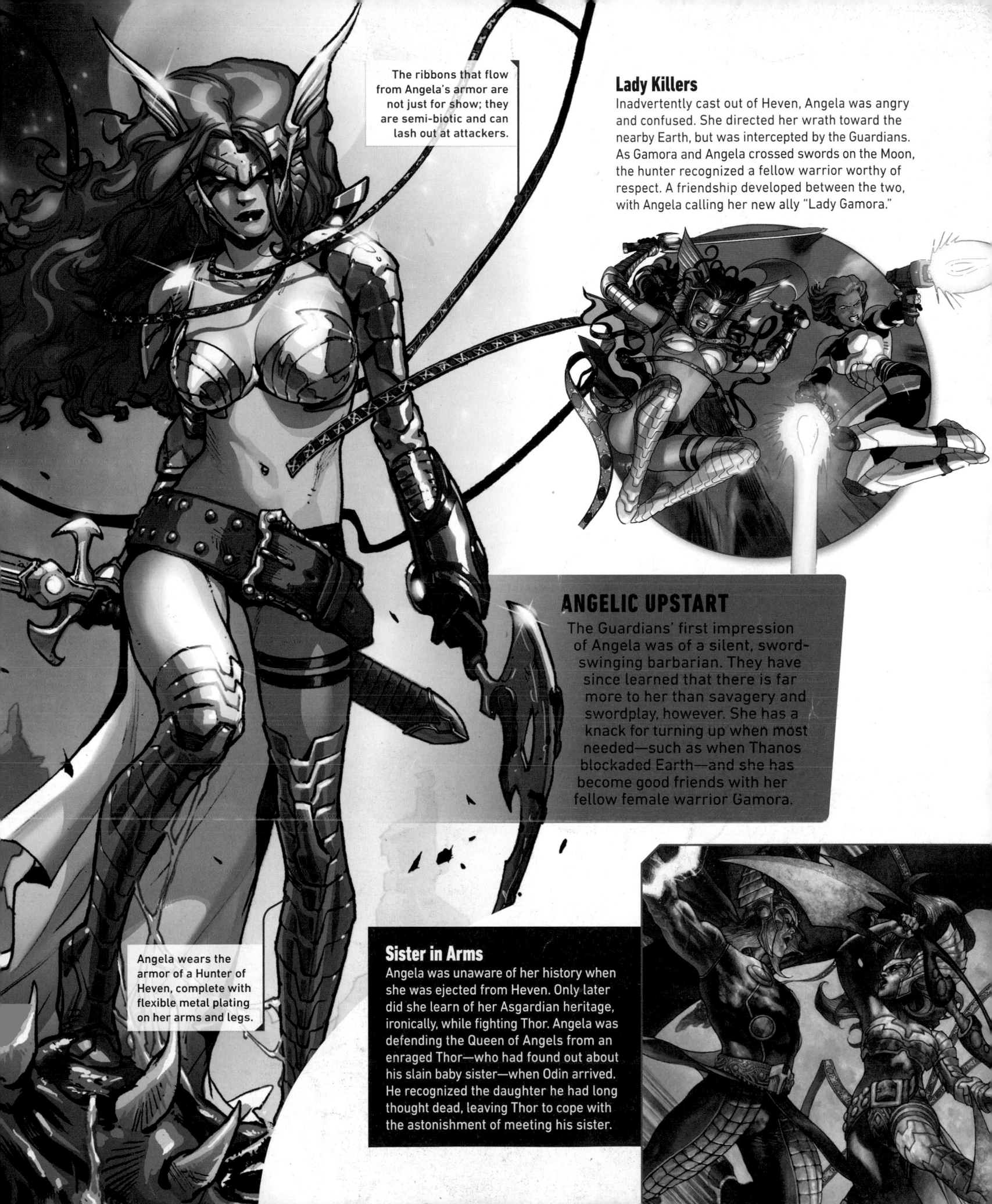

The ribbons that flow from Angela's armor are not just for show; they are semi-biotic and can lash out at attackers.

Lady Killers

Inadvertently cast out of Heven, Angela was angry and confused. She directed her wrath toward the nearby Earth, but was intercepted by the Guardians. As Gamora and Angela crossed swords on the Moon, the hunter recognized a fellow warrior worthy of respect. A friendship developed between the two, with Angela calling her new ally "Lady Gamora."

ANGELIC UPSTART

The Guardians' first impression of Angela was of a silent, sword-swinging barbarian. They have since learned that there is far more to her than savagery and swordplay, however. She has a knack for turning up when most needed—such as when Thanos blockaded Earth—and she has become good friends with her fellow female warrior Gamora.

Angela wears the armor of a Hunter of Heven, complete with flexible metal plating on her arms and legs.

Sister in Arms

Angela was unaware of her history when she was ejected from Heven. Only later did she learn of her Asgardian heritage, ironically, while fighting Thor. Angela was defending the Queen of Angels from an enraged Thor—who had found out about his slain baby sister—when Odin arrived. He recognized the daughter he had long thought dead, leaving Thor to cope with the astonishment of meeting his sister.

INFINITY

A sprawling interplanetary conflict sees many Avengers departing planet Earth for deep space. Sensing an opportunity, Thanos of Titan prepares an all-out assault on Earth—and the Guardians of the Galaxy are sucked into the conflict.

BLACK ORDER ASSEMBLED

Thanks to the spies of his trusted lieutenant, Corvus Glaive, Thanos learns that there is discord among the Inhumans and also a schism between the X-Men. Taking advantage of the Avengers being off-world, he convenes his nefarious Black Order: Proxima Midnight, Black Dwarf, Ebony Maw, and Supergiant. Thanos tasks them and their army of cutthroat mercenaries with blockading and enslaving the Earth.

Guardians of the Galaxy (Vol. 3) #8 (Dec. 2013) Under heavy fire from Thanos' forces, Star-Lord, Agent Brand, and Rocket fight a running battle on orbital station the Peak.

PEAK PERFORMANCE

Star-Lord receives a message from Abigail Brand, Director of Earth agency S.W.O.R.D. (Sentient World Observation and Response Department). She explains that Thanos' armada has captured the Peak—a heavily armed orbital station—and it could be used to prevent the Avengers from returning. Gamora, Groot, Drax, and a new recruit named Angela tackle the armada in space. Star-Lord and Rocket Raccoon fight their way through the Peak to free Brand, and Star-Lord lowers the Peak's defenses, letting the returning Avengers' shuttle through.

Infinity (Vol. 1) #1 (Oct. 2013) Corvus Glaive has scoured the galaxy for his master's son, murdering any young men who fit the bill.

Hidden Agenda

The machinations of Thanos are rarely straightforward. While Earth's subjugation is tempting in itself, the despot has another goal in mind. On Thanos's orders, Corvus Glaive has been searching for his master's son, whom the Mad Titan views as a threat to his power and wants dead. It appears this individual is somewhere on Earth.

Guardians of the Galaxy (Vol. 3) #9 (Feb. 2014) To keep the Peak out of Thanos' hands, Brand sets the auto-destruct button, and the station explodes shortly after she and the Guardians make their escape.

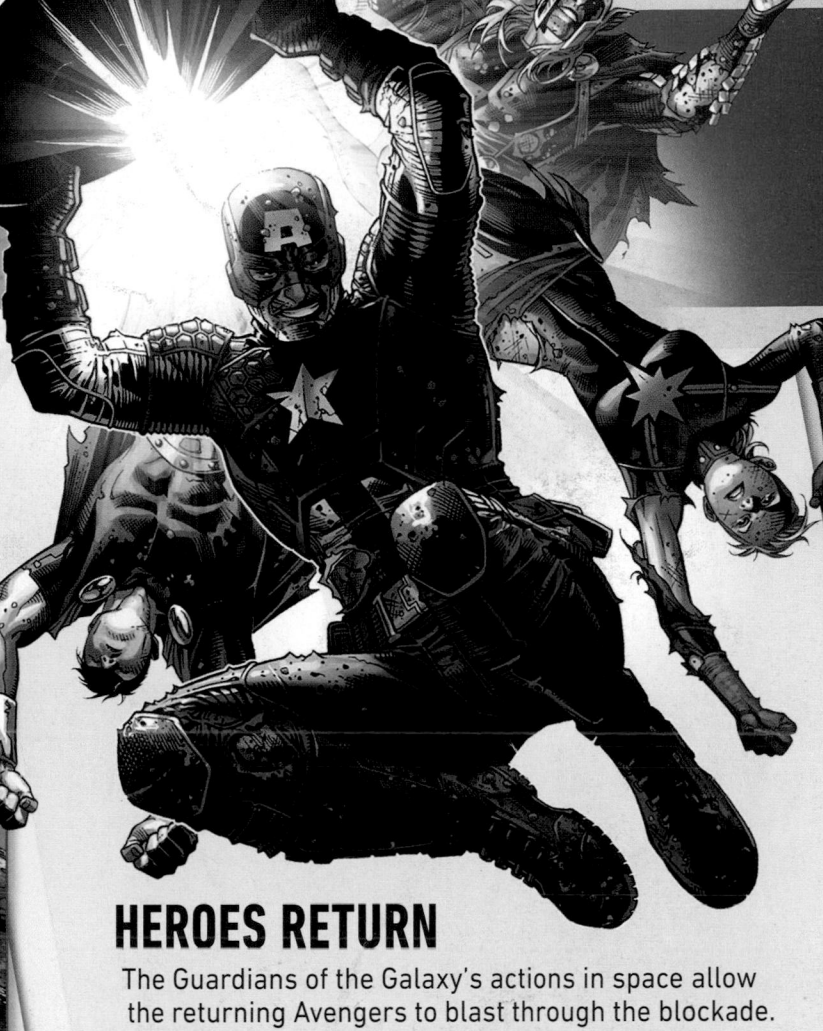

Infinity (Vol. 1) #6 (Jan. 2014) *Thanks to the Guardians breaking Thanos' blockade, the Avengers make it back to Earth. Led by Captain America and Captain Marvel, they launch a frontal assault on Thanos and his Black Order.*

> "Kind of a mess ya got here, Brand."
>
> ROCKET RACCOON

Infinity (Vol. 1) #5 (Dec. 2013) *Ebony Maw locates Thane, Thanos' son, in the smoking ruins of the community the young man has been hiding in, and starts manipulating him for his own devious purposes...*

HEROES RETURN

The Guardians of the Galaxy's actions in space allow the returning Avengers to blast through the blockade. Landing on terra firma, they take the fight to Thanos and his Black Order. Corvus Glaive and Proxima Midnight fall, but not even Thor can bring down Thanos. The duplicitous Ebony Maw frees Thane and urges him to usurp his father. Thane unleashes his newfound powers, and seals Thanos in an unbreakable amber prison.

AN INHUMAN ACT

On Earth, in a desperate last act against Thanos' army, Black Bolt of the Inhumans sets off a Terrigen Bomb, activating all latent Inhumans on the planet. One of these is Thane, Thanos' half-Inhuman son. The activation of his destructive powers results in the extinction of the secretive community in which he's been hiding. Ebony Maw locates Thane and captures him.

Infinity (Vol. 1) #6 (Jan. 2014) *Encasing his father (and Proxima Midnight) in amber, Thane consigns Thanos to a living death. Unseen by the Avengers, Thane is then spirited away by Ebony Maw.*

IRON MAN

A founding Avenger and one of Earth's greatest heroes, Iron Man has found allies beyond Earth in the shape of the Guardians. Wearing a special suit of space armor, he has become a trusted team member, starting a new era of cooperation between the Guardians and Avengers.

ORIGIN

Billionaire industrialist Tony Stark made his fortune designing weapons for the US military. Overseeing the deployment of one of his inventions in an active war zone, Tony tripped a booby-trap and was badly injured. Captured by the insurgent leader Wong-Chu, he was told to design powerful weapons if he wanted to survive. Using these demands as cover, Tony instead built an electronically powered suit of armor fitted with a device to prevent the shrapnel lodged near his heart from killing him. He used the suit to make his escape, then began a crime-fighting career as Iron Man!

Iron Man's space armor can travel at Mach 10 within the atmosphere of a planet and has a warp drive for faster-than-light travel in space.

The armor has a built-in Artificial Intelligence named P.E.P.P.E.R. after Tony's multi-talented assistant, Pepper Potts.

Iron Guardian

Iron Man first met the Guardians when they teamed up with the Avengers to stop Thanos, who had acquired a Cosmic Cube. After the two teams defeated the Mad Titan, Iron Man told the Guardians he envied their freedom to explore space, so Star-Lord invited him to join them. Soon after, Tony did just that, helping them take on the Badoon, the Spartoi, and others. He eventually returned to Earth, but his example has inspired other Avengers to become Guardians, too.

DATA FILE

REAL NAME: Anthony "Tony" Stark

OCCUPATION: Industrialist, inventor, Avenger

BASE: Stark Industries

HEIGHT: 6ft 1in

WEIGHT: 225 lbs

EYES: Blue

HAIR: Black

FIRST APPEARANCE: *Tales of Suspense* (Vol. 1) #39 (Mar. 1963)

US Air Force intelligence officer Carol Danvers was in charge of security at a top-secret base when she first met the Kree hero Mar-Vell, alias Captain Marvel. During a battle between Mar-Vell and the Kree villain Yon-Rogg, Carol was knocked into the power-granting Psyche-Magnitron machine, and then caught in the blast when it exploded. As a result she developed superhuman strength, the ability to fly, and invulnerability. She donned a costume to fight evildoers, first as Ms. Marvel, then as Warbird, and finally as the new Captain Marvel!

Carol's Captain Marvel costume echoes the look of Mar-Vell's, but with the red and blue color scheme inverted.

Catch a Falling Star-Lord

Iron Man's recommendation that the Avengers establish a presence in space prompted Captain Marvel to head out into the galaxy. She first met the Guardians during a planetary refugee crisis, and joined the team soon after. She raced to Star-Lord's aid when he was taken prisoner by the Spartoi, arriving just in time to save him as he fell from a tower. An amazed Star-Lord asked her to marry him, but she simply told him not to ruin the moment!

The sash around Carol's waist was originally a scarf, worn as part of her very first Ms. Marvel costume.

CAPTAIN MARVEL

As the Avenger and galactic hero Captain Marvel, Carol Danvers carries on the legacy of the late Kree warrior Mar-Vell. Super-strong and super-fast with incredible energy abilities, she is perhaps the greatest powerhouse the Guardians have ever had on their team.

DATA FILE

REAL NAME: Carol Danvers

OCCUPATION: Adventurer, Avenger

BASE: Alpha Flight Low-Orbit Space Station

HEIGHT: 5ft 11in

WEIGHT: 165 lbs

EYES: Blue

HAIR: Blonde

FIRST APPEARANCE: (as Carol Danvers) *Marvel Super-Heroes* (Vol. 1) #13 (Mar. 1968); (as Captain Marvel) *Captain Marvel* (Vol. 7) #1 (Sep. 2012)

SWORN ENEMIES OF SPARTAX

Peter Quill's refusal to become a prince in the empire of his father, J'Son of Spartax, has repeatedly propelled the Guardians into conflict with Spartax. Time and again the Spartoi have tried to capture Quill—and time and again the Guardians have foiled them.

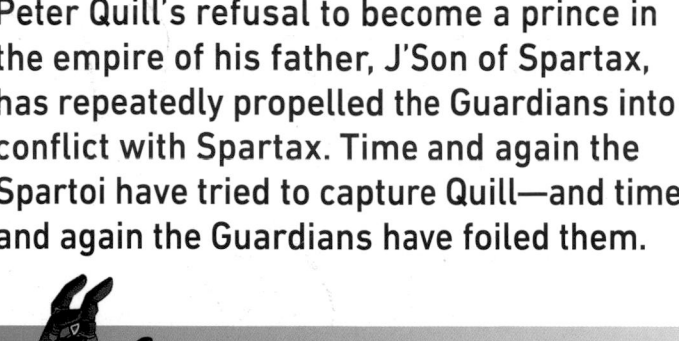

SPARTOI'S MOST WANTED

Having proclaimed Earth off-limits to extraterrestrials, J'Son orchestrated a Badoon attack to lure his son and the Guardians to Earth, then sent a Spartoi force to arrest them. After the Guardians vanquished the troops, Peter Quill broadcast a message detailing J'Son's duplicity.

Guardians of the Galaxy (Vol. 3) #2 (Jun. 2013)

ESCAPE FROM SPARTAX

In order to rid the galaxy of the Guardians once and for all, J'Son set the forces of Spartax, plus an array of headhunters, upon them. When Star-Lord was eventually captured, J'Son had him taken to Spartax and put on trial as an enemy of the empire—answerable for the actions of all his teammates. Refusing to play by his father's rules, Star-Lord jumped through a window to certain death. Fortunately, however, the Guardians' ally, Captain Marvel, who had been tracking Star-Lord, caught him.

Guardians of the Galaxy (Vol. 3) #16 (Aug. 2014)

REVOLUTION NOW

In an attempt to put an end to J'Son and Spartax's pursuit of the Guardians, Star-Lord forced his father to admit to the devious things he had done during the course of his vendetta. The exchange was caught on video camera, and Spartax erupted into riots. As Star-Lord made his escape, a furious mob overran the palace and deposed J'Son.

Guardians of the Galaxy (Vol. 3) #17 (Sep. 2014)

SISTER ACT

On a solo mission, Star-Lord was apprehended by the Spartax Royal Guard, commanded by Captain Victoria—J'Son's daughter, and Peter's half-sister! Victoria blamed Star-Lord for deposing J'Son and leaving the Spartax Empire in ruins, and Peter had to convince her not to turn him over to a bounty hunter.

Guardians of the Galaxy (Vol. 2) #18 (Nov. 2009)

RIGHTFUL HEIR

With J'Son gone, the people of Spartax voted for a new king. To the surprise of almost everyone, they elected the man who had shown them the real J'Son: Star-Lord! When Peter learned of the people's decision, he was faced with a difficult choice: remain a part of the Guardians of the Galaxy, or leave the team and take responsibility for bringing peace and democracy to an entire Empire.

Guardians of the Galaxy (Vol. 3) #24 (Apr. 2015)

THE TRIAL OF JEAN GREY

Years ago, Jean Grey became the Dark Phoenix and destroyed 11 planets in Shi'ar space. One of the original X-Men, Jean later died, but has now been brought forward from the past—along with her fellow mutants—to answer for her crimes...

Guardians of the Galaxy (Vol. 3) #11 (Mar. 2014) *The Galactic Council watches footage of Jean Grey and her transformation into the world-destroying Phoenix.*

*"The Earth is under **our** protection, Gladiator. Next time you won't get **near** it."*

STAR-LORD

NEW ALLIANCES

The Guardians arrive on Earth too late: the Shi'ar have already abducted Jean. The other displaced young X-Men—and their mentor Kitty Pryde—join the Guardians on board their ship. As they come to terms with being on a spacecraft with a talking raccoon and a tree, Star-Lord pilots them to the Shi'ar Empire. As soon as they enter Shi'ar space, they come under attack, but as they battle a Shi'ar warship, another vessel comes to their aid, putting paid to the Shi'ar. This timely intervention comes courtesy of the Starjammers—the band of brigands led by X-Man Cyclops' father, Corsair.

CRIMES OF THE PAST

Gladiator, Emperor of the Shi'ar, tells the Galactic Council that Jean Grey must pay for her crimes (though, as other council members point out, she has yet to commit them). The Guardians learn that the Shi'ar intend to kidnap Jean to put her on trial. Deciding to get involved, they make for Earth.

All-New X-Men (Vol. 1) #23 (Apr. 2014) *On board the Guardians' spaceship, the X-Men become acquainted with their new out-of-this-world friends.*

Guardians of the Galaxy (Vol. 3) #13 (May 2014) The Guardians and the X-Men join forces in battle against the Shi'ar Imperial Guard.

THE TRIAL BEGINS

On the Shi'ar throne world, Jean's trial begins. Gladiator accuses her of genocide and presents footage of the Phoenix causing millions of deaths. Before she can enter a plea, Galactic Council member J'Son of Spartax— Star-Lord's father—interjects, saying that it is ridiculous to try someone for something they haven't yet done. He reveals that the Shi'ar had Jean's family killed, to prevent any of them becoming the Phoenix— something that Jean was unaware of. The trial is paused as Gladiator and J'Son argue. Escorted from the tribunal hall, Jean seizes the opportunity and escapes.

SHI'AR SHOWDOWN

The Guardians, the Starjammers, and the X-Men arrive on the Shi'ar throne world, leading to a battle. Jean displays a new level of power, even fighting the mighty Gladiator to a standstill. The Guardians and their allies escape with Jean, telling Gladiator to keep away from Earth. When the Guardians drop the X-Men off on Earth, a smitten Star-Lord gives Kitty Pryde a communicator, telling her to use it anytime—even just to say hi. She kisses him and runs off. Peter smiles as she goes.

All-New X-Men (Vol. 1) #24 (May 2014) Above and right: On the Shi'ar homeworld, Jean Grey is subjected to a show trial and expected to answer for crimes that she has yet to commit.

Guardians of the Galaxy (Vol. 3) #13 (May 2014) Safely returned to Earth, Kitty Pryde acts on the bond that has formed between her and Peter Quill, kissing him on the cheek.

X-Mentor

Following in the footsteps of her mentor, Professor Charles Xavier, Kitty took it upon herself to tutor her own team: the young versions of the original X-Men line-up, who had been brought from the past to the present day. Kitty's guidance proved invaluable to this team of "All-New X-Men"—not least the youthful Jean Grey, who relied on Kitty to help her get to grips with her ever-increasing telepathic abilities.

ORIGIN

Young Katherine "Kitty" Pryde had no idea why she'd begun to suffer from increasingly bad headaches—until she learned that she could phase through solid objects! Kitty discovered that she was a mutant and was recruited by Professor X and the X-Men. Joining the Xavier School for Gifted Youngsters, she quickly earned the X-Men's respect by helping them fight off attacks from the shadowy Hellfire Club. Taking the name Shadowcat, Kitty became the X-Men's youngest ever recruit. She was instrumental in their victories over many enemies of mutant-kind and mankind, including the Brotherhood of Evil Mutants and the Brood.

> "I'm a teacher, a scholar, a warrior, and a **galactic** Guardian."
>
> KITTY PRYDE

KITTY PRYDE

Brave, resourceful, and level-headed, Kitty Pryde is a mutant who can disrupt and phase through solid matter. Her time with the X-Men meant that Kitty was no stranger to planet-sized perils, or indeed to space travel. As a result, she was well prepared for life as a Guardian of the Galaxy—and for dealing with her roguish boyfriend, Star-Lord.

New Alliances

Kitty first met the Guardians of the Galaxy when the All-New X-Men's Jean Grey was abducted by the Shi'ar. Kitty quickly struck up a flirtatious friendship with Peter Quill, which would later blossom into romance. When Peter's father, J'Son, harnessed the power of the Black Vortex for villainous ends, it was Kitty who succeeded in turning the power of the Vortex against him, earning Peter's deeply smitten respect.

DATA FILE

REAL NAME: Katherine Pryde

OCCUPATION: X-Man, adventurer, teacher

BASE: Mobile, formerly New Charles Xavier School for Mutants

HEIGHT: 5ft 6in

WEIGHT: 110 lbs

EYES: Hazel

HAIR: Brown

FIRST APPEARANCE: *Uncanny X-Men* (Vol. 1) #129 (Jan. 1980)

A sturdy red jacket echoes Peter Quill's Star-Lord costume and is engineered to withstand harsh environments.

Kitty has twin blasters in her hip holster, but is just as likely to use her mutant phasing powers to disrupt opponents' weaponry or even their internal biology.

Star-Lord's Successor

After fighting alongside the Guardians to defeat J'Son in his guise as Mister Knife, Kitty became a full member of the team. She even took on the title of Star-Lord for a while, when Peter Quill was serving as the president of Spartax. She soon earned the respect of the other Guardians, thanks to her daring exploits in space.

STAR-LADY

Kitty Pryde got to know the Guardians when they came to the aid of the All-New X-Men she was mentoring. Kitty and Peter Quill fell in love, and she joined the Guardians, becoming a key member of the team. Wise beyond her years, she was a source of sage advice for her X-Men wards, and has remained so for the Guardians. She also has a fiery temperament—handy in the heat of battle, and when bringing the errant Peter to heel.

ORIGINAL SIN

Not long after Star-Lord, Drax, Nova, and Thanos were thought lost in the Cancerverse, Star-Lord and Drax were back in action, and Thanos was at large again. Now, Gamora wants answers from Star-Lord about how they escaped certain doom.

STAR-LORD'S STORY

Tired of waiting for him to spill the beans, Gamora confronts Peter about his time in the Cancerverse. She demands to know what happened to her ex-lover, Nova, and whether Peter struck a deal with her hated adoptive father, Thanos. He says that when he and Nova trapped Thanos in the collapsing Cancerverse, it was with full knowledge that they would both die, too. However, Thanos revealed a way that they could all escape: with a damaged Cosmic Cube that Thanos alone knew how to use.

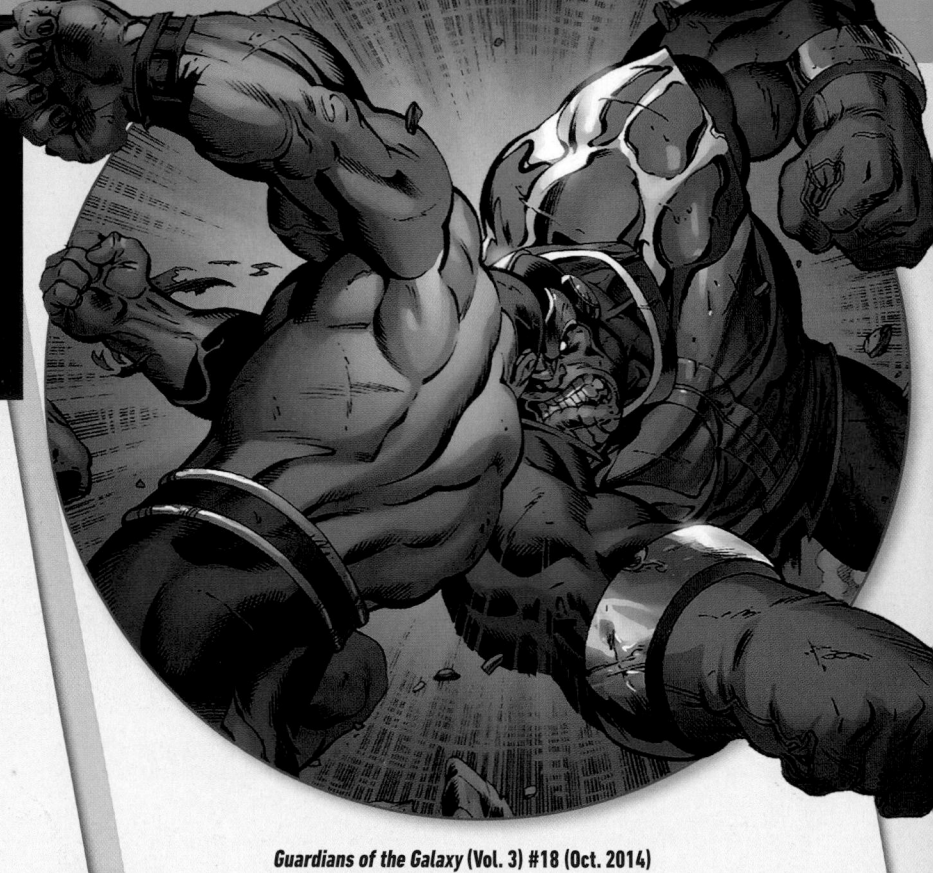
Guardians of the Galaxy (Vol. 3) #18 (Oct. 2014)
Drax hits back at his would-be killer, Thanos.

Guardians of the Galaxy (Vol. 3) #18 (Oct. 2014) In the Cancerverse, Star-Lord and Nova attack Thanos.

DESTROYER REBORN

Peter explains to Gamora that he and Nova turned Thanos down—but then Drax appeared. Drax had been killed by Thanos earlier in their mission to the Cancerverse, yet now he was alive once more. As nothing could stay dead in the Cancerverse at the time when Drax was killed, he had eventually been resurrected. Swearing to finish Thanos for good, Drax attacked his old enemy.

*"How did you survive a suicide mission into **an imploding nightmare universe**?"*

GAMORA TO STAR-LORD

Guardians of the Galaxy (Vol. 3)
#19 (Nov. 2014) *Thanos kills Star-Lord with a fist through the chest, but Peter is soon brought back to life.*

DEATH BECOMES THEM

Drax and Thanos traded blows, but neither could best the other. Taking a chance, Star-Lord blasted Thanos with the Cosmic Cube. To his surprise, it worked: Thanos was obliterated. However, he was swiftly resurrected, and punched a hole through Star-Lord, killing him! Nova then destroyed Thanos, but before he could mourn his friend, both Peter and Thanos returned to life. It was stalemate: even now, none of them could die in the Cancerverse.

Revengers Assemble

Led by Lord Mar-Vell, who had corrupted them in his pursuit of a universe without death, the Revengers featured warped, evil versions of Scarlet Witch, Ms. Marvel, Giant-Man, Captain America, Thor, Iron Man, and other familiar Avengers heroes. (*Guardians of the Galaxy* (Vol. 3) #19 (Nov. 2014))

Guardians of the Galaxy (Vol. 3) **#20 (Dec. 2014)** *Nova takes the Cosmic Cube from Thanos.*

NOVA CUBED

As Star-Lord and the others debated what to do, they were surrounded by the Revengers—the Cancerverse's evil Avengers. Star-Lord, Drax, and Nova had no choice but to ally with Thanos to keep the Cube out of the Revengers' hands. Thanos defeated the Revengers, and a gravely injured Nova seized the Cube from him, using it to transform himself into a living portal. He sent Star-Lord and Drax home—but unwittingly sent Thanos back, too. His story over, Peter tells Gamora that Nova's final message was for her: he loved her, and he hoped she would find happiness.

DATA FILE

REAL NAME: Eugene "Flash" Thompson

OCCUPATION: Soldier, adventurer

BASE: Mobile

HEIGHT: 4ft 1in

WEIGHT: 160 lbs

EYES: Blue

HAIR: Strawberry blond

FIRST APPEARANCE: (as Flash Thompson) *Amazing Fantasy* (Vol. 1) #15 (August 1962); (as Agent Venom) *Amazing Spider-Man* (Vol. 1) #654 (April 2011)

ORIGIN

Growing up, Flash Thompson idolized Spider-Man. Little did he realize that his classmate, "puny" Peter Parker, was the wall-crawler! Flash bullied Peter mercilessly, but as he got older, he developed a sense of responsibility. He enlisted in the US Army and saved the life of a fellow soldier in Iraq, but sustained wounds that led to both his legs being amputated. He was then enrolled in a program to become the new host for the alien symbiote Spider-Man had once worn as a costume, and was transformed into the super-powered Agent Venom.

This spider design is a holdover from the symbiote's connection with Peter Parker, as are Agent Venom's Spidey-like powers.

Avenging Agent

After losing both his legs, bonding with the Venom symbiote was the start of a new life for Flash. Not only could he walk again, he also acquired a variety of superpowers. He fought crime on Earth, before the Avengers assigned him to the Guardians. In space he has found friendship and adventure, and discovered more about the origins of his alien symbiote.

AGENT VENOM

Assigned by Iron Man, Venom is the Avengers' representative on the Guardians' team. He has become a valued member of the line-up thanks not only to the superhuman abilities granted by his alien symbiote, but also his courage, heroism, and trustworthiness.

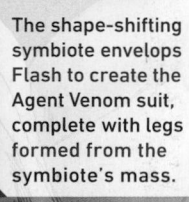

The shape-shifting symbiote envelops Flash to create the Agent Venom suit, complete with legs formed from the symbiote's mass.

THANE

The last son of Thanos, Thane may be even more powerful than his father. His left hand kills on contact, while the right confers living death encased in amber. Under the influence of Mister Knife and Ebony Maw, he has become a threat to the Guardians—and the universe.

Thane's monstrous face is a result of his Terrigenesis, caused by Black Bolt's bomb. Before this, he was a good-looking, seemingly human man with thick brown hair.

ORIGIN

When Thanos encountered a tribe of Inhumans living on a distant world, only one woman lived to tell the tale. She went to Earth bearing Thanos' child, who grew up in Greenland, becoming his community's healer. Later, when Thanos invaded Earth, Black Bolt set off a Terrigen Bomb, activating all latent Inhumans across the planet. Thane was transformed in an instant, taking on a look similar to his father's, and gaining terrible powers that wiped out the community in which he'd grown up.

Thane wears a containment suit provided by Ebony Maw that gives him greater control of his powers.

Like Father, Like Son

When Thane's powers manifested, his father planned to kill him. However, the Avengers attacked Thanos before he could do so. Seeing an opportunity, Thanos' manipulative lieutenant, Ebony Maw, freed Thane and urged him to turn his power on his father. Ebony Maw has been a malign influence on Thane ever since, as has Mister Knife—alias J'Son, former Emperor of Spartax. Knife sought Thane out and told him lies to turn him against the Guardians, whom he then tried to destroy.

DATA FILE

REAL NAME: Thane

OCCUPATION: Healer

BASE: Mobile

HEIGHT: Unknown

WEIGHT: Unknown

EYES: Purple

HAIR: None

FIRST APPEARANCE: *New Avengers* (Vol. 3) #10 (Nov. 2013)

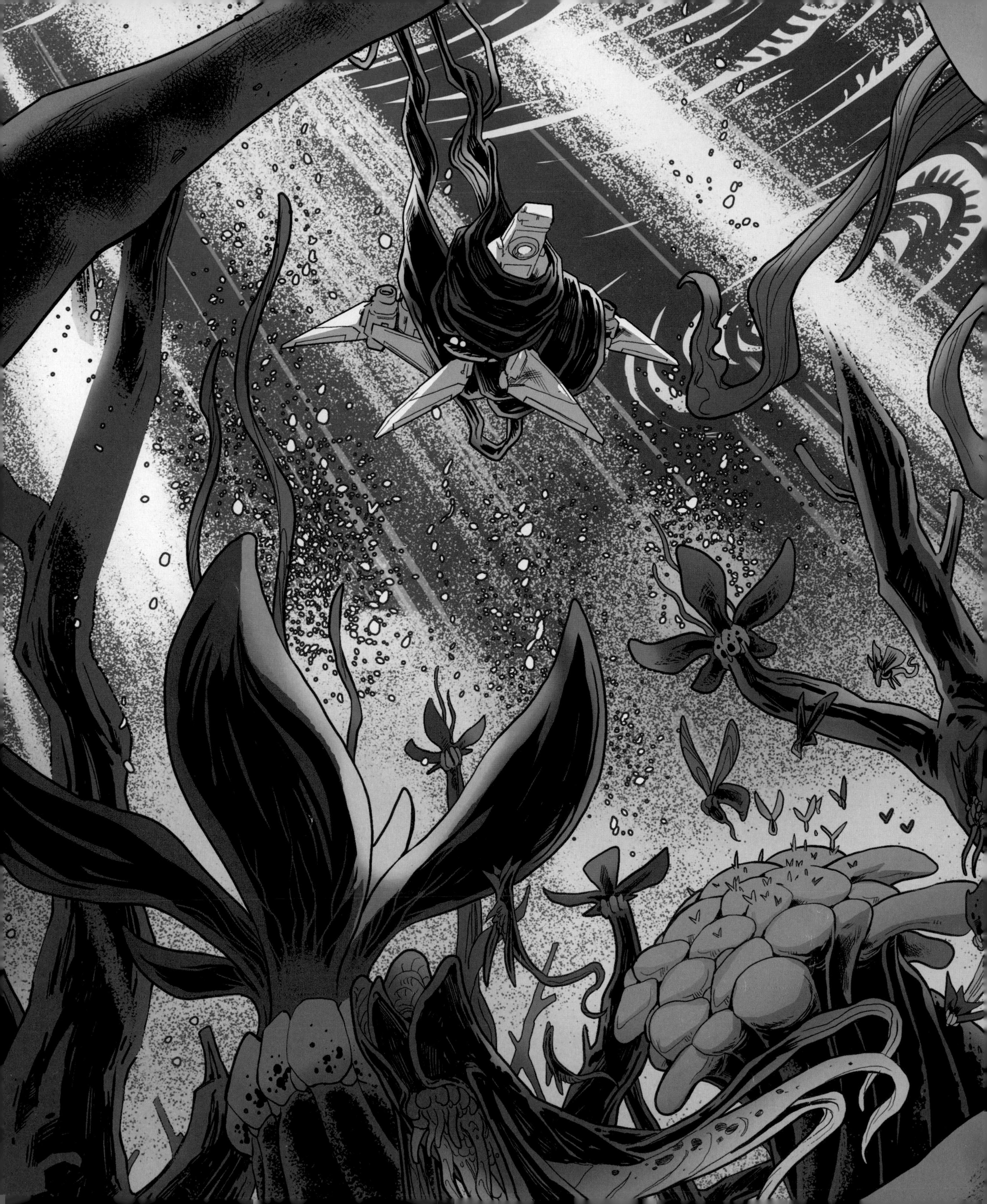

GUARDIANS OF THE GALAXY (VOL. 3) #23
MARCH 2015

When Venom lost control of his symbiote, the parasitic alien possessed each Guardian in turn, guiding their ship to its homeworld, the Planet of the Symbiotes. Once there, the ship was captured by the amorphous natives, the Klyntar. They explained that they had brought the Guardians there in order to help Venom, whose symbiote had become corrupted.

THE BLACK VORTEX

Mister Knife—alias J'Son, Peter Quill's father—has acquired the Black Vortex, an artifact that can grant incredible powers. Peter thinks J'Son is the last person who should have it, and decides to steal it from him with his girlfriend, Kitty Pryde.

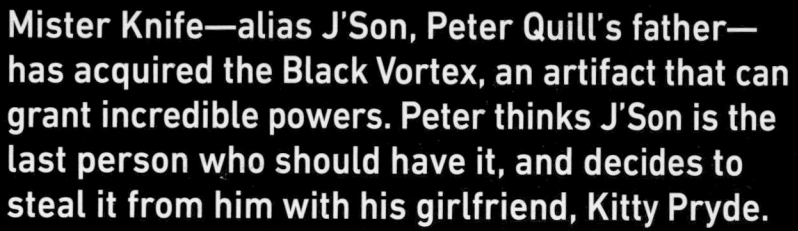

Guardians of the Galaxy & X-Men:
The Black Vortex Alpha (Feb. 2015)
The mirror-like Black Vortex itself.

SUBMIT TO THE VORTEX

After sneaking aboard Mister Knife's Flying Fortress, Peter and Kitty see J'Son's allies —the Slaughter Squad and Thane, son of Thanos—submitting to the Black Vortex to gain its cosmic power. Peter and Kitty escape with the Vortex, then call together the Guardians and the X-Men (including Kitty's former students) on Spartax. As the two teams debate what to do with the Vortex, the Slaughter Squad attack—now cosmically powered and renamed the Slaughter Lords!

Guardians of the Galaxy & X-Men: The Black Vortex Alpha **(Feb. 2015)**
Heroes unite against the Slaughter Lords.

All-New X-Men #38 (Feb. 2015)
Angel, Beast, and Gamora are all transformed by the Black Vortex.

COSMIC TEMPTATION

Czar-Doon of the Slaughter Lords grabs hold of the Vortex, but is run-through by Gamora, who now looks very different. While everyone else was distracted, she submitted to the Vortex, and has now taken on a new cosmic countenance! The X-Men's Magik transports the two teams to Spartax's moon, where the X-Men's Beast and the young Angel both submit and gain cosmic powers.

"We are the new cosmic protectors of the galaxy!"
GAMORA

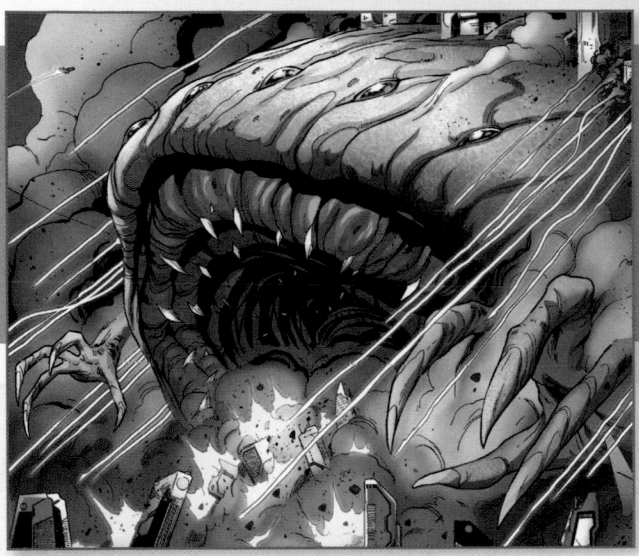

Guardians of the Galaxy (Vol. 3) #25 (May 2015) *Mr. Knife's Flying Fortress—a citadel on the back of a space-whale—rains down destruction on the Kree homeworld.*

Legendary Star-Lord
(Vol. 1) #10 (Mar. 2015)
Thane, son of Thanos, flexes his new powers alongside Mr. Knife and a representative of the virus-like Brood.

COSMIC KITTY

Forced into drastic action to even the odds, Groot and the X-Men Cyclops and Iceman submit to the Vortex and gain cosmic powers, joining forces with the repentant Gamora, Beast, and Angel. Finally, Kitty also submits, and uses her new powers to rid Spartax of Thane's amber and the Brood. With Knife's plans thwarted, Groot, Cyclops, Iceman, and Beast surrender their Vortex powers—but Gamora, Angel, and Kitty decide to keep theirs.

THE FALL OF HALA

Gamora, Beast, and Angel leave with the Black Vortex, intent on reshaping the universe in their own image. But before they get that chance, the Vortex is stolen by Ronan the Accuser, who intends to use it to enhance his fellow Kree. The trio attack the Kree homeworld, Hala, and the Guardians and the X-Men follow them there. J'Son also attacks the planet in his Flying Fortress—blasting it into pieces! The Guardians and the X-Men barely escape in time.

Guardians of the Galaxy & X-Men: The Black Vortex Omega (Apr. 2015) *Kitty Pryde literally holds the fate of Spartax in her hands.*

J'SON'S REVENGE

The Vortex is once more in the hands of Mister Knife. He gets Thane to turn his new powers on Spartax—the planet J'Son once ruled—encasing its people in amber. To complete his revenge on the Spartoi, he turns Spartax over to the virus-like species the Brood. They will infect everyone on Spartax—turning them into hosts for a new Brood—then build a new empire, with J'Son as their ally.

Legendary Star-Lord
(Vol. 1) #10 (Mar. 2015)
Mr. Knife raises a fist in triumph as he wreaks his revenge upon the Spartoi.

SLAUGHTER SQUAD

Gathered together by the villainous Mister Knife (Star-Lord's father, J'Son), the Slaughter Squad are a band of interstellar cutthroats and mercenaries. On Knife's orders they hunted down the powerful Black Vortex, which turned them into the cosmically charged Slaughter Lords.

> "Serve me well, and I will reward you well."
> MISTER KNIFE

DELPHINIA

Hailing from the Centauri system, Delphinia derives her skill with a bow and arrow from her people's innate abilities as hunters. (In a thousand years' time, in an alternative timeline, Yondu, another Centaurian, would use those skills for good rather than evil.) Delphinia was the first to attack Star-Lord when the Slaughter Squad set out to capture him, firing arrows at Peter Quill while he was at the opera on a holo-date with Kitty Pryde. Like her Slaughter Squad teammates, Delphinia submitted to the Black Vortex, and gained the ability to send her arrows vast distances as a result.

FATHER DIABLO

Known as the Priest from Planet X (no relation to Groot's home planet), Father Diablo's "body" is composed of a dark, gaseous substance that he is able to manipulate. When the Slaughter Squad located the Black Vortex, it was Father Diablo who gave them access to it, using his gaseous abilities to lift the incredibly dense globe, which sealed the chamber that held the artifact.

RASKOR

Before he joined the Slaughter Squad, the shape-shifting Skrull Raskor spent months locked in fierce battle with a Kree warrior called Bel-Dann. Their fight was so epic that each was chosen to be champion of their respective people in the Kree-Skrull War, and were ultimately responsible for ending the conflict.

NUX VOMICO

A member of the reptilian Zn'rx species, also known as Snarks, Nux Vomico's time as one of the Slaughter Lords was somewhat brief. When the Slaughter Squad located the Black Vortex, it gave him cosmic powers—but he was swiftly shot dead by Mister Knife, who had expressly ordered that no one tamper with the artifact.

MISA

Shi'ar hunter Misa can destroy living matter with her sonic screech. When Kitty Pryde rescued Star-Lord from Mister Knife and the Slaughter Squad, Misa used her formidable tracking skills to follow Peter Quill and Kitty to Ma Savage's orphanage on Spartax, relaying their location to Mister Knife. As a result, the Slaughter Lords—as they renamed themselves after becoming cosmically empowered—were able to find the Guardians and the X-Men when Peter and Kitty stole the Black Vortex from Mister Knife.

CZAR-DOON

Not long after he first left Earth (long before he faced the Slaughter Squad) Peter Quill met the Badoon mercenary Czar-Doon as a member of the space pirate Yondu's motley crew of Ravagers. He wasn't the only Guardian to have a formative encounter with Czar, either. The mercenary was assisting Thanos when the Titan destroyed the car carrying Arthur Douglas—who died and was reborn as Drax—and his daughter, Heather—who survived and grew up to become Moondragon. The faces of Thanos and Czar-Doon were the last thing Arthur saw before he died. Years later, as part of the Slaughter Squad, Czar-Doon was cosmically empowered by the Black Vortex.

BROTHER BLOOD

Brother Blood was originally one half of the Blood Brothers—psionically linked twins in the service of Thanos. The two toughs did battle with Drax, as well as Iron Man, during the Destroyer's pursuit of Thanos, before winding up as Drax's fellow detainees on a prison transport. When that ship crash-landed on Earth, Drax was reborn in a new form and killed one of the twins. The other brother later joined the Slaughter Squad.

STAR-LORD LOVES KITTY

Over the years, Star-Lord had developed a well-earned rep as a ladies' man—never happier than when in a bar trying to pick up exotic maidens. That was until he met the X-Men's Kitty Pryde. The mutant girl from Earth managed the impossible: taming the previously incorrigible casanova.

A CONNECTION IS MADE

Star-Lord and Kitty Pryde first met when the Guardians came to the aid of the young X-Men she was mentoring. The pair grew close over the course of the encounter and, when they went their separate ways, Star-Lord gave Kitty a holographic communicator. He told her she could call him anytime—even if it was just to have a moan—and that she was one of the coolest people he'd met in the galaxy. Her response was to give the surprised Star-Lord a kiss.

Guardians of the Galaxy (Vol. 3) #13 (May 2014)

LONG-DISTANCE LOVERS

Peter and Kitty chatted often using the communicator he'd given her. On one occasion, she was less than impressed to find that he was calling her from a Badoon jail cell. Soon after, Peter wound up in jail again, and called Kitty up so that she could help him escape. Another time, Peter told Kitty that before they had met, he had been involved with hundreds of women. He swore that he was now a changed man, and that all he wanted to do now was see Kitty's face and talk to her.

Legendary Star-Lord (Vol. 1) #1 (Sep. 2014)

DATE CRASHERS

After a series of flirtatious holo-chats, Peter and Kitty went on a holo-date to Spartax. Peter took the holo-Kitty to the opera, ice-skating, and to dinner. Unfortunately, he was distracted by a series of assaults by the Slaughter Squad, whom his father, J'Son, had sent to capture him. Unaware of the attacks, Kitty started to think Peter wasn't interested in her—until he was kidnapped by the Squad right before her eyes!

Legendary Star-Lord (Vol. 1) #6 (Feb. 2015)

DUDE IN DISTRESS

When Peter was abducted by J'Son, Kitty left Earth again to rescue him. After she used her mutant phasing power to free him, Peter asked her if she wanted to stay with him in space. She pointed out that she had responsibilities on Earth, while he spent all his time stealing stuff. But when Kitty found out that he gave all his money to an orphanage on Spartax, her heart melted, and she agreed to stay with him.

Legendary Star-Lord (Vol. 1) #8 (Mar. 2015)

MATCH MADE IN THE HEAVENS

The battle over the Black Vortex saw Kitty gain new cosmic powers. After she used them to save all of Spartax, she took Peter on a flight through space. She expressed worries that her new powers might change her, but Peter told her he would love her all the same. Then, as the other Guardians and X-Men watched from nearby, Peter got down on one knee and proposed. To everyone's delight, Kitty said yes.

Guardians of the Galaxy & X-Men:
The Black Vortex Omega (Jun. 2015)

MA SAVAGE AND THE ORPHANS

Peter Quill knows how it feels to grow up as an orphan. Abandoned by his father before he was born, then deprived of his mother by the Badoon, he has given his life as Star-Lord meaning by stealing money and valuables on his adventures—then funneling his ill-gotten gains into orphanages across the galaxy.

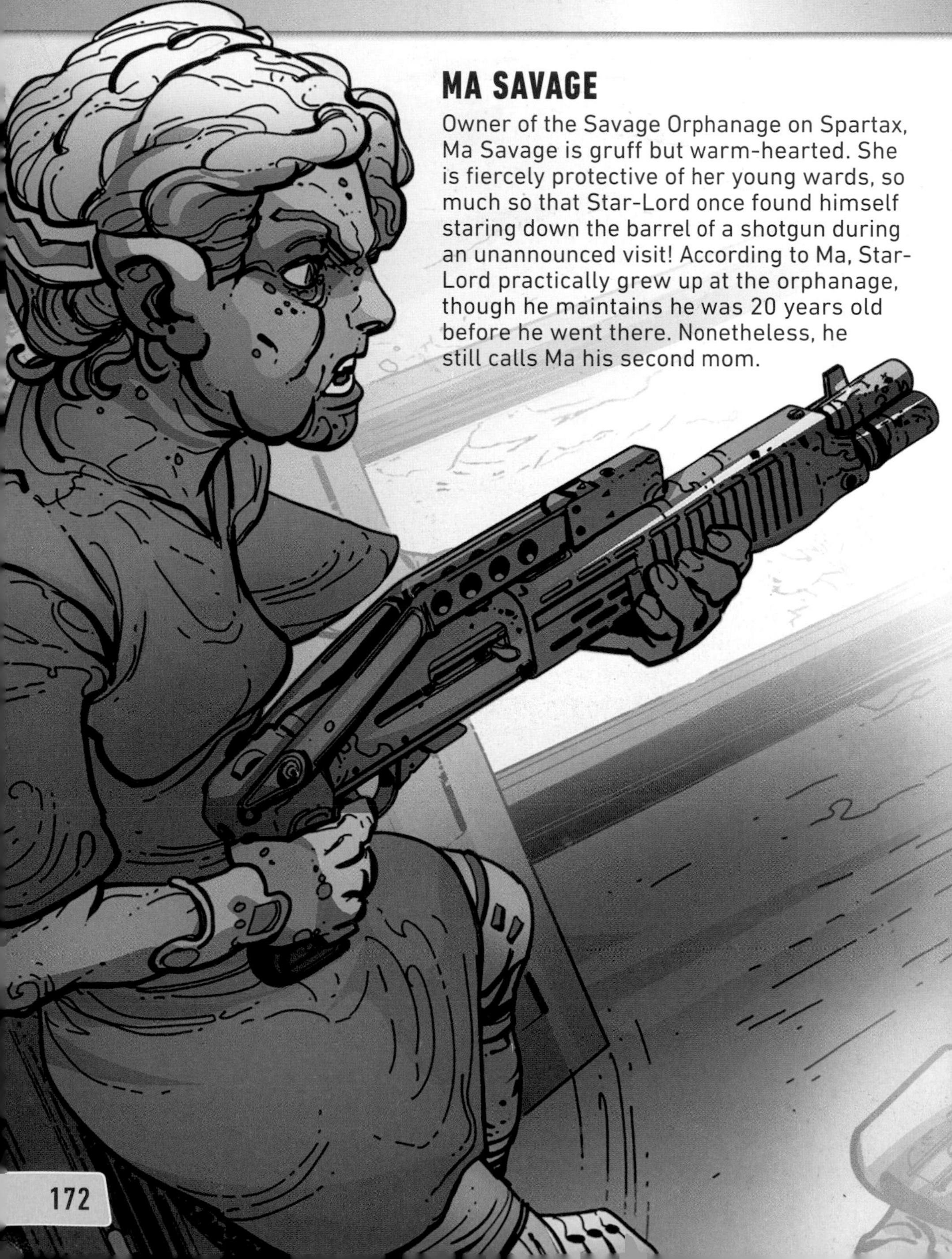

MA SAVAGE

Owner of the Savage Orphanage on Spartax, Ma Savage is gruff but warm-hearted. She is fiercely protective of her young wards, so much so that Star-Lord once found himself staring down the barrel of a shotgun during an unannounced visit! According to Ma, Star-Lord practically grew up at the orphanage, though he maintains he was 20 years old before he went there. Nonetheless, he still calls Ma his second mom.

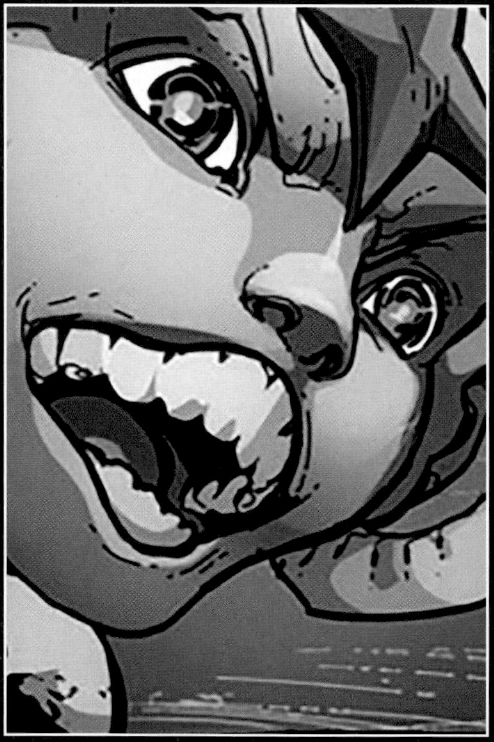

LULA

When Star-Lord took Kitty Pryde to the Savage Orphanage for the first time, the pair sat next to Lula at dinner. One of Ma Savage's young wards, Lula was angry that Peter hadn't been to visit in a while and told him she wasn't supposed to talk to strangers. She relaxed when the meal deteriorated into a food fight, and was later in the thick of a water fight between Peter and the other kids. Peter's hijinks with Lula and the children endeared him to Kitty more than ever.

DONNA

The Savage Orphanage isn't the only orphanage that Star-Lord funds. He donates money to many similar institutions across the galaxy, including an orphanage in the Spartax fringe territories. Its owner, Donna, was suspicious of Star-Lord when he first came to visit—understandably given that he was there to steal a valuable Spartax Mandalay Gem that was stashed there! However, she soon learned that he wanted the Gem so that bad guys wouldn't target the orphanage. Once Star-Lord had it, he sold it through a fence and gave all the proceeds to Donna.

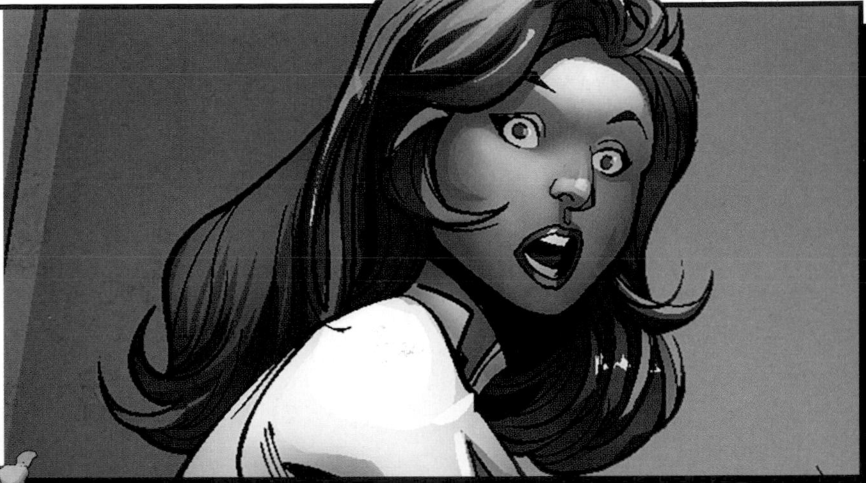

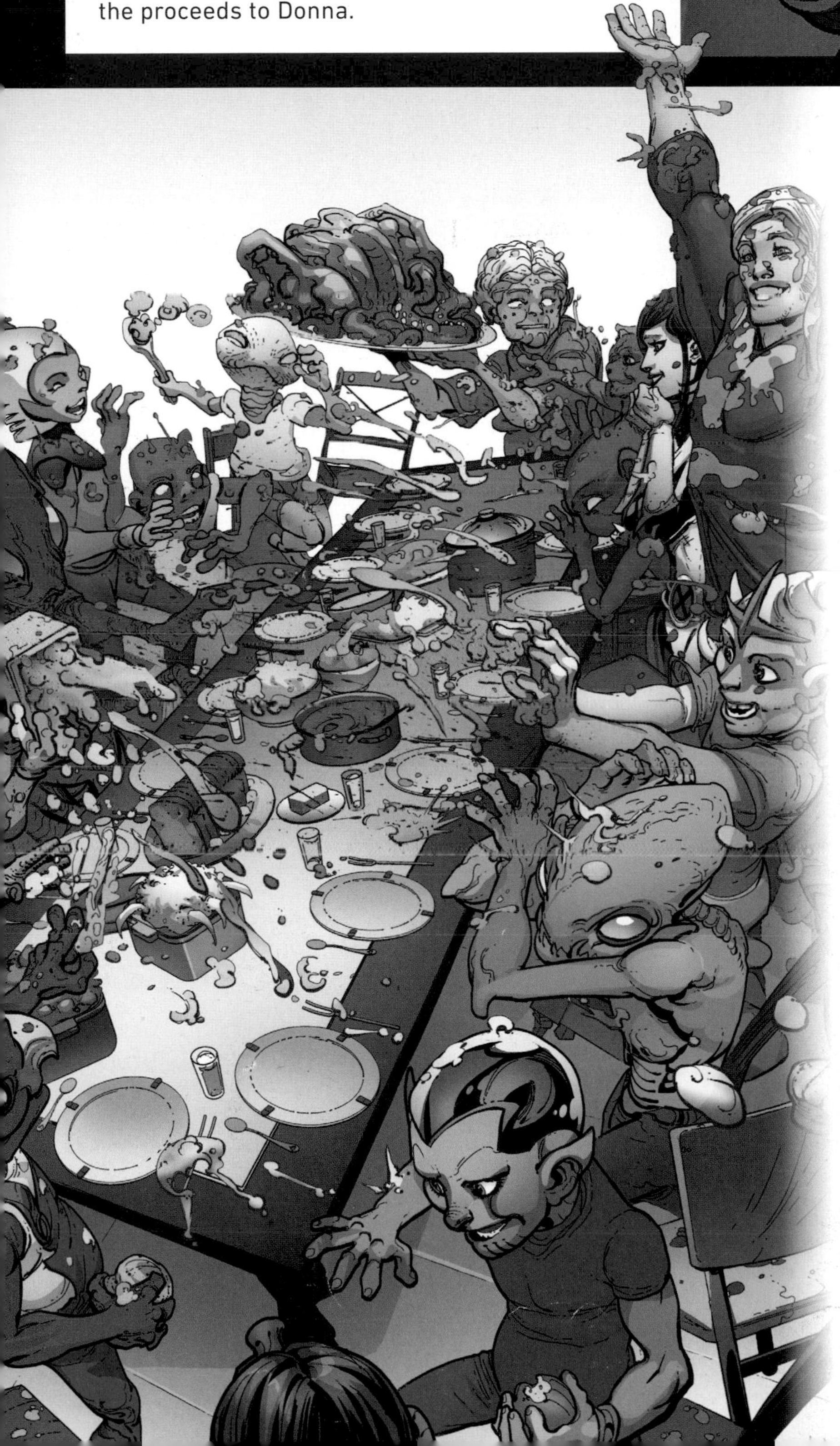

SAVAGE ORPHANAGE

Located on the planet Spartax, the Savage Orphanage is run by Ma Savage and is home to more than a dozen kids from throughout the Spartoi Empire and beyond. Whenever Star-Lord visits, fun and chaos ensue, with at least one food or water fight guaranteed!

"***Everyone*** *needs a home. Even in* ***space****.*"

STAR-LORD

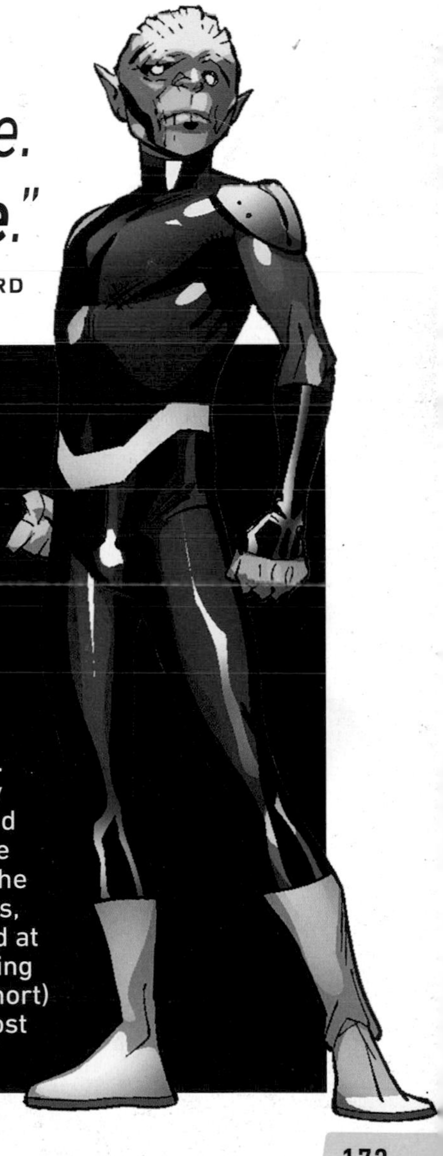

TIBERIUS

When he was thrown into a jail cell aboard a Badoon destroyer, Star-Lord saw that one of his cellmates was a silent Badoon boy. He had no idea why the kid was in jail—he didn't even know his name—but when their chance came to escape, he took the boy with him. The child pointed the way to a small spacecraft, and together the pair fled the destroyer. On reaching the Spartax fringe territories, Star-Lord dropped the kid at Donna's orphanage, naming him Tiberius (or Ty for short) "after Earth's coolest, most awesome space captain."

GUARDIANS OF THE GALAXY (Vol. 3) #27

A DEVASTATING PLANETARY STRIKE LEAVES THE TEAM AT A CROSSROADS.

Star-Lord has been elected President of Spartax, and now he must make a decision. With cheering crowds of Spartoi imploring him to accept the role, Peter Quill has to choose between the Guardians and his people. As he deliberates, the ground beneath him begins to shake—and a planet appears in the sky above Spartax!

JULY 2015

MAIN CHARACTERS
Peter Quill—Star-Lord • Gamora • Rocket Raccoon • Kitty Pryde • Drax • Groot • Venom

SUPPORTING CHARACTERS
Kindun • Chitauri

MAIN LOCATIONS
Spartax • Kindun

1 As the gravitational pull of the new planet begins to tear Spartax apart, Gamora identifies it as Kindun: the planet named after its ruler, who is also Gamora's sworn enemy. To make matters even worse, a swarm of Chitauri then descends from Kindun and attacks Spartax.

2 Proclaiming that she will end this, Gamora —cosmically powered in the wake of the Black Vortex episode—takes flight toward Kindun. On the ground, Star-Lord commands the rest of the Guardians to engage the enemy. Venom, who has never done battle with the Chitauri before, carries out the order enthusiastically.

3 In the narrowing space between Spartax and Kindun, Gamora carves her way through the Chitauri and reaches the planet's surface. There she is met by Kindun himself and his Chitauri guard. The Chitauri are no match for the unimaginably powerful Gamora. She gives her old enemy an ultimatum: leave or die!

4 Star-Lord, Rocket, Kitty Pryde, and Venom seize a Chitauri flyer and head for Kindun—but are surprised to see the Chitauri fleeing, and Gamora coming toward them. Having sent Kindun running, she tells her friends that she too must leave. Her immense new powers pose a threat to the Guardians, and she loves them too much to allow that.

> *"Listen, we need to make a plan. Plan number one: **no one die**."*
>
> **STAR-LORD**

5 Back on Spartax, the Spartoi congratulate Star-Lord on his victory and tell him he acted like a true leader. Peter seeks Kitty's advice: should he remain a Guardian, or take up the role of President? She says she will stand by him whether he's a king, a janitor, or a space-pirate. It's his decision to make alone.

GUARDIANS 3000

In the year 3014, Humanity has been conquered by the Badoon. In Labor Camp 347, new arrival Geena Drake doesn't expect to live long, but then the camp is liberated by Vance Astro, Martinex, Charlie-27, Yondu, and Starhawk—the Guardians of the Galaxy!

FUTURE UNWRITTEN

After liberating Camp 347, Vance Astro reveals to a startled Geena that the Guardians were looking for her. Starhawk has determined that Geena will play a vital role in saving the future—and she and the Guardians must travel into the distant past to do so. Shortly after, Geena and the Guardians are killed fleeing from cyborg-like Badoon. Half an hour in the past, in another timeline, Geena has a premonition of an impending Badoon attack. Picking up a blaster, she tells the Guardians they must fight or die!

Guardians 3000 (Vol.1) #3 (Feb. 2015) *The future Star-Lord comes to the rescue when Geena, Yondu, and Charlie-27 are attacked by the cyborg Stark.*

Guardians 3000 (Vol.1) #1 (Dec. 2014)
Major Victory and Geena fight off the Badoon.

STARK VS. STAR-LORD

With the Badoon driven back, Geena tells Vance Astro about the other version of events, and explains that the Badoon are controlled by a malevolent cyborg intelligence. Later, the Guardians' ship is crippled by a cyborg craft belonging to the Stark, an aggressive species descended from Iron Man's technology. Geena, Charlie-27, and Yondu escape in a life-pod and capture one Stark unit, before being attacked by others. Fortunately, Star-Lord—a distant descendant of Peter Quill—intervenes!

> "Starhawk believes we've been **fighting this war forever**. Every time we win, time starts over."
> VANCE ASTRO

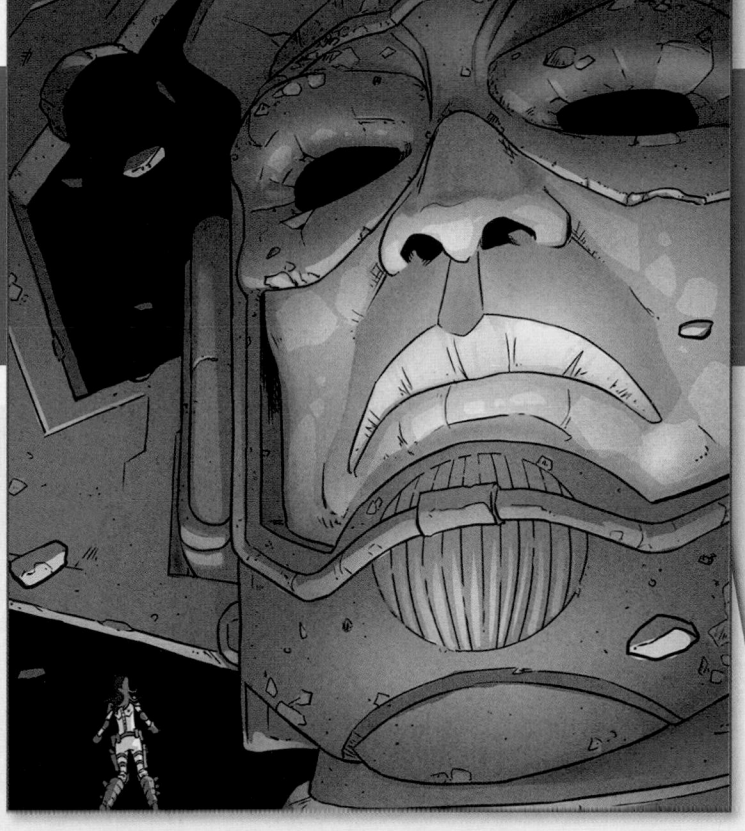

Guardians 3000 (Vol.1) #5 (Apr. 2015) By the 31st century, the long-dormant planet-eater Galactus has come to be known as "Old Hunger".

GUARDIANS UNITED

Star-Lord, Charlie-27, Yondu, and Geena arrive on 21st-century Earth with their captured Stark unit—then run straight into the Guardians of that era! There is barely time for introductions or explanations before the Stark unit replicates itself many times over and launches an attack. The rest of the 31st-century Guardians arrive, making for a more even fight, but then the Stark units suddenly retreat. Starhawk tracks them to a seemingly ordinary house in the suburbs, inside of which a glowing figure awaits—the villainous cyborg, Korvac!

Guardians 3000 (Vol.1) #7 (Jun. 2015) The Guardians track down their old enemy Korvac, living in an unexpectedly suburban setting.

JOURNEY TO GALACTUS

In space, Vance, Martinex, and Starhawk have survived the loss of their ship. They board a Stark vessel and learn that the Stark are trying to protect reality—and the Guardians have been identified as anomalies to be eradicated! At the same time, Geena, Charlie-27, and Yondu journey with Star-Lord to the dormant world-devourer Galactus, intending to use his massive gravity well to travel to the past. Galactus wakes and tells Geena that, while he will help her and the Guardians, their mission is doomed.

REALITY CHECK

Once, Korvac almost conquered the universe, but he was defeated by the Avengers and the 31st-century Guardians. Now he is back and has taken control of the Stark. As two teams of Guardians come under attack from Stark units, Korvac tells Geena he is trying to create order in the universe by reformatting reality. She does her best to reason with him, but it's too late: reality is ending, and Korvac cannot stop it. What happens next will be decided in the Secret Wars...

Guardians 3000 (Vol.1) #8 (Jul. 2015) In the 21st century, both teams of Guardians are surrounded by Stark units controlled by Korvac.

Relaunched in 2016, in the wake of the universe-destroying Secret Wars event, the Guardians of the Galaxy got a new first issue and a new team member in the shape of Thing from the Fantastic Four. Otherwise it was business as usual: big battles, even bigger explosions, and a big showdown with the original Guardians big bad, the Badoon.

GUARDIANS FOR THE FUTURE

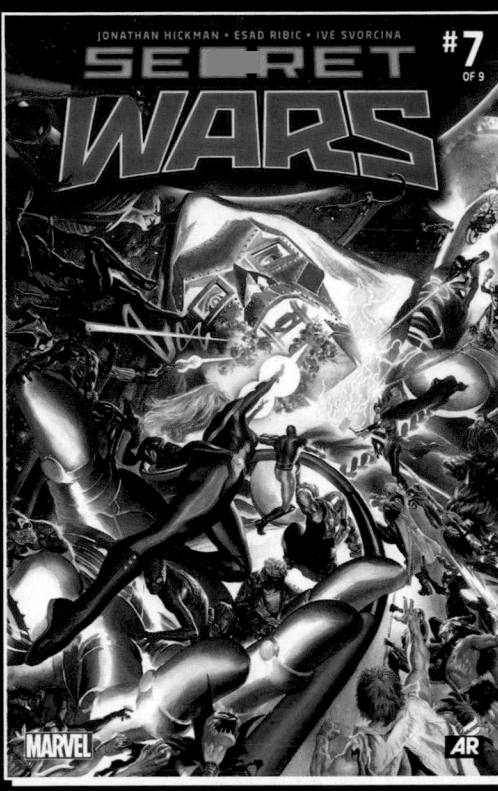

***SECRET WARS* (VOL. 1) #7 (JAN. 2016)**
Star-Lord plays a vital role in a
high-stakes pan-dimensional war, helping take on
Doctor Doom in a battle to save reality.

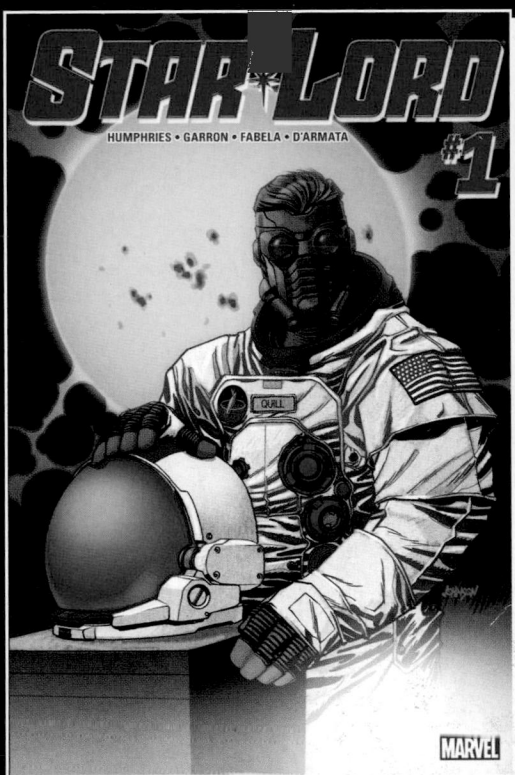

***STAR-LORD* (VOL. 1) #1 (JAN. 2016)**
Peter Quill's second solo series begins with a look
back at his earliest exploits in space, as he steals
a ship and sets out for the stars.

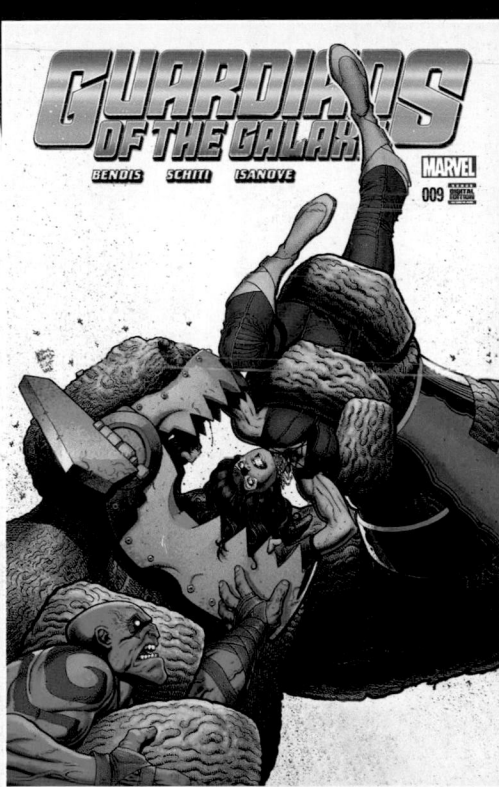

GUARDIANS OF THE GALAXY
(VOL. 4) #9 (AUG. 2016)
Drax and Gamora take on an army of
Badoon (and a Badoon Monster) on a
prison planet in a bid to rescue Angela.

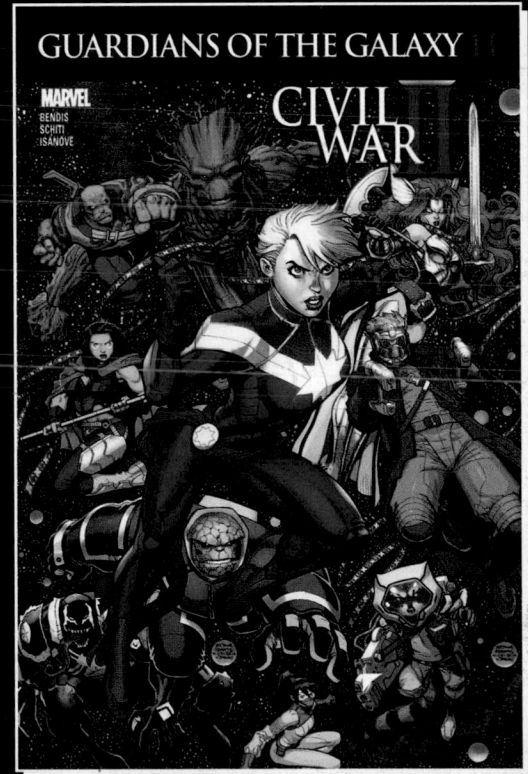

GUARDIANS OF THE GALAXY
(VOL. 4) #11 (OCT. 2016)
The Guardians get mixed up in the second
Super Hero Civil War, as Captain Marvel asks for
backup... against their teammate Iron Man.

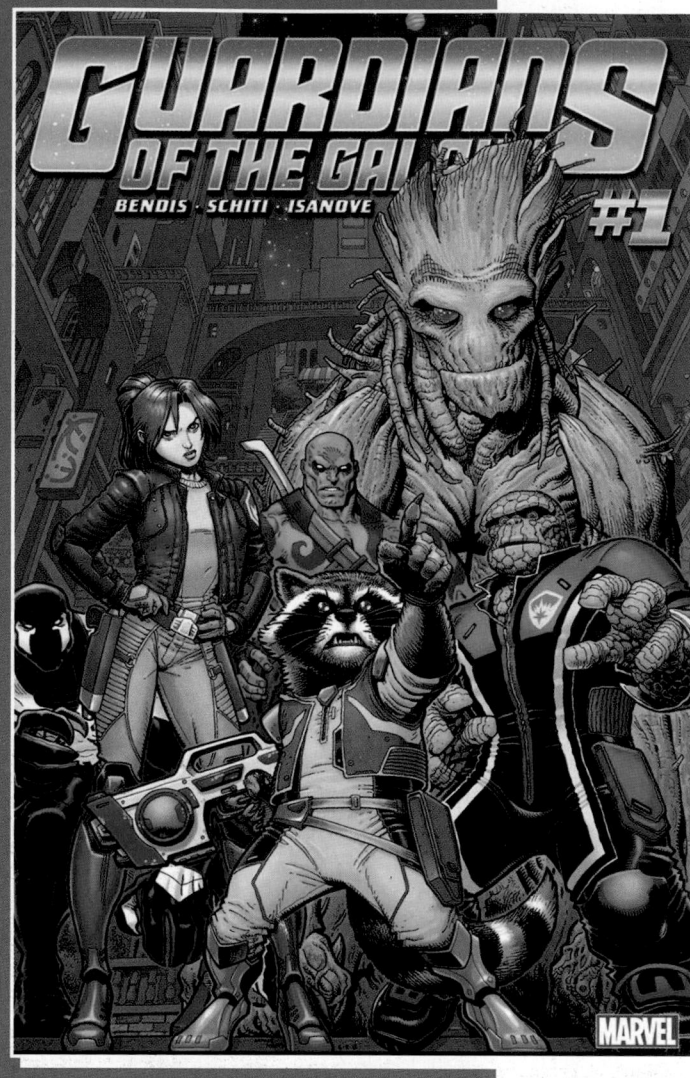

GUARDIANS OF THE GALAXY (Vol. 4) #1

IT'S A BOLD NEW ERA FOR THE GUARDIANS—WITH A BRAND NEW STAR-LORD.

DECEMBER 2015

Peter Quill has accepted the responsibility thrust upon him by his fellow Spartoi and become the Emperor of Spartax. The Guardians have regrouped around a new Star-Lord—Kitty Pryde, a member of Earth's X-Men and Peter's girlfriend. Ben Grimm, alias the Thing of the Fantastic Four, is also on the team, seeking new adventures in space.

MAIN CHARACTERS
Kitty Pryde—Star-Lord • Rocket Raccoon • Groot • Drax • Flash Thompson— Venom • Ben Grimm—the Thing • Emperor Peter Quill

SUPPORTING CHARACTERS
Gamora • Hala the Accuser

MAIN LOCATIONS
Spartax

1 As an ex-astronaut, the Thing loves being among the stars—well, apart from the fact that everyone seems to be trying to kill him! A case in point is the warlike Chitauri, though—to be fair—the Thing and the rest of the Guardians have decided to steal a valuable device from them. Though exactly what that device is, they have yet to figure out...

2 On Spartax, Peter Quill is bored. As Emperor, he has to endure endless meetings on military expenditure and other such riveting matters. Taking an all-too-rare break, he is cornered by an amorous alien delegate who proposes that they build a bridge between their societies by procreating—right here, right now.

"I *like* our new Star-Lord."

ROCKET RACCOON ON KITTY PRYDE

3 In the nick of time, the Guardians' ship arrives on Spartax. Kitty is far from impressed to find Peter in the arms—and tendrils—of a large pink alien. For his part, Peter is baffled by the mysterious Chitauri device the Guardians have brought with them. He suggests that they let the Spartax Science Council have a little "looky-loo."

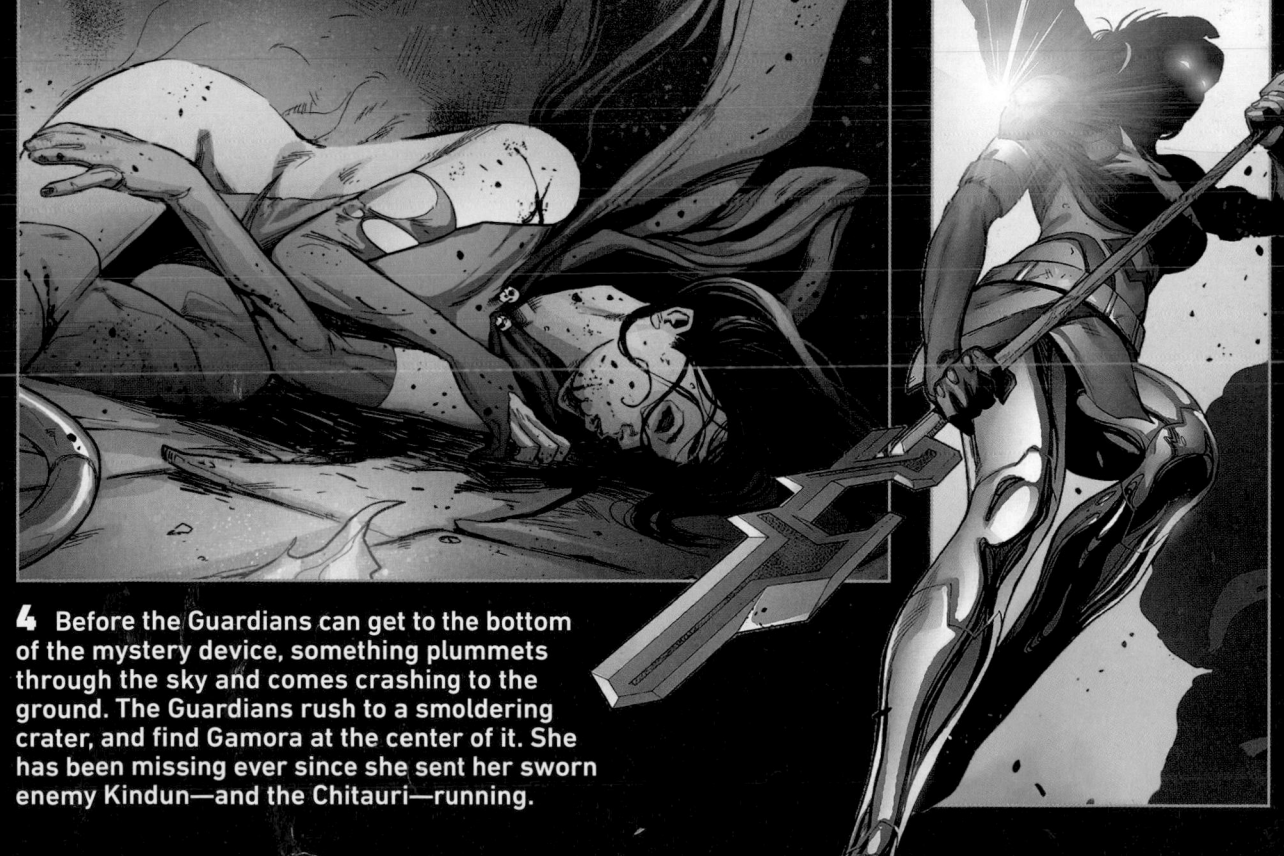

4 Before the Guardians can get to the bottom of the mystery device, something plummets through the sky and comes crashing to the ground. The Guardians rush to a smoldering crater, and find Gamora at the center of it. She has been missing ever since she sent her sworn enemy Kindun—and the Chitauri—running.

5 Bloodied and beaten, Gamora barely has the strength to utter a warning: that she's sorry; that she tried to stop something; that it took all her power just to escape; and that the destroyer of worlds is here. Hala the Accuser descends from the sky. The last of the Kree warriors, she has arrived to kill the Guardians!

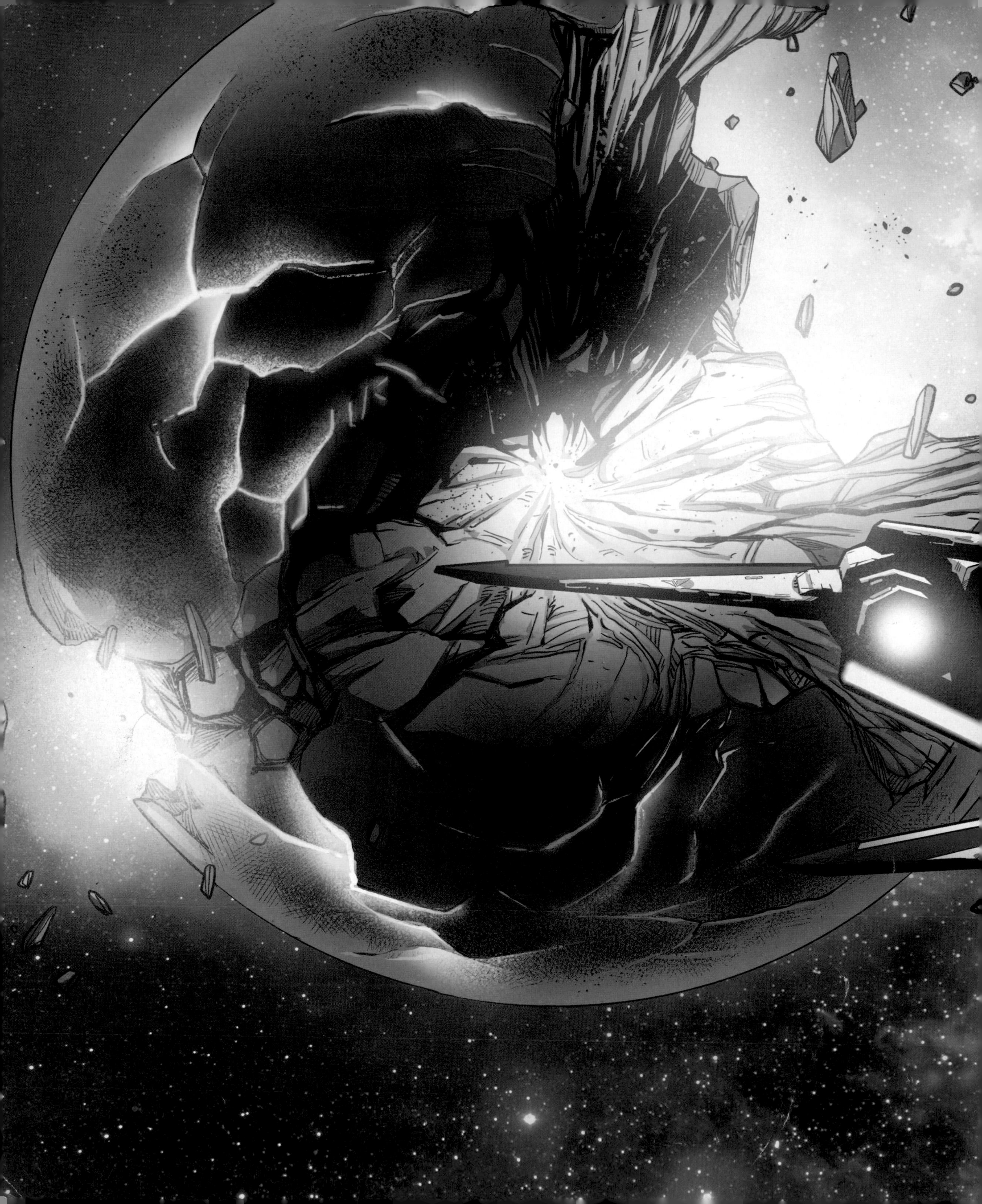

GUARDIANS OF THE GALAXY (VOL. 4) #2
JANUARY 2016

During his struggle with the Guardians over possession of the Black Vortex, J'Son (Mister Knife) used the ancient artifact to destroy the Kree homeworld, Hala. The Guardians barely escaped with their lives. Hala, the last Kree Accuser, then sought vengeance on those she blamed for the death of her world: the Guardians of the Galaxy.

SECRET WARS

The ancient, godlike Beyonders are bringing reality to an end in a grand experiment. As a result, Earths from other realities have been colliding in events called Incursions, destroying entire universes. Now, just two universes—and their Earths—remain.

Secret Wars (Vol. 1) #1 (Jul. 2015) *Star-Lord vanishes as Drax and Gamora see Rocket die.*

EARTH'S LAST STAND

Learning that Earth is the focal point for the impending destruction of the universe, the Galactic Council opts to destroy the planet. The Shi'ar, Kree, Skrull, Brood, and others send a vast battle fleet toward Earth—and the Guardians intercept its communications. They realize that they must warn Earth, but its heroes—including the Avengers, the Fantastic Four, and the X-Men—insist that they won't be evacuating. Rocket tells them in no uncertain terms that they are idiots.

The Avengers (Vol. 5) #42 (May 2015) *Rocket questions the wisdom of Earth's greatest heroes.*

Secret Wars (Vol. 1) #1 (Jul. 2015) *X-Man Cyclops is one of the Earth heroes teleported onto a life raft.*

EVERYTHING ENDS

The final Incursion begins, as another Earth appears in the sky above New York, and the heroes of that world try to save their planet by launching an attack. The Guardians join the fray, fighting alongside the Earth heroes from their own universe. Rocket and Drax manage to bring down the other Earth's Iron Man, but Rocket is then shot and killed. Before he even has a chance to register this, a shocked Star-Lord is teleported away against his will. The rest of the Guardians fight on, but the two Earths collide, and all of reality blinks out of existence.

***Secret Wars* (Vol. 1) #3 (Sep. 2015)** *Star-Lord, Spider-Man, Thor, and Captain Marvel emerge from a life raft, after somehow surviving the end of reality.*

***Secret Wars* (Vol. 1) #8 (Feb. 2016)**
"Say hello to my little friend," says Star-Lord as he reveals that he has been carrying a tiny shard of Groot all along.

BEYOND REALITY

Star-Lord finds himself on a ship—a life raft crewed by Reed Richards (Mr. Fantastic), Captain Marvel (Carol Danvers), and other heroes. The raft survives the end of reality and lands on Battleworld—a patchwork planet assembled from the remnants of other Earths by Doctor Doom—where it is joined by a second life raft bearing Thanos and a cabal of other villains. Battleworld's many domains are ruled by Doom, who has stolen the power of the Beyonders and established himself as "God".

THE BATTLE FOR BATTLEWORLD

When Doom tries to impose his will on the new arrivals, his Sheriff, Doctor Strange, spirits them to Battleworld's most distant domains to keep them out of his reach. A furious Doom kills Strange, and begins to hunt his prey. Star-Lord and the others regroup and seek to depose Doom and restore reality. As battle rages, Star-Lord unveils his secret weapon: a toothpick-sized piece of Groot, which grows to a colossal size. Groot's intervention helps to turn the tide, helping Reed Richards to confront his nemesis Doom and take his power, before using it to restore every Earth and its attendant universe.

> *"Center of the universe **my ass**... This place is a giant, stinkin' pile of—"*
>
> ROCKET RACCOON
> DESCRIBES EARTH

Doom's Domain

Doctor Doom ruled over Battleworld for eight years before the last two Earths were destroyed. By the time Star-Lord arrived, the inhabitants of the different domains no longer remembered the worlds they had come from, and believed they had always lived under Doom's despotic rule.

***Secret Wars* (Vol. 1) #8 (Feb. 2016)**
Combined with Yggdrasill—the World Tree—a tiny splinter of Groot swells to a colossal size.

BATTLEWORLD TALES

All of reality has been destroyed—except for one patchwork version of Earth made by Doctor Doom. Star-Lord is one of the few to survive the end of everything. On Battleworld, he will meet familiar but different versions of his fellow Guardians...

Star-Lord and Kitty Pryde (Vol. 1) #2 (Aug. 2015)
Kitty makes clear her affection for Peter Quill.

STAR-LORD SINGS

On the run from Doom, Battleworld's ruler, Star-Lord hides out in one of the planet's many bizarre domains—a stylish version of New York. He gets a job as a crooner (using the name Steve Rogers) in a nightclub owned by a version of Drax with a fetching quiff. It's here that he meets Kitty Pryde—but this Kitty is an agent for Doom, with claws like Wolverine's! She doesn't know Star-Lord, but once she finds out he's not from around here, she becomes very interested indeed...

Star-Lord and Kitty Pryde (Vol. 1) #1 (Jul. 2015)
Star-Lord tries out a new career as a nightclub singer—named after Captain America!

A TAIL OF LOVE

Kitty plans to take Star-Lord to Doom, but when he helps her to fight a group of killer robots, she relents. He also lends a hand with her mission to track down an object that doesn't belong in this domain. When this turns out to be Rocket's tail, Star-Lord is reminded of everyone he lost when his universe ended. Kitty and Star-Lord share a tender kiss before she departs on a new mission.

> *"**Doctor Doom** is God. That should give you an idea of how **twisted** this place is."*
> — STAR-LORD

Guardians of Knowhere (Vol. 1) #2 (Oct. 2015) *The Battleworld mercenary Yotat starts to get the better of Drax.*

GUARDIANS OF KNOWHERE

Above Battleworld, a more familiar Drax is protecting Knowhere—a severed Celestial head, home to myriad outcasts. With him are Rocket, Mantis, and Gamora, who is dimly aware that Battleworld is artificial. She is being hunted by one of Doom's agents, Angela, but when Drax finds himself in combat with a mercenary named Yotat, Angela dispatches his attacker.

WARRIOR WOMEN

Angela and Gamora call a truce, and Gamora explains that she doesn't believe that Doom is God, or that Battleworld is even real. The two warriors come to blows once more, but then are attacked by another female warrior, whom neither of them recognizes.

REALITY BITES

The newcomer kills Angela before Gamora and the other Guardians succeed in repelling her. In time—when the universe has been restored—they will meet her again and learn that she is Hala the Accuser. But for now, they are left to ponder the fragments of a life that Gamora has started to recall—names such as Thanos, Groot, and Quill. Right on cue, Star-Lord arrives. He explains that the world as they know it is a sham, and he needs their help to vanquish Doom and restore reality...

Guardians of Knowhere (Vol. 1) #4 (Nov. 2015) *Gamora and the other Guardians are reunited with Star-Lord.*

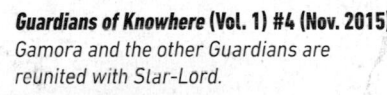

Guardians of Knowhere (Vol. 1) #4 (Nov. 2015) *Angela and Gamora join forces to stab the mysterious warrior.*

THE THING

Supremely strong and almost invulnerable, Ben Grimm is one quarter of the Fantastic Four, and now a vital member of the Guardians. Trained as a pilot and astronaut, Ben has always seen outer space as his ultimate goal, and being a Guardian gives him the perfect way to explore it.

This rocket pack belongs to Rocket Raccoon, who has given the Thing permission to use his cast-offs!

ORIGIN

Ben Grimm was an experienced test pilot when his old college friend Reed Richards approached him about flying a new kind of craft into space. Despite his concerns about the dangers posed by Cosmic Rays, Ben reluctantly agreed. In the event, Ben's fears were confirmed as he, Reed, and their two fellow astronauts, Sue and Johnny Storm, were all bathed in Cosmic Rays. Yet, instead of being harmed, all of them gained incredible powers. Ben was transformed into the super-strong, rock-like Thing, joining his friends in the Earth-defending super-team the Fantastic Four.

The Thing's rock-like body can withstand most things, but he is not impervious to the ravages of space, so he wears a special flight suit.

Space is the Place

Since joining the Guardians, the Thing has found a new lease of life beyond the confines of Earth and his usual team, the Fantastic Four. It hasn't been a trouble-free existence, however. From the day he signed up, he was pitched into battle with a series of awesome threats, from Hala the Accuser to the Brotherhood of Badoon. Ben's superhuman strength has helped to win the day on more than one occasion, and his gruff but genial nature has made him a natural fit as a Guardian. Though delighted to have finally become a full-time spaceman, he stills finds plenty of time for clobbering bad guys.

DATA FILE

REAL NAME: Benjamin J. Grimm

OCCUPATION: Adventurer

BASE: Mobile; formerly New York

HEIGHT: 6ft

WEIGHT: 500 lbs

EYES: Blue

HAIR: None

FIRST APPEARANCE: *Fantastic Four* (Vol. 1) #1 (Nov. 1961)

When the Guardians of the Galaxy fought Mister Knife and the Slaughter Lords for possession of the Black Vortex, their conflict resulted in the destruction of the Kree homeworld Hala. In a stroke, the entire population of the planet was wiped out, along with its entire Accuser Corps—with one exception. A single Accuser had been on a mission in deep space and returned home to find that everything she loved was gone. She renamed herself Hala in honor of her lost world, and set out to have her revenge.

J'Accuse the Guardians!

After learning of the Guardians' part in the obliteration of her homeworld, Hala began her mission of vengeance by tracking down Gamora and beating her severely. When Gamora tried to warn the other Guardians, Hala followed her to Spartax and attacked the team. Her onslaught proved so powerful that it took the 500 lbs Thing dropping on her from orbit to bring her down. As well as trying to kill the Guardians, she has also tried to destroy the worlds they hold dear, including Spartax and Earth. She remains at large, despite an arrest by Spartoi forces, and is still a major threat.

Kree Accuser Corps armor features built-in defenses, including the ability to fire energy bolts from the eyes.

Hala the Accuser wields a powerful energy staff that she can summon from a distance, and which cannot be used by others.

HALA
THE ACCUSER

Rising from the ruins of the Kree homeworld, the last of the Accuser Corps is one of the few survivors of her planet's destruction. She holds the Guardians responsible for the loss of her world, and has named herself after it, swearing vengeance on those she holds responsible.

DATA FILE

REAL NAME: Hala

OCCUPATION: Accuser

BASE: Mobile; formerly Hala

HEIGHT: Unknown

WEIGHT: Unknown

EYES: Blue

HAIR: Black

FIRST APPEARANCE: *Guardians of Knowhere* (Vol. 1) #3 (Oct. 2015)

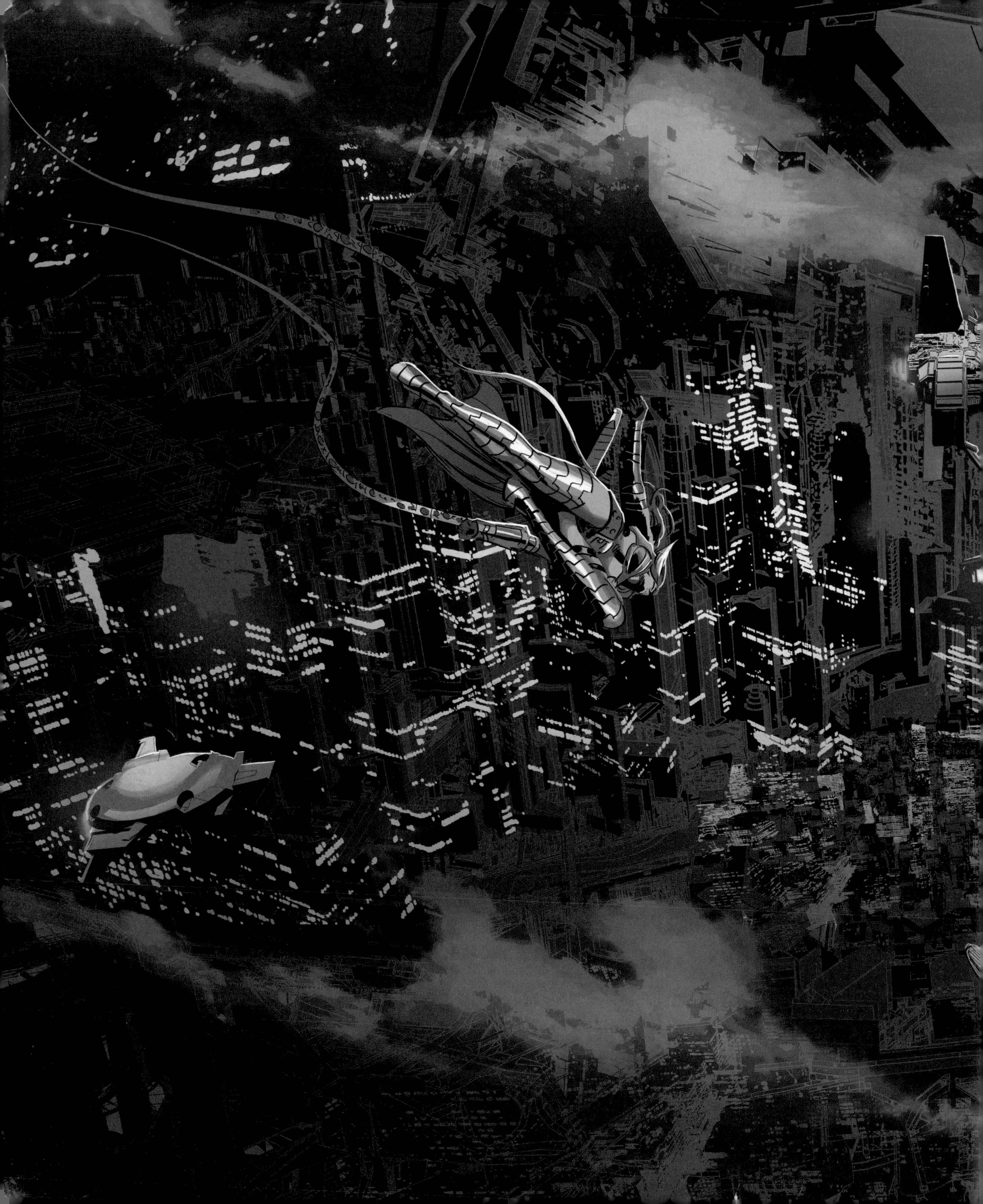

GUARDIANS OF KNOWHERE (VOL. 1) #1
SEPTEMBER 2015

After all of reality was destroyed by the Beyonders, most of the Guardians wound up on a recreated Knowhere, orbiting Battleworld—a planet created by Doctor Doom from the remnants of alternate Earths. Angela, however, was turned into one of Doom's Thor Corps enforcers, charged with keeping the rebellious Guardians confined to Knowhere.

GUARDIANS OF INFINITY

Uttering the immortal words, "Seriously, since when have I ever led you astray?" Rocket Raccoon does precisely that to Drax and Groot, convincing them to join him on a mission to explore a massive, mysterious vessel floating in space...

GUARDIANS GALORE!

The two sets of Guardians are suddenly attacked by armored troops. Charlie-27 is captured, but the others escape through a doorway that turns out to be a portal through time. They emerge in Iraq in the year 1016 and are immediately confronted by... yet another team of Guardians of the Galaxy! This iteration is led by a Kree woman named Stella Nega, and its members refuse to believe that the new arrivals are Guardians as well. However, after coming to blows, the three teams call an uneasy truce.

Guardians of Infinity (Vol. 1) #2 (Mar. 2016) *Stella Nega finds herself at the center of three teams of warring Guardians!*

Guardians of Infinity (Vol. 1) #1 (Feb. 2016)
The Guardians' ship is dwarfed alongside the vastness of the mysterious so-called "Structure."

STRUCTURAL SURVEY

Arriving at the Structure (as the vessel quickly becomes known), Rocket, Groot, and Drax are unable to determine its size, because it is so vast. The three Guardians board the Structure and start to explore it. They are surprised when they bump into the Guardians of the Galaxy from the 31st century—Vance Astro, Martinex, Charlie-27, and Nikki—who are also exploring the Structure, having entered it from their own era. It seems the Structure is so big it ranges across time as well as space!

*"I am Stella Nega. I **lead** the Guardians of the Galaxy."*
STELLA NEGA

Guardians of Infinity (Vol. 1) #3 (Apr. 2016) Inside the Structure, a vast invasion fleet awaits the orders of Hermetikus.

SECRET INVASION

Stella Nega explains that the Structure belongs to the Newcomers, a species that is plundering worlds and harvesting their populations—"gene-cruiting" them to become Newcomer Highbreeds. This is the fate that has probably befallen Charlie-27, and which also claims Skytower— one of Stella's team—when the Highbreeds attack again. After fighting them off, all three teams of Guardians return to the Structure. There they find a network of chambers, each hundreds of miles square, containing regiments of Highbreed and warships—an invasion fleet with the ability to strike anywhere across 2,000 years of history!

BRAINS TRUST

The Guardians come under assault from the Highbreed once more and all three teams are captured. They are taken to the Newcomers' leader, Hermetikus, who was once a member of Stella's Guardians. He is intent on controlling the galaxy, drawing on the knowledge he gains by stealing the brains of genius individuals. Noting Rocket's tactical brilliance, Hermetikus removes Rocket's brain and adds it to the store in his armor. The rest of the Guardians are imprisoned, but Nikki breaks free and releases them.

Guardians of Infinity (Vol. 1) #5 (Jun. 2016) Hermetikus addresses his captive audience.

Guardians of Infinity (Vol. 1) #8 (Sep. 2016) Charlie-27 strikes back!

SUCKER PUNCH

Hermetikus' plan goes awry when Rocket's brain assumes control of his captor's body, causing Hermetikus to punch himself in the face! Rocket's brain then raises the shields of the Structure—destroying the invasion fleet as it departs—and breaks Hermetikus' control of the Newcomers. They all start returning to normal, including Charlie-27, who fells Hermetikus with a single punch. Rocket's brain is reunited with his body— while Hermetikus' is removed and put in a jar! Three sets of Guardians go their separate ways, each wondering exactly when the Guardians were founded...

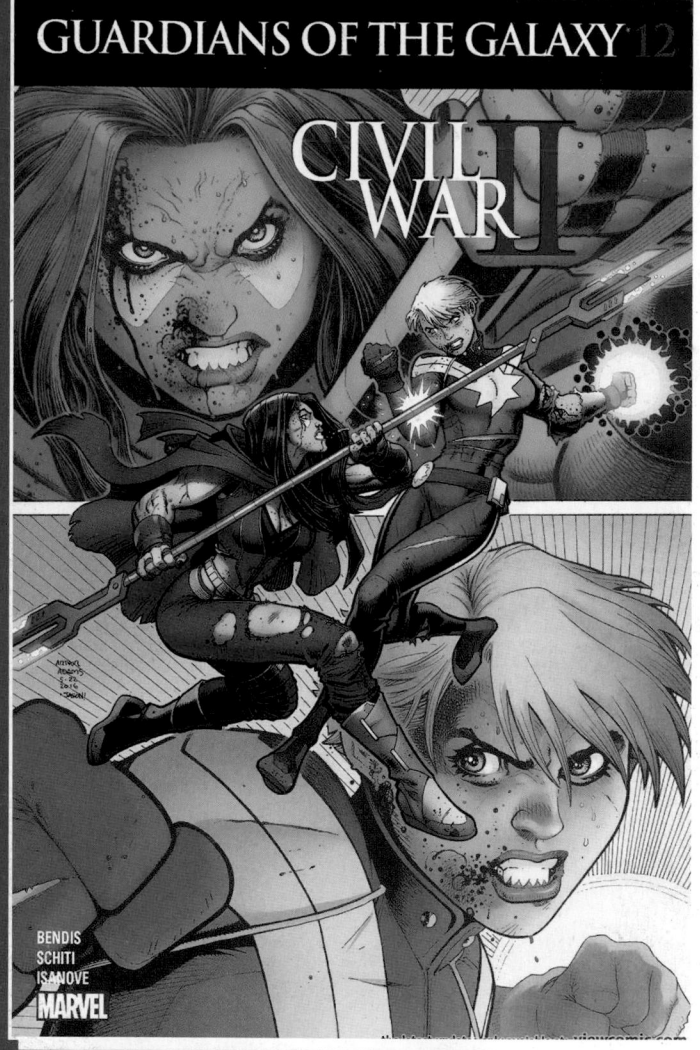

GUARDIANS OF THE GALAXY 12

CIVIL WAR II

BENDIS
SCHITI
ISANOVE
MARVEL

GUARDIANS OF THE GALAXY (Vol. 4) #12

THE GUARDIANS ARE DRAWN INTO A WAR OF SUPER HERO AGAINST SUPER HERO.

One of the most divisive conflicts in recent memory was Earth's superhuman Civil War, which saw hero pitted against hero over the Superhuman Registration Act. Now, history is about to repeat itself, as Earth's Super Hero community splits down the middle. Even worse, the two sides are led by two Guardians: Iron Man and Captain Marvel!

NOVEMBER 2016

MAIN CHARACTERS
Peter Quill—Star-Lord • Rocket Raccoon • Kitty Pryde • Groot • Drax • Gamora • Flash Thompson—Agent Venom • Ben Grimm—the Thing • Angela

SUPPORTING CHARACTERS
Captain Marvel • Iron Man

MAIN LOCATIONS
Earth—New York

1 The Guardians have responded to a request from Captain Marvel (Carol Danvers) for help. The Inhuman Ulysses has the power to foresee events and this has caused a schism among Super Heroes. While Carol believes Ulysses' visions can be utilized to prevent disasters by arresting criminals in advance, Iron Man sees this as a form of profiling.

2 As the Guardians wait for Carol's signal, they debate whether they're on the right side of the conflict. Gamora states that she's with Captain Marvel: If she had the opportunity to stop her nemesis, Thanos, before he did any harm, she would seize it. Agent Venom asks himself what if he, as Flash, were arrested for something he hadn't yet done?

3 The Guardians watch on screen as Iron Man's forces assemble on the roof of the Triskelion, headquarters of S.H.I.E.L.D. Super Hero task force the Ultimates. Flash notes that Iron Man's team represents a lot of firepower, including two Captain Americas, Thor, Luke Cage, and Doctor Strange. Kitty's former students, the young All-New X-Men, are also on Iron Man's side.

4 As Carol gathers her forces—including her team Alpha Flight and various X-Men and Inhumans—the Guardians ready themselves. Carol tells Iron Man he's under arrest. Iron Man replies that she's seriously out-powered. Knowing she has friends all over the place, Carol gives the signal. The Guardians de-cloak their ship and leap into the fray.

5 During the ensuing battle, a blast from the Avenger Vision slices through the Guardians' ship, exploding it in a ball of fire! A furious Rocket laments the loss of his ship, and also that the Guardians are now stuck on Earth—a place he despises. Gamora overhears a S.H.I.E.L.D. soldier ordering the battle-damaged Triskelion's sub-basement checked... and requesting an update on its prisoner, Thanos!

"We just lost everything we own!"

ROCKET RACCOON

INDEX

Page numbers in **bold** are main entries.

N

O

P

Q

R

S

T

U

V

W

X

Y

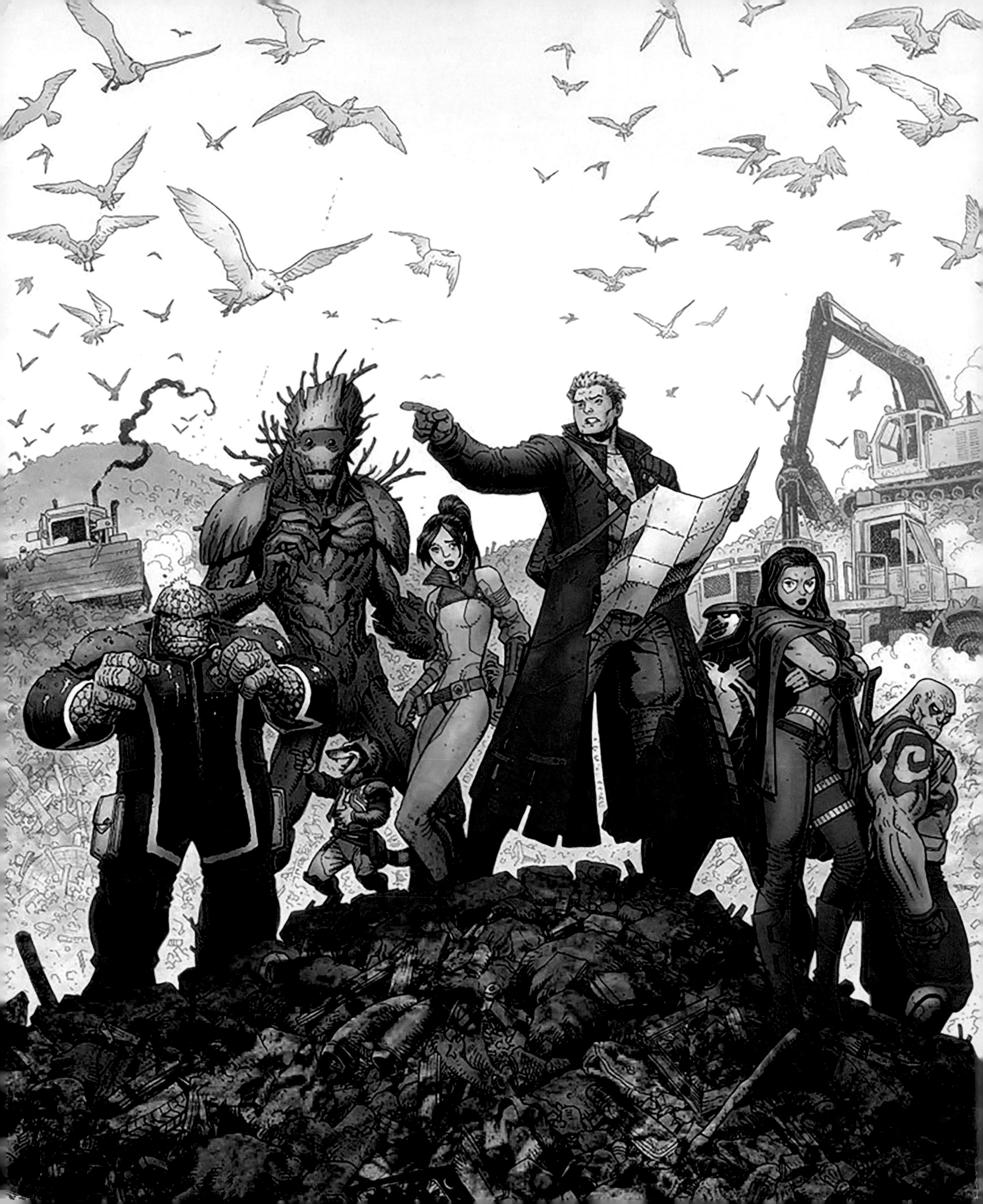